T0176703

MODERN MACHINE LEARNING TECHNIQUES AND THEIR APPLICATIONS IN CARTOON ANIMATION RESEARCH

MODERN MACHINE LEARNING TECHNIQUES AND THEIR APPLICATIONS IN CARTOON ANIMATION RESEARCH

Jun Yu
Computer Science Department
Xiamen University, Xiamen

Dacheng Tao
Centre for Quantum Computation and Intelligent Systems
Faculty of Engineering and Information Technology
University of Technology, Sydney

Systems, Man, & Cybernetics Society

IEEE Press

WILEY

A JOHN WILEY & SONS, INC., PUBLICATION

Published by John Wiley & Sons, Inc., Hoboken, New Jersey

Published simultaneously in Canada

For general information on our other products and services or for technical support, please contact our Customer Care Department within the United States at (800) 762-2974, outside the United States at (317) 572-3993 or fax (317) 572-4002.

Wiley also publishes its books in a variety of electronic formats. Some content that appears in print may not be available in electronic formats. For more information about Wiley products, visit our web site at www.wiley.com.

Library of Congress Cataloging-in-Publication Data:

Yu, Jun.
  Modern machine learning techniques and their applications in cartoon animation research / Jun Yu, Dacheng Tao. — First edition.
    pages cm
  Includes bibliographical references.
  ISBN 978-1-118-11514-5 (cloth)
1. Machine learning. 2. Computer animation. 1. Tao, Dacheng, 1978– II. Title.
  Q325.5.Y83 2013
  006.6'96—dc23   2012037690

Printed in the United States of America.

10 9 8 7 6 5 4 3 2 1

To our parents

CONTENTS

PREFACE

Machine learning techniques have been widely used in many fields including computer vision, natural language processing, image and signal processing, document analysis, video surveillance, and multimedia. In recent years, many modern machine learning techniques have been proposed, and this book introduces a number of those techniques, such as patch alignment framework; spectral clustering, graph cuts, and convex relaxation; ensemble manifold learning; multiple kernel learning; multiview subspace learning, and multiview distance metric learning. We also discusses applications of these modern machine learning techniques to animation research. Based on these techniques, users can efficiently utilize graphical materials, such as cartoons and 2D contours, to generate animations in practice including virtual reality, video games, animated films, and sport simulations. In respect of manifold learning, we introduce a novel framework called patch alignment framework, which includes most of the existing manifold learning methods [98] as special cases. For spectral clustering, graph cuts, and convex relaxation, we present a group of state-of-the art techniques. For ensemble manifold learning, multiple-kernel learning, multiview subspace learning, and multiview distance metric learning, we explain how to learn an efficient subspace or distance metric from multiview features. Specifically, we consider the application of manifold learning in correspondence construction. Correspondence construction of objects in keyframes is the pre-condition for inbetweening and coloring in computer-assisted animation production. In this book, we introduce a semi-supervised patch alignment framework for complex object correspondence construction. The new framework constructs local patches for each point on an object and aligns these patches in a new feature space, in which correspondences between objects can be detected by the subsequent clustering. This book also introduces the application of multiview learning (or learning from multiple features) in cartoon production. To effectively and efficiently create cartoons by reusing existing cartoon clips, it is essential to have proper visual features to represent cartoon characters. We detail several visual features to represent the color, shape, and motion structure information of a cartoon character. A variety of multiview learning methods are carefully explored to learn the complementary nature of these features, which are critical for cartoon generation. Organization of this book is presented below:

- The first chapter reviews the uses of machine learning methods and concepts in recent computer animation and related fields. Many existing computer animation techniques are categorized according to our insight into their characteristics, which not only illuminates how these techniques are related but also reveals possible ways in which they may be improved.

- Chapter 2 presents several recently proposed representative machine learning techniques for cartoon animation research, including patch alignment framework; spectral clustering, graph cuts, and convex relaxation; ensemble manifold learning; multiple kernel learning; multiview subspace learning and multiview distance metric learning. It is impossible to include all related works in this Chapter. We hope readers can find other possibly useful works from recently published journals and conference proceedings.

- Chapter 3 summarizes animation research. We introduce the history of traditional animation production, procedures of animation production, and the relationship between traditional animation and computer animation. Afterward, we detail the computer animation techniques in computer-assisted systems and present a novel computer animation approach which synthesizes new animations from an existing cartoon library. Techniques involving the reuse of graphical material are also introduced.

- Chapter 4 describes how we apply machine learning techniques in the computer animation field. We present the automatic correspondence construction method based on patch alignment framework, the novel cartoon synthesis approach based on constrained spreading activation network, and the efficient cartoon retrieval algorithm based on multiview subspace learning.

CHAPTER 1

INTRODUCTION

Machine learning has experienced explosive growth in the last few decades. It has achieved sufficient maturity to provide efficient techniques for a number of research and engineering fields including machine perception, computer vision, natural language processing, syntactic pattern recognition, and search engines. Machine learning provides a firm theoretical basis upon which to propose new techniques that leverage existing data to extract interesting information or to synthesize more data. It has been widely used in computer animation and related fields, e.g. rendering, modeling, geometry processing, and coloring. Based on these techniques, users can efficiently utilize graphical materials, such as models, images, and motion capture data to generate animations in practice, including virtual reality, video games, animation films, and sport simulations.

In this chapter, we introduce the uses of machine learning methods and concepts in contemporary computer animation and its associated fields. We also provide novel insights by categorizing many existing computer animation techniques into a common learning framework. This not only illuminates how these techniques are related, but also reveals possible ways in which they may be improved. The details of these potential improvements are presented in subsequent chapters.

1.1 PERCEPTION

Computer animation has become a prevalent medium for science, art, education, communication, and entertainment. The production of computer animation involves multidisciplinary skills, and the special effects for film are generated by the collaboration of animators, excellent artists, and engineers.

Generally, in animation production, the time-consuming and tedious work is artistic, not technical [111, 244]. This means that the efficiency of the artists is the bottleneck in animation production, due to the fact that computer animation algorithms are eminently reusable, but the data they operate on are often customized and highly stylized. This bottleneck is exemplified by computer-generated film production where the human workload is usually more than 80% artistic (e.g., modeling, texturing, animating, etc.) [79].

To remove the bottleneck in animation data generation, data transformation and modeling techniques have been adopted to synthesize or generalize data. Machine learning techniques are utilized based on the existing data because of two specific merits: structural information extraction and new data synthesizing. Thus, time can be saved in animation production by using machining learning techniques to reuse existing data. Allen et al. [16] proposed a novel technique which generates meshes of new human bodies based on a small set of example meshes through regression.

Even when the computation workload is more important than the human workload, clever synthesis and reuse of data can still often be beneficial. Schödl et al. [245] provided a new type of video production technique which synthesizes videos from a finite set of images. This allows for the rapid generation of convincing videos that do not exhibit discernible noise. Tang [279] et al. proposed a framework for generating video narrative from existing videos in which the user only needs to conduct two steps: selecting the background video and avatars, and setting up the movement and trajectory of avatars. By using this approach, realistic video narratives can be generated from the chosen video clips and the results will be visually pleasing.

In this chapter, recent uses of machine learning techniques in computer animation are presented. Techniques such as manifold learning and regression are reviewed, and we introduce important and popular topics in computer animation and related fields, discussing how machine learning has been leveraged in each. We also provide suggestions for future work on enhancing computer animation through machine learning.

1.2 OVERVIEW OF MACHINE LEARNING TECHNIQUES

In this section, we provide an overview of modern machine learning techniques. A more thorough introduction to machine learning is provided in Ref. [190, 199]. Machine learning [266] is concerned with the problem of how to build computer programs that acquire and utilize information to effectively perform tasks. One successful example is the field of computer vision [266]. Many vision techniques rely on, and are even designed around, machine learning. For example, machine learning through Bayesian inference has proven extremely powerful at analyzing surveillance video to automatically track humans [357, 352] and label human activities [185].

Unfortunately, the computer animation community has not utilized machine learning as widely as computer vision. Nevertheless, we can expect that integrating machine learning techniques into the computer animation field may create more effective methods. Suppose that users wish to simulate life on the streets of Bei Jing in ancient China, or in a mysterious alien society. They have to generate all the 3D models and textures for the world, the behaviors of animations for the characters. Although tools exist for all of these tasks, the scale of even the most prosaic world can require months or years of labor. An alternative approach is to create these models from existing data, either designed by artists or captured from the world. In this section, we introduce the idea that fitting models from data can be very useful for computer graphics, along with the idea that machine learning can provide powerful tools.

To consider the problem of generating motions for a character in a movie, it is important to realize that the motions can be created procedurally, i.e. by designing algorithms that synthesize motion. The animations can be created "by hand" or captured from an actor in a studio. These "pure data" approaches give the highest-quality motions, but at substantial cost in time and effort of artists or actors. Moreover, there is little flexibility: If it is discovered that the right motions were not captured in the studio, it is necessary to retrack and capture more. The situation is worse for a video game, where all the motions that might conceivably be needed must be captured. To solve this problem, machine learning techniques can be adopted to promise the best of both worlds: Starting with an amount of captured data, we can procedurally synthesize more data in the style of the original. Moreover, we can constrain the synthetic data, for example, according to the requirements of an artist. For such problems, machine learning offers an attractive set of tools for modeling the patterns of data. These data-driven techniques have gained a steadily increasing presence in graphics research. Principal components analysis and basic clustering algorithms are commonly used in SIGGRAPH, the world's premier conference on computer graphics and interactive techniques. Most significantly, the recent proliferation of papers on cartoon and motion synthesis suggests a growing acceptance of learning techniques. In this section, we introduce modern machine learning techniques from which the animations can deeply benefit. Furthermore, we introduce the applications of these techniques in computer animation.

1.2.1 Manifold Learning

Techniques of manifold learning are important and have been popularly applied in computer animation [49, 16, 131, 183]. Manifold learning [313] can be defined as the process of transforming measurements from a high-dimensional space to a low-dimensional subspace through the spectral analysis on specially constructed matrices. It aims to reveal the intrinsic structure of the distribution of measurements in the original high-dimensional space.

Manifold learning has a close relationship with computer animation research. For example, Principal Components Analysis (PCA) [116] is an extremely simple, linear manifold learning method which is primarily used as a preprocess for high-dimensional problems. PCA has been used as a preprocess in "Style Machines" [49] which addresses the problem of stylistic motion synthesis by learning motion patterns from a highly varied set of motion capture sequences. The human body pose data typically contain 30-40 degrees of-freedom (DOFs); however, the proposed method would learn very slowly on such a large number of DOFs. Applying linear manifold learning is very fast, and the resulting 10-dimensional space maintains the important underlying structure of the motion data. More sophisticated non-linear manifold learning approaches [241, 287, 31, 353] have been developed and applied in the computer animation field. For example, Shin and Lee [253] proposed a low-dimensional motion space constructed by ISOMAP, in which high-dimensional human motion can be effectively visualized, synthesized, edited, parameterized, and interpolated in both spatial and temporal domains. This system allows users to create and edit the motion of animated characters in several ways: The user can sketch and edit a curve on low-dimensional motion space, directly manipulate the character's pose in three-dimensional object space, or specify key poses to create inbetween motions.

Representative manifold learning can be classified into linear and nonlinear manifold learning groups. Principal Component Analysis (PCA) [116] and Linear Discriminant Analysis(LDA) [83] are two typical linear manifold learning techniques. PCA, which is unsupervised, maximizes the mutual information between original high-dimensional Gaussian distributed measurements and projected low-dimensional measurements. LDA finds a projection matrix that maximizes the trace of the between-class scatter matrix and minimizes the trace of the within-class scatter matrix in the projected subspace simultaneously. LDA is supervised because it utilizes class label information. Representative nonlinear manifold learning includes Locally Linear Embedding (LLE) [241], ISOMAP [287], Laplacian Eigenmaps (LE) [31], Hessian Eigenmaps (HLLE) [78], and Local Tangent Space Alignment (LTSA) [353]. Locally Linear Embedding (LLE) [241] uses linear coefficients, which reconstruct a given measurement by its neighbors, to represent the local geometry, and then seeks a low-dimensional embedding in which these coefficients are still suitable for reconstruction. ISOMAP, a variant of MDS, preserves global geodesic distances of all pairs of measurements. LE preserves proximity relationships by manipulations on an undirected weighted graph, which indicates neighbour relations of pairwise measurements. LTSA exploits the local tangent information as a representation of the local geometry, and this local tangent information is then aligned to provide a global coordinate. HLLE obtains the final low-dimensional representations by applying eigen-analysis to a matrix which is built by estimating the Hessian over neighbourhood. All of these algorithms suffer from the out-of-sample problem. One common response to this problem is to apply a linearization procedure to construct explicit maps over new measurements. Examples of this approach include Locality Preserving Projections (LPP) [108], a linearization of LE; neighborhood preserving embedding (NPE) [107], a linearization of LLE; orthogonal neighborhood preserving projections (ONPP) [142], a linearization of LLE with the orthogonal constraint over the projection matrix; and linear local tangent space alignment (LLTSA) [351], a linearization of LTSA. The above analysis shows that all the aforementioned algorithms are designed according to specific intuitions, and solutions are given by optimizing intuitive and pragmatic objectives. That is, these algorithms have been developed based on the experience and knowledge of field experts for their own purposes. As a result, the common properties and intrinsic differences of these algorithms are not completely clear. The framework of "Patch Alignment" [350, 99] is therefore proposed for better understanding the common properties and intrinsic differences in algorithms. This framework consists of two stages: part optimization and whole alignment. The details of this framework will be introduced in Chapter 2.

1.2.2 Semi-supervised Learning

In computer animation, the interaction between computer and artist has already been demonstrated to be an efficient way [120]. Some researchers have explored the close relationship between SSL and computer animation; for example, in character animation, Ikemoto [120] has found what the artist would like for given inputs. Using these observations as training data, the input output mapping functions can be fitted to generalize the training data to novel input. The artist can provide feedback by editing the output. The system uses this feedback to refine its mapping function, and this iterative process continues until the artist is satisfied. This framework has been applied to address important character animation problems. First, sliding foot plants are a common artifact resulting from almost any attempt to modify character motion. Using an artist-trained oracle, it can be demonstrated that the animation sequences can be accurately annotated with foot plant markers. Second, all motion synthesis algorithms sometimes produce character animation that looks unnatural (i.e., contains artifacts or is otherwise distinguishable as synthesized motion by a human observer). It can be demonstrated that these methods can be successfully adopted as the testing parts of hypothesize-and-test motion synthesis algorithms. Furthermore, artists can create compelling character animations by manipulating the details of a character's motion. This process is labor-intensive and repetitive. It has been found that the character animation can be made efficient by generalizing the edits an animator makes on short sequences of training data to other sequences. Another typical example is in cartoon animation. Correspondence construction of objects in keyframes is the pre-condition for inbetweening and coloring in cartoon animation production. Since each frame of an animation consists of multiple layers, objects are complex in terms of shape and structure; therefore, existing shape-matching algorithms, specifically designed for simple structures such as a single closed contour, cannot perform well on objects constructed by multiple contours with an open shape. Yu et al. [338] proposed a semi-supervised learning method for complex object correspondence construction. In particular, the new method constructs local patches for each point on an object and aligns these patches in a new feature space, in which correspondences between objects can be detected by the subsequent clustering. For local patch construction, pairwise constraints, which indicate the corresponding points (must link) or unfitting points (cannot link), are introduced by users to improve the performance of the correspondence construction. This kind of input is conveniently available to animation software users via user friendly interfaces. Furthermore, the feedback [280, 285] provided by users can enhance the results of correspondence construction.

Based on the above analysis, semi-supervised learning (SSL) [365, 303, 304, 305, 307] could be an appropriate technique for designing novel tools for computer animation. SSL is halfway between supervised and unsupervised learning [306]. Based on the unlabeled data, the algorithm is enhanced by supervision information. Generally, this information will be the targets associated with some of the examples. In this case, the data set $\mathbf{X} = [\mathbf{x}_1, \ldots, \mathbf{x}_n]$ will be divided into two parts: The data points $\mathbf{X}_l = [\mathbf{x}_1, \ldots, \mathbf{x}_l]$ with labels $\mathbf{Y}_l = [\mathbf{y}_1, \ldots, \mathbf{y}_l]$ are provided, and the data points $\mathbf{X}_u = [\mathbf{x}_{l+1}, \ldots, \mathbf{x}_{l+u}]$ whose labels are not known. Other forms of partial supervision are possible. For example, there may be constraints such as "these points have (or do not have) the same target." The different setting corresponds to a different view of semi-supervised learning, in which SSL is perceived as unsupervised learning guided by constraints. By contrast, in most other approaches, SSL is assumed to be supervised learning with additional information on the distribution of the data samples. A problem related to SSL is transductive learning [296], which was introduced by Vapnik. In this problem, there is a (labeled) training set and an (unlabeled) test set. The idea of transduction is to perform predictions only for the test points. This is in contrast to inductive learning, where the goal is to output a prediction function which is defined on the entire space. Next, we will introduce several semi-supervised learning methods in detail.

Self-training is a commonly used technique for semi-supervised learning. In self-training, a classifier is first trained with a small amount of labeled data. The classifier is then used to classify the unlabeled data. Typically, the most confident unlabeled points, together with their predicted labels, are added to the training set. Then, the classifier is re-trained and the procedure repeated. This procedure is also called self-teaching or bootstrapping. Yarowsky [332] adopts self-training for word sense disambiguation. Riloff et al. [236] use it to identify subjective nouns. Maeireizo et al. [188] classify dialogues as 'emotional' or 'non-emotional' with a procedure involving two classifiers.

In co-training, several assumptions are made: (1) Features can be classified into two sets; (2) each subfeature set is sufficient to train a good classifier; (3) the two sets are conditionally independent given the class. Initially, two separate classifiers are trained with the labeled data on the two sub-feature sets respectively. Each classifier then classifies the unlabeled data and 'teaches' the other classifier with the few unlabeled examples (and the predicted labels) about which they feel most confident. Each classifier is retrained with the additional training examples given by the other classifier, and the process repeats. Nigam and Ghani [213] perform extensive empirical experiments to compare co-training with generative mixture models and EM. The result shows that co-training gives excellent performance if the conditional independence assumption indeed holds. Jones [128] also used co-training, co-EM and other related methods for information extraction from text. Balcan and Blum [27] show that co-training can be quite effective in an extreme case where only one labeled point is needed to learn the classifier. Zhou et al. [363] give a co-training algorithm using Canonical Correlation Analysis, which also needs only one labeled point.

In graph-based semi-supervised learning, the nodes in the graph are labeled and unlabeled samples in the dataset, and the edges in the graph represent the similarity of samples. These methods usually assume label smoothness over the graph. In general, graph-based methods can be seen as estimation of a function $\mathbf{f}$ on the graph. Two issues of $\mathbf{f}$ should be satisfied: it should be close to $\mathbf{y}_l$ on the labeled data and it should be smooth on the whole graph. Thus, these two issues can be represented in a regularization framework where the first term is a loss function and the second term is a regularizer. It is more important to construct a good graph than to choose among the methods. Blum and Chawla [45] adopt the graph mincut problem to solve semi-supervised learning. In this method, the positive labels act as sources and the negative labels act as sinks. The objective is to find a minimum set of edges whose removal blocks all flow from the sources to the sinks. The nodes connecting to the sources are then labeled positive, and those to the sinks are labeled negative. The Gaussian random fields and harmonic function method [366] is a continuous relaxation to the difficulty of discrete Markov random fields. It can be viewed as having a quadratic loss function with infinity weight, so that the labeled data are clamped, and a regularizer based on the graph combinatorial Laplacian $\triangle$ can be

$$\sum_{i \in L} (\mathbf{f}_i - \mathbf{y}_i)^2 + \frac{1}{2} \sum_{i,j} \mathbf{w} \left(\mathbf{f}_i - \mathbf{f}_j\right)^2 = \sum_{i \in L} (\mathbf{f}_i - \mathbf{y}_i)^2 + \mathbf{f}^{\mathbf{T}} \triangle \mathbf{f}, \qquad (1.1)$$

where $\mathbf{f}_i \in \mathbf{R}$ is the key relaxation to Mincut. Zhou et al. [361] proposed the local and global consistency method where the loss function is $\sum_{i=1}^{n} (\mathbf{f}_i - \mathbf{y}_i)^2$, and the normalized Laplacian $\mathbf{D}^{-1/2} \triangle \mathbf{D}^{-1/2} = \mathbf{I} - \mathbf{D}^{-1/2} \mathbf{W} \mathbf{D}^{-1/2}$ in the regularizer as

$$1/2 \sum_{i,j} \mathbf{w}_{i,j} \left(\mathbf{f}_i / \sqrt{\mathbf{D}_{ii}} - \mathbf{f}_j / \sqrt{\mathbf{D}_{jj}}\right)^2 = \mathbf{f}^{\mathbf{T}} \mathbf{D}^{-1/2} \triangle \mathbf{D}^{-1/2} \mathbf{f} \qquad (1.2)$$

The manifold regularization framework [32] employs two regularization terms

$$\frac{1}{l} \sum_{i=1}^{l} V\left(\mathbf{x}_i, \mathbf{y}_i, \mathbf{f}\right) + \lambda \|\mathbf{f}\|_K^2 + \beta \|\mathbf{f}\|_I^2 \qquad (1.3)$$

where V is an arbitrary loss function, K is a "base kernel", e.g., a linear or RBF kernel. I is a regularization term induced by the labeled and unlabeled data.

In general, there are no explicit rules for choosing hyperparameters for graph-based semi-supervised learning, because it is nontrivial to define an objective function to obtain these hyperparameters. Usually, cross-validation is utilized for parameter selection. However, this grid-search technique tries to select parameters from discrete states in the parameter space, and lacks the ability to approximate the optimal solution. To deal with the parameter configuration problem, an ensemble manifold regularization (EMR) framework [87, 86] is proposed to combine the automatic intrinsic manifold approximation and the semi-supervised classifier learning. By providing a series of initial guesses of graph Laplacian, the framework learns to combine them to approximate the intrinsic manifold.

Besides, Yu et al. [341] adopt hypergraph [362] to address the problem of parameters selection in graph-based semi-supervised learning. Unlike a graph that has an edge between two vertices, a set of vertices is connected by a hyperedge in a hypergraph. Each hyperedge is assigned a weight. In hypergraph learning, the weights of the hyperedges are empirically set according to certain rules. In practice, a large number of hyperedges will usually be generated, and these hyperedges have different effects. In Ref.[341], an adaptive hypergraph learning method is proposed. For hypergraph construction, the hyperedges are generated based on data samples and their nearest neighbors. Specifically, the size of the neighborhood is varied to produce multiple hyperedges for each sample. Thus, a large set of hyperedges will be generated in this process. This makes the approach much more robust, because the neighborhood size dose not need to be tuned. Since it is difficult to choose a suitable strategy to heuristically weight hyperedges, a principled approach, termed regularized loss minimization, is considered based on statistical learning theory. The loss minimization ensures that the learned weights are optimal for the training set. Since the size of the training set is not large in practice, the regularization item ensures that the learned weights do not overfit to the training samples. This scheme essentially achieves improved classification performance compared to the scheme that uses fixed weights for different hyperedges.

1.2.3 Multiview Learning

Multiview learning has a long history [242]. It has been applied to semi-supervised regression [259, 50, 343] and the more challenging structured output spaces [51]. In computer animation, it is normal to use multiple features from different views to describe the character. For instance, to describe a character well in cartoons, it is elementary to extract a set of visual features to define its color, texture, motion and shape information. A set of vectors can be obtained in different spaces to represent the character. In this case, one possible method is to concatenate these vectors as a new vector. This concatenation is not physically meaningful because each feature has a specific statistical property.

Long et al. [181] proposed a distributed spectral embedding (DSE) to construct a subspace learning with multiple views. To give a multiview datum with n objects having m views, i.e., a set of matrices $\mathbf{X} = \{\mathbf{X}^{(i)} \in \mathbf{R}^{m_i \times n}\}$, each representation $\mathbf{X}^{(i)}$ is a feature matrix from view i. DSE assumes that the low-dimensional representation of each view $\mathbf{X}^{(i)}$ is already known, i.e., $\mathbf{A} = \{\mathbf{A}^{(i)} \in \mathbf{R}^{n \times k_i}\}_{i=1}^{m}, k_i < m_i (1 \leq i \leq m)$. DSE aims to learn a consensus low-dimensional subspace $\mathbf{B} \in \mathbf{R}^{n \times k}$ based on A; the objective function of DSE can be formulated as

$$\min_{\mathbf{B},\mathbf{P}} \sum_{i=1}^{m} \left\| \mathbf{A}^{(i)} - \mathbf{B}\mathbf{P}^{(i)} \right\|^2 \text{ s.t. } \mathbf{B}^{\mathrm{T}}\mathbf{B} = \mathbf{I}, \tag{1.4}$$

where $\mathbf{P} = \{\mathbf{P}^{(i)} \in \mathbf{R}^{k \times k_i}\}_{i=1}^m$ is a set of mapping matrices. The optimal solution to DSE is given by performing eigendecomposition of the matrix $\mathbf{CC}^{\mathbf{T}}$, $\mathbf{C} = [\mathbf{A}^{(1)}, \ldots, \mathbf{A}^{(m)}]$. Furthermore, a novel multiview subspace learning method [324] is proposed based on the patch alignment framework. The details are presented in Chapter 2.

1.2.4 Learning-based Optimization

In this section, we present an overview of mathematical optimization, which will be used in the subsequent contents of this book.

The form of a mathematical optimization problem can be written as

$$\min \, f_0(\mathbf{x}), \text{ s.t. } f_i(\mathbf{x}) \leq b_i, \; i = 1, \ldots, m, \qquad (1.5)$$

where the vector $\mathbf{x} = (\mathbf{x}_1, \ldots, \mathbf{x}_n)$ is the optimization variable for the problem. The function $f_0 : \mathbf{R}^n \to \mathbf{R}$ is the objective function, and the function $f_i : \mathbf{R}^n \to \mathbf{R}, i = 1, \ldots, m$, are the constraint functions. The constants $b_1, \ldots, b_m$ are the bounds for the constraints. A vector $\mathbf{x}'$ is called a solution of the problem in Eq. (1.5), if it has the smallest objective value among all vectors which satisfy the constraints. In general, the optimization problems can be characterized by particular forms of the objective and constraint functions. Next, we present the optimization methods of least-squares, linear programming and convex optimization.

Least-Squares Problems: The least-squares problem can be formulated as an optimization problem with no constraints and the objective function is formulated by summing the squares of terms of the form $\mathbf{a}_i^{\mathbf{T}} \mathbf{x} - \mathbf{b}_i$:

$$\min \, f_0(\mathbf{x}) = \|\mathbf{Ax} - \mathbf{b}\|_2^2 = \sum_{i=1}^k (\mathbf{a}_i^{\mathbf{T}} - \mathbf{b}_i)^2, \qquad (1.6)$$

where $\mathbf{A} \in \mathbf{R}^{k \times n}$ (with $k \geq n$), $\mathbf{a}_i^{\mathbf{T}}$ is the rows of $\mathbf{A}$, and the vector $\mathbf{x} \in \mathbf{R}^n$ is the optimization variable. The solution of the least-squares problem, Eq. (1.6), can be reduced to solving a set of linear equations

$$(\mathbf{A}^{\mathbf{T}} \mathbf{A}) = \mathbf{A}^{\mathbf{T}} \mathbf{b}. \qquad (1.7)$$

Thus, the analytical solution is $\mathbf{x} = (\mathbf{A}^{\mathbf{T}} \mathbf{A})^{-1} \mathbf{A}^{\mathbf{T}} \mathbf{b}$. The least-squares problem can be solved in a time approximately proportional to $n^2 k$ with a known constant. In many cases, the least-squares problem can be solved by exploiting some special structure in the coefficient matrix $\mathbf{A}$. For instance, by investigating sparsity, we can usually solve the least-squares problem much faster than order $n^2 k$.

The least-squares problem is the basis for regression analysis, optimal control, and many parameter estimation and data fitting methods. It has a number of statistical interpretations, e.g., as the maximum likelihood estimation of a vector $\mathbf{x}$. It is straightforward to recognize the optimization problem as a least-squares problem. We only need to verify whether the objective function is a quadratic function. Recently, several standard techniques have been used to increase the flexibility of least-squares in applications. For example, the weighted least-squares cost can be formulated as

$$\sum_{i=1}^{k} \mathbf{w}_i(\mathbf{a}_i^{\mathrm{T}}\mathbf{x} - \mathbf{b}_i)^2, \tag{1.8}$$

where $\mathbf{w}_1, \ldots, \mathbf{w}_k$ are positive. In a statistical setting, weighted least-squares arise in estimation of a vector $\mathbf{x}$, given linear measurements corrupted by errors with unequal variances.

Another technique in least-squares is regularization, in which extra terms are added to the cost function. In the simplest case, a positive multiple of the sum of squares of the variables is added to the cost function:

$$\sum_{i=1}^{k} \mathbf{w}_i(\mathbf{a}_i^{\mathrm{T}}\mathbf{x} - \mathbf{b}_i)^2 + \alpha \sum_{i=1}^{n} \mathbf{x}_i^2, \tag{1.9}$$

where $\alpha > 0$. Here, the extra terms penalize large values of $\mathbf{x}$, and result in a sensible solution in cases when minimizing the first sum only does not. The parameter α is selected by the user to provide the right trade-off.

Linear Programming: Another important group of optimization methods is linear programming, in which the objective function and all constraints are linear.

$$\min \ \mathbf{c}^{\mathrm{T}}\mathbf{x} \ \text{s.t.} \ \mathbf{a}_i^{\mathrm{T}}\mathbf{x} \le \mathbf{b}_i, i = 1, \ldots, m, \tag{1.10}$$

where the vectors $\mathbf{c}, \mathbf{a}_1, \ldots, \mathbf{a}_m \in \mathbf{R}^n$ and scalars $\mathbf{b}_1, \ldots, \mathbf{b}_m \in \mathbf{R}$ are problem parameters which specify the objective and constraint functions.

There is no simple analytical formula for the solution of a linear program. However, there is a variety of very effective methods for solving them, including Dantzig's simplex method [235]. We can easily solve problems with hundreds of variables and thousands of constraints on a small desktop computer. If the problem is sparse, or has some other exploitable structure, we can often solve problems with tens or hundreds of thousands of variables and constraints, as shown in Ref. [364].

Convex Optimization: The convex optimization problem [267, 127] can be formulated as

$$\min \ f_0(x) \ \text{s.t.} \ f_i(\mathbf{x}) \le \mathbf{b}_i, \ i = 1, \ldots, m, \tag{1.11}$$

where the functions $f_0, \ldots, f_m : \mathbf{R}^n \to \mathbf{R}$ are convex, and satisfy

$$f_i(\alpha\mathbf{x} + \beta\mathbf{y}) \le \alpha f_i(\mathbf{x}) + \beta f_i(\mathbf{y}), \tag{1.12}$$

for all $\mathbf{x}, \mathbf{y} \in \mathbf{R}^n$ and all $\alpha, \beta \in \mathbf{R}$ with $\alpha + \beta = 1, \alpha \ge 0, \beta \ge 0$.

The use of convex optimization is very much like using least-squares or linear programming. If a problem can be described as a convex optimization problem, it can be solved efficiently, like solving the least-squares problem, but there are also some important differences. The recognition of a least-squares problem is straightforward, but recognizing a convex function is more difficult. Additionally, there are many more tricks for transforming convex problems than for transforming linear programs.

1.3   RECENT DEVELOPMENTS IN COMPUTER ANIMATION

In this section, we introduce the application of machine learning techniques into computer animation and its related fields. It can be seen that animation has thus far benefited considerably from the application of machine learning [22]. Excellent introductions to the field of computer animation are presented by Parent [218] and Pina et al. [231]. Computer animation is a time-intensive process, and this is true for both the 3D virtual character and 2D cartoon character. As a result, there has long been interest in partially automating animation [218, 231]. Some well-known approaches include keyframing and inverse kinematics, but these techniques still require significant animator input. In the following content, we will present some efficient and effective techniques in automatic animation generation.

1.3.1   Example-Based Motion Reuse

An efficient approach to motion synthesis is to create novel motions using some example motion data, as shown in Figure 1.1 and Figure 1.2. Intuitively, example-based motion synthesis can more easily produce realistic motion than entirely artificial approaches.

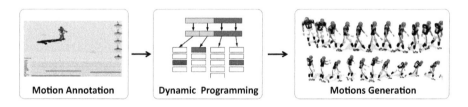

Motion Annotation   **Dynamic Programming**   **Motions Generation**

Figure 1.1   Example-based motion synthesis guided by annotations.

1.3.1.1   Introduction of Motion Capture Systems   The prerequisite of example-based motion synthesis is obtaining the motion data using specified techniques. These techniques were first proposed in the 1970s. In general, the motion capture can be achieved by adopting specific equipment to record the 3D motion data in real time. In the 1990s, a number of typical motion capture systems have been proposed, the details of which are presented in Table 1.1.

Motion capture systems to date can be classified into the following categories:

- Electronic mechanical system: The advantage of this system is the unconstrained motion capture place, and the avoidance of self-occlusion in the motion capture procedure. The Gypsy5 system from the Animazoo Company [2] can be bought in the market (as shown in Figure 1.3(a)).

- Electromagnetic system: This system adopts multiple sensors to record the joint positions and angles of real objects (as shown in Figure 1.3(b)). The

Figure 1.2 Slide show of example-based motion synthesis. The character transitions from walking to jogging to looking over her shoulder. Example-based techniques have proven quite effective because they synthesize motion that complies with real example motion.

Table 1.1 Motion Capture Systems

Date	Name of Systems
1980-1983	Goniometers [58]
1982-1983	Graphical marionette [88]
1988	Mike the Talking Head [198]
1988	Waldo C. Graphic [300, 301]
1989	Dozo [139]
1991	Mat the Ghost [286]
1992	Mario [238]

deficiencies can be summarized as: First, this system is sensitive to metal objects in a motion capture scene; second, because the sensors are fastened to the actors, some complicated actions cannot be performed; third, the low sampling rates of this system cannot meet the requirements of sports analysis, besides which the cost of the system is very high.

- Optical system: This kind of system has been widely adopted in motion capture. Representative products are Hawk, Eagle [3] from MotionAnalysis and Vicon MX system from the Vicon Company [4]. These systems record motion by sticking markers onto the human body's joints. A group of specialized cameras are adopted to take videos and human motions are then extracted from the videos. In general, this system requires 4-6 cameras. This technique can provide high sampling rates, which can record the motion data for tracking and

3D modeling reconstruction in computer vision. The optical systems are also very expensive.

(a)   (b)

Figure 1.3   (a) Electronic mechanical motion capture system (b) Electromagnetic motion capture system.

Based on the above elaborations, the available motion capture systems have the disadvantages of high price, complicated operating procedure, and more. In recent years, therefore, scientists and engineers have been exploring novel motion capture devices which are cheap and easy to operate. The video-based motion capture system is an emergent topic, which we will discuss below.

In terms of motion capture devices, video-based motion capture systems can be divided into the single camera system and multiple camera system. The techniques of feature tracking, modeling matching, statistical learning, and silhouette analysis are widely used in video-based motion capture. The following paragraphs offer more detail on these techniques.

Feature Tracking-Based Motion Capture Techniques: Most video-based motion capture techniques are based on a single camera which takes a series of frames for human characters and adopts feature tracking methods to extract the motions. Here, the adopted features are feature points and motion patches. Segen and Pingali [248] proposed a contour-based motion capture system. They adopt the points' position and curvature to match two successive frames' feature points and to estimate the motion parameters. Bregler and Malik [54] proposed a novel vision-based motion capture technique which can recover human motion from single-view video frames with complicated backgrounds. Pekelny and Gotsman [226] proposed a novel motion capture system which acquires the motion of a dynamic piecewise-rigid object using a single depth video camera. This system identifies and tracks the rigid components in each frame while accumulating the geometric information acquired over time, possibly from different viewpoints. The algorithm also reconstructs the dynamic skeleton of the object and thus can be used for markerless motion capture. Fossati et al. [84] proposed a motion capture approach which combines detection and tracking techniques to achieve robust 3D motion recovery of people seen from arbitrary viewpoints by a single and potentially moving camera. This approach depends on detecting key postures and can be done reliably, using a motion model to infer 3D poses between consecutive detections, finally refining them over the whole sequence using a generative model. Wang et al. [312] proposed a motion capture system built from commodity components, as shown in Figure 1.4. This approach uses one or more webcams and a color shirt to track the upper-body at interactive rates. In their system, a robust color calibration procedure is described to enable color-based tracking to work against cluttered backgrounds and under multiple illuminants.

(a) Devices   **(b) Motion Capture**   **(c) Application of Motion Capture**

Figure 1.4   (a) A lightweight color-based motion capture system that uses one or two commodity webcams and a color shirt (b) Performance capture in a variety of natural lighting environments, such as the squash court (c) Application of motion capture data in video games.

Model Matching and Silhouette Analysis-based motion capture techniques: In the field of motion capture research, some scientists adopt model matching and silhouette analysis to recover the human motion parameters from the images/videos. The basic idea is to fix a search space for human gesture [281] and build the correspondence between the extracted image features (feature points, silhouette) and the 3D human model. Normally, this procedure is conducted by solving an optimization problem. The details of this procedure are shown in Figure 1.5.

Zhao and Li [354] adopted Genetic Algorithm to match the feature points from the 2D image with an optimal 3D gesture retrieved from 3D human gesture space. However, the matching accuracy of this method depends heavily on the tracking accuracy of the 2D feature points. Thus, satisfactory results cannot be achieved in videos with complicated backgrounds and self-occlusions. Chen et al. [68] proposed a novel method to recover 3D human motion. First, the 3D human gestures are parameterized and projected onto a 2D plane by using different configurations. Then, the silhouette of the character in the video frame is input into the system and its corresponding optimal 3D human gesture can be retrieved. The major deficiency of this approach is that the adopted 3D human model is general and simple, thus it cannot be perfectly matched to the silhouetted extracted from the videos. Micilotta et al. [196] proposed an upper body motion capture system which extracts motion by building correspondence between silhouette and Edge Map; however, this approach can only capture upper body motion. Agarwal and Triggs [10] presented a learning-based method for recovering a 3D human body pose from single images and monocular image series. This approach does not require an explicit body model and prior labeling of the body parts in the image. Instead, it recovers the pose by direct nonlinear regression against shape descriptor vectors extracted automatically from image silhouettes. For robustness against local silhouette segmentation errors, the silhouette shape is encoded by a histogram-of-shape-contexts descriptors. To handle the problems of depth and labeling information loss, this method is integrated into a novel regressive tracking framework, using dynamics from the previous state estimate together with a learned regression value to disambiguate the pose. Recently, Aguiar et al. [13] proposed a new marker-less approach to capturing human performances from multiview video (as shown in Figure 1.5). This algorithm can jointly reconstruct spatio-temporally coherent geometry, motion and textural surface appearance of actors that perform complex and rapid moves. This algorithm is purely mesh-based and makes as few prior assumptions as possible about the type of subject being tracked; it can even capture performances of people wearing wide apparel, such as a dancer wearing a skirt. In Figure 1.5(c) small-scale time-varying shape detail is recovered by applying model-guided multiview stereo to refine the model surface. Xu et al. [326] presented a method to synthesize plausible video sequences of humans according to user-defined body motions and viewpoints. First, they captured a small database of multiview video sequences of an actor performing various basic motions. They applied a marker-less model-based performance capture approach to the entire database to obtain the pose and geometry of the actor in each database frame. To create novel video sequences of the actor from the database, a user animates a 3D human skeleton with novel motion and viewpoints. This technique then synthesizes a realistic video sequence of the actor performing the specified motion, based only on the initial database. Stoll et al. [269] presented a motion capture approach that incorporates a physically based cloth model to reconstruct the real person in loose apparel from multiview video recordings. This algorithm requires little manual interaction. Without the use of optical markers, this algorithm can reconstruct the skeleton motion and detailed time-varying surface geometry of a real person from a reference video sequence. Wei and Chai [316] provided a novel method to capture physically realistic human motion from monocular video sequences. This approach first computes camera parameters, human skeletal size, and a small number of 3D key poses from video and then uses 2D image measurements at intermediate frames to automatically calculate the "in between" poses. During reconstruction, Newtonian physics, contact constraints, and 2D image measurements are leveraged to simultaneously reconstruct full-body poses, joint torques, and contact forces. Li et al. [171] presented a framework and algorithms for robust geometry and motion reconstruction of complex deforming shapes. This method makes use of a smooth template that provides a crude approximation of the scanned object and serves as a geometric and topological prior for reconstruction. Large-scale motion of the acquired object is recovered using a space-time adaptive, nonrigid registration method. Fine-scale details such as wrinkles and folds can be successfully synthesized with an efficient linear mesh deformation algorithm.

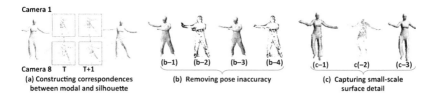

Camera 1

Camera 8   T   T+1
(a) Constructing correspondences
between modal and silhouette

(b-1)   (b-2)   (b-3)   (b-4)
(b) Removing pose inaccuracy

(c-1)   c(-2)   (c-3)
(c) Capturing small-scale
surface detail

Figure 1.5 (a) 3D correspondences are extracted from corresponding SIFT features in respective input camera views at t and t+1. These 3D correspondences, two of them illustrated by lines, are used to deform the model into a first pose estimate for t+1. (b) Model (b-1) and the silhouette overlap (b-2) after the refinement step; slight pose inaccuracies in the leg and the arms appear black in the silhouette overlap image. (b-3) and (b-4) show that after key vertex optimization, these pose inaccuracies are removed and the model strikes a correct pose. (c) First, deformation constraints from the silhouette contours, shown as red arrows, are estimated in (c-1). Additional deformation handles are extracted from a 3D point cloud that is computed via model-guided multi-view stereo in (c-2). Together, both sets of constraints deform the surface scan to the highly accurate pose shown in (c-3).

Other Motion Capture Techniques: In general, motion capture techniques require the task to be performed in a specified lab or closed stage setting with controlled lighting. Thus, the capture of motions is constrained by the outdoor setting or the traversal of large areas. Recently, T. Shiratori et al. [254] adopted body-mounted cameras to reconstruct the motion of a subject, as shown in Figure 1.6. In this system, outward-looking cameras are attached to the limbs of the subject, and the joint angles and root pose are estimated through nonlinear optimization. The optimization objective function incorporates terms for image matching error and temporal continuity of motion. Structure-from-motion is used to estimate the skeleton structure and to provide initialization for the non-linear optimization procedure. Global motion is estimated and drift is controlled by matching the captured set of videos to reference imagery. For nonrigid object motion capture, Yan and Pollefeys [328] proposed an approach which is based on the modeling of the articulated non-rigid motion as a set of intersecting motion subspaces. Here, a motion subspace is the linear subspace of the trajectories of an object. It can model a rigid or non-rigid motion. The intersection of two motion subspaces of linked parts models the motion of an articulated joint or axis. Bradley et al. [47] described a marker-free approach to capturing garment motion that avoids these downsides. Temporally coherent parameterizations are established between incomplete geometries that are extracted at each timestep with a multiview stereo algorithm. Holes in the geometry are then filled, using a template. This method allows users to capture the geometry and motion of unpatterned off-the-shelf garments made from a range of different fabrics.

In this section, we present various kinds of motion capture systems capable of capturing realistic motions. In the next section, we shall introduce the reuse of motion data in the computer animation field. In general, motion reuse can be separated into three categories: motion retargeting, motion editing and motion synthesis.

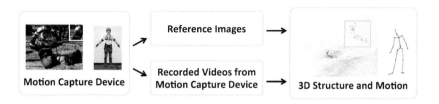

Figure 1.6 A novel motion capture system which captures both relative and global motion in natural environments using cameras mounted on the body.

1.3.1.2 Motion Retargeting Motion retargeting can be defined as transferring the captured motion data onto a new character with a different skeleton. This procedure is presented in Figure 1.7.

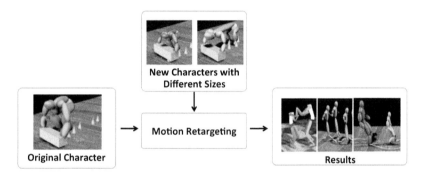

Figure 1.7 Motion of picking up an object is retargeted onto differently sized characters.

In 1997, Hodings and Pollard [113] proposed an automatic method which retargeted existing human motion onto a new character whose skeleton had different length and mass. The presented algorithm adapts the control system to a new character in two stages. First, the control system parameters are scaled based on the sizes, masses, and moments of inertia of the new and original characters. A subset of the parameters is then fine-tuned using a search process based on simulated annealing. In addition to adapting a control system for a new model, this approach can also be used to adapt the control system in an on-line fashion to produce a physically realistic metamorphosis from the original to the new model while the morphing character is performing the behavior. Similarly, Gleicher [91] proposed a constraint-based motion retargeting algorithm. Their focus is on adapting the motion of one articulated figure to another figure having identical structure but different segment lengths. This approach creates adaptations that preserve the desirable qualities of the original motion. In addition, specific features of the motion as constraints are identified and preserved in the retargeting procedure. A time constraints solver computes an adapted motion that reestablishes these constraints while preserving the frequency characteristics of the original signal. To solve the motion retargeting problem between characters that have different structures, Park and Shin [220] proposed a novel example-based motion retargeting approach. Provided with a set of example motions, this method automatically extracts a small number of representative postures called source key-postures. The animator then creates the corresponding key-postures of the target character, breathing his/her imagination and creativity into the output animation. Exploiting this correspondence, each input posture is cloned frame by frame to the target character to produce an initial animation, which is further adjusted in space and time for retargeting and time warping and then finalized with interactive fine tuning. Hecker et al. [110] provided a real-time motion retargeting system for animating characters whose morphologies are unknown at the time the animation is created. The proposed technique allows describing the motion using familiar posing and key-framing methods. The system records the data in a morphology-independent form, preserving both the animation's structural relationships and its stylistic information. At runtime, the generalized data are applied to specific characters to yield pose goals that are supplied to a robust and efficient inverse kinematics solver.

More complicated motion retargeting tasks have recently been achieved in the research field. For example, Ho et al. [112] presented a novel motion retargeting method which reused the motion involving close interactions between body parts of single or multiple articulated characters, such as dancing, wrestling, and sword fighting, or between characters and a restricted environment, such as getting into a car. In such motions, the implicit spatial relationships between body parts/objects are important for capturing the scene semantics. A simple structure called an interaction mesh is adopted to represent the spatial relationships. The interaction mesh representation is general and applicable to various kinds of close interactions. Yamane et al. [327] proposed an approach for producing animations of nonhumanoid characters from human motion capture data. Characters considered in this work (as shown in Figure 1.8) have proportion and/or topology significantly different from humans, but are expected to convey expressions and emotions through body language that are understandable to human viewers. Keyframing is most commonly used to animate such characters. This method provides an alternative for animating nonhumanoid characters that leverages motion data from a human subject performing in the style of the target character. The method consists of a statistical mapping function learned from a small set of corresponding key poses, and a physics-based optimization process to improve the physical realism.

1.3.1.3 Motion Editing

1.3.1.3 Motion Editing   Based on the existing motion capture data, the techniques of motion editing allow users to modify the features of the motion to meet their new requirements. In general, the input of the motion editing system is in single motion clips. In the following section, we shall review these techniques. **Motion Signal Processing:** In 1995, Bruderlin and Williams [55] successfully applied techniques from the image and signal processing domain to designing, modifying, and adapting animated motion. In their opinion, the multiresolution motion filtering, multitarget motion interpolation with dynamic timewarping, waveshaping and motion displacement mapping are well suited to the reuse and adaptation of existing motion data such as joint angles, joint coordinates or higher level motion parameters

Figure 1.8   Nonhumanoid characters animated using human motion capture data.

of articulated figures with many degrees of freedom. Thus, existing motions can be modified and combined interactively and at a higher level of abstraction than supported by conventional systems. Unuma et al. [295] presented a method for modeling human figure locomotion. In this approach, Fourier expansions of experimental data of actual human behaviors serve as a basis from which the method can interpolate or extrapolate human locomotion. This means, for instance, that transition from a walk to a run is smoothly and realistically performed by the method. Moreover, an individual's character or mood appearing during the human behaviors is also extracted by the method. For example, the method gets "briskness" from the experimental data for a "normal" walk and a "brisk" walk. Then the "brisk" run is generated by the method, using another Fourier expansion of the measured data of running. The superimposition of these human behaviors is shown as an efficient technique for generating rich variations of human locomotion. In addition, step-length, speed, and hip position during locomotion are also modeled, and interactively controlled to get a desired animation.

Keyframe Editing and Motion Deformation: The basic idea of keyframe editing is to put constraints on the keyframes from original motion data. The gestures of these characters in keyframes are deformed according to the specification of users, and the inbetween frames are generated by using an interpolation algorithm. In using these techniques, the results of motion editing are affected by the keyframe selection.

If sufficient and appropriate keyframes are selected, smooth and natural motions can be generated. The motion editing technique proposed in [44] is based on the idea of keyframe editing. In real application, it might be not easy to edit the keyframes; thus, Witkin and Popovic [322] proposed a novel technique called motion warping. Unlike the technique of keyframe editing, motion warping conducts interpolation between the difference of the task motion and the source motion. One typical procedure of the motion warping system can be divided into two steps [221]: First, the inverse kinematics is adopted to achieve the constrained optimization of the keyframes, and interpolation is conducted to obtain the variance. In recent years, Sok et al. [260] proposed an integrated framework for interactive editing of the momentum and external forces in a motion capture sequence. This framework allows users to control the momentum and forces, which provides a powerful and intuitive editing tool for dynamic motions. Neff and Kim [209] proposed a system for editing motion data that is particularly well suited to making stylistic changes. This approach transforms the joint angle representation of animation data into a set of pose parameters more suitable for editing. These motion drives include position data for the wrists, ankles, and center of mass, as well as the rotation of the pelvis. In this system, an animator can interactively edit the motion by performing linear operations on the motion drives or extracted correlations, or by layering additional correlations.

Motion Path Editing: The motion capture data have a specified trajectory (motion path), and path modification is a necessary step for animation production. Michael Gleicher [92] introduced the motion path editing algorithm, which records the trajectory of the skeleton's joints as the character's motion path and adopts B-spline to describe it. After the user has interactively changed the formation of the path, the parameters of the original path curve are adopted to resample and recalculate the transition and rotation parameters for each frame. Thus, the spatial-time constraint of the original motion data can be preserved; meanwhile, the purpose of changing the path formation can be achieved. Recently, Lockwood and Singh [180] presented a system for interactive kinematic editing of motion paths and timing that employs various biomechanical observations to augment and restrict the edited motion. Realistic path manipulations are enforced by restricting user interaction to handles identified along a motion path using motion extrema. An as-rigid-as-possible deformation technique modified specifically for use on motion paths is used to deform the path to satisfy the user-manipulated handle positions. After all motion poses have been adjusted to satisfy the new path, an automatic time-warping step modifies the timing of the new motion to preserve the timing qualities of the original motion.

Spatial-Time-Constraint-Based Motion Editing: The difference between spatial-time-constraint-based motion editing and other motion editing techniques is that this method does not handle isolated frames. Here, the spatial-time constraint means that a group of motion frames are simultaneously processed. In early research work, the spatial-time constraints were initially used to denote the positions of characters in the specified time. The optimal postures of the characters were then obtained in these positions. In the early research work [321, 71], the physical rules are used as constraints of the motion, and the objective function of changing the character's motion is constructed to take the consumption of energy into consideration. Finally, the minimization of the objective function is conducted to obtain the new motion. In Ref. [93], Gleicher and Litwinowicz made improvements in spatial-time constraint-based motion editing by using a novel objection function, and they provided real-time interactive editing functions in this approach. In recent years, novel motion editing techniques have been proposed to achieve complex motion reuse. Complex acrobatic stunts, such as double or triple flips, can be performed only by highly skilled athletes. On the other hand, simpler tricks, such as single-flip jumps, are relatively easy to master. Majkowska and Faloutsos [189] presented a method for creating complex, multi-flip ballistic motions from simple, single-flip jumps. This approach allows an animator to interact with the system by introducing modifications to a ballistic phase of a motion. This method automatically adjusts motion trajectories to ensure the physical validity of the motion after the modifications. The presented technique is efficient and produces physically valid results without resorting to computationally expensive optimization. Hsu et al. [117] provided a time-warping technique which allows users to modify timing without affecting poses. This technique has many motion editing applications in animation systems, such as refining motions to meet new timing constraints or modifying the action of animated characters. The proposed approach simplifies the whole process by allowing time warps to be guided by a provided reference motion. Given few timing constraints, it computes a warp that both satisfies these constraints and maximizes local timing similarities to the reference. Compared with existing methods, this algorithm is fast enough to incorporate into standard animation workflows. Similar ideas of using time constraints in motion editing can be found in Ref. [168, 121, 205].

1.3.1.4 *Motion synthesis*

The task of motion synthesis is to combine multiple motion clips into novel motion. It is very challenging because it is not obvious how many data may be generalized. For example, an unrealistic animation may be generated by blending two motion clips. In this case, researchers have tried to apply machine learning to make example-based motion synthesis possible.

Motion Transition and Motion Blending: Motion transition seamlessly integrates two motion clips into one long motion. The typical technique for motion transition is verbs and adverbs [240]. Based on machine learning theory, this technique is proposed to create a generative model of motion through regression. The motion clips representing a class of motion (e.g., walking, waving, etc.) are collected by users. These clips are then manually placed in an n-dimensional parameter space determined by the user, and the technique of scattered data interpolation is adopted to synthesize the novel motions.

In such an approach of motion transition, the location of good transition points in the motion stream is critical. Wang and Bodenheimer [308] proposed a method to evaluate the cost function for determining such transition points. A set of optimal weights for the cost function is compared using a constrained least-squares technique. The weights are then evaluated in two ways: first, through a cross-validation study and second, through a medium-scale user study. The cross-validation shows that the optimized weights are robust and work for a wide variety of behaviors. The user study demonstrates that the optimized weights select more appealing transition points than the original weights.

Motion blending can be defined as averaging multiple motion clips to obtain the novel motion data. The importance of motion blending is that it achieves time registration of the motion clips. The techniques of time warping [222, 223] have been commonly used. In motion transition, the technique of motion blending has been used. Menardais et al. [194] proposed a real-time motion blending algorithm, which achieves smooth motion blending by averaging multiple motions. Furthermore, Wang and Bodenheimer [309] adopted linear blending to determine visually appealing motion transitions.

Motion-Graph-based Motion Synthesis: Motion graph modeling, initially proposed in Ref.[145], consists both of pieces of original motion and automatically generated transitions. Motion can be generated simply by building walks on the graph. A general framework for extracting particular graph walks is presented to meet a user's specification. Details of motion graph are presented in Figure 1.9. In recent years, a group of novel motion synthesis methods have been proposed based on this technique. Gleicher et al. [94] applied this technique to virtual environments and games. In their research, an approach called Snap-Together Motion (STM) preprocesses a corpus of motion capture examples into a set of short clips which can be concatenated to make continuous streams of motion. The result process is a simple graph structure that facilitates efficient planning of character motions. A user-guided process selects "common" character poses and the system automatically synthesizes multiway transitions that connect through these poses. In this manner, well-connected graphs can be constructed to suit a particular application, allowing for practical interactive control without the effort of manually specifying all transitions. Li et al. [336] adopted a statistical technique called a linear dynamic system (LDS) to perform linear function approximation. A graph is constructed to model the transitions that can occur between the LDS's.

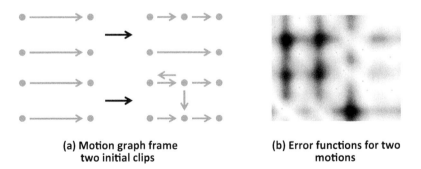

(a) Motion graph frame
two initial clips

(b) Error functions for two
motions

Figure 1.9   (a) Motion graph built frame with two initial clips. A node can be trivially inserted to divide an initial clip into two smaller clips. (b) An example error function for two motions. The entry at *(i; j)* contains the error for making a transition from the *i*th frame of the first motion to the *j*th frame of the second. White values correspond to lower errors and black values to higher errors. The dots represent local minima.

Motion-graph-based methods are popularly used to synthesize long motions by playing back a sequence of existing motion clips. However, motion graphs only support transitions between similar frames. In Ref.[234], an optimization-based graph was introduced to combine continuous constrained optimization with motion-graph-based motion synthesis. The constrained optimization is used to create a vast number of complex realistic-looking transitions in the graph. The graph can then be used to synthesize long motions with nontrivial transitions that for example allow the character to switch its behavior abruptly while retaining motion naturalness. Beaudoin et al. [30] presented a technique called motion-motif graph, which represents clusters of similar motions. Together with their encompassing motion graph, they lend understandable structure to the contents and connectivity of large motion datasets. They can be used in support of motion compression, the removal of redundant motions, and the creation of blend spaces. This research develops a string-based motif-finding algorithm which allows for a user-controlled compromise between motif length and the number of motions in a motif.

The above motion-graph-based approaches have shown great promise for novice users due to their ability to generate long motions and the fully automatic process of motion synthesis. The performance of motion-graph-based approaches, however, relies heavily on selecting a good set of motions to build the graph. The motion set needs to contain enough motions to achieve good connectivity and smooth transitions. At the same time, the motion set needs to be small enough for fast motion synthesis. Manually selecting a good motion set that achieves these requirements is difficult; hence, Zhao et al. [355] proposed an automatic approach to select a good motion set. Here, the motion selection problem is presented as a search for a minimum-size subgraph from a large motion graph representing the motion capture database. This approach especially benefits novice users who desire simple and fully automatic motion synthesis tools. To obtain better motion graphs, Reitsma and Pollard [217] described a method for using task-based metrics to evaluate the capability of a motion graph to create the set of animations required by a particular application. This capability is examined for typical motion graphs across a range of tasks and environments. The results of this approach can be used to evaluate the extent to which a motion graph will fulfill the requirements of a particular application, lessening the risk of the data structure performing poorly at an inopportune moment. The method can also be used to characterize the deficiencies of this technique whose performance will not be sufficient, as well as to evaluate the relative effectiveness of different options for improving those techniques. A similar idea has been applied in Ref.[356].

Subspace Learning-Based Motion Synthesis: The basis of subspace-learning-based motion synthesis is to project the original high-dimensional motion data into a simple low-dimensional subspace. Motion editing and synthesis are conducted in this new space, and the results are projected back to the high-dimensional space. It is a typical integration of machine learning techniques and computer animation. Alex and Muller [15] adopted principle component to represent the animation frames, while Mori and Hoshino [201] used the Independent Component Analysis (ICA) to obtain the sparse gesture subspace for realistic human motion synthesis. First, independent motion features are extracted from the original high-dimensional motion capture data to construct the ICA subspace. Then, the new human motion data are generated through interpolation in the ICA subspace. Similarly, Glardon et al. [90, 89] adopted PCA to project the motion data into the low-dimensional space. The operations of interpolation/extrapolation are conducted in this new space to obtain new motions with different speed. It can also be reused in new characters with different skeletons. Safonova et al. [243] utilized manifold learning and regression to combine motor controller-based motion synthesis and data-driven synthesis (as shown in Figure 1.10). In this method, a small number of similar motion clips are connected by the user, and dimensionality reduction is then performed on the data using PCA. The synthesis is guided through optimization, seeking useful paths on the manifold. A similar idea can be found in [61].

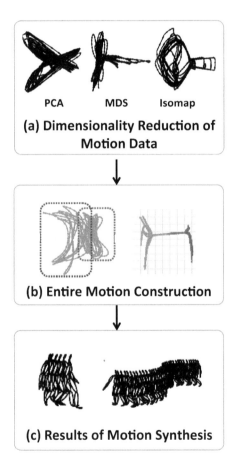

Figure 1.10 Projection of walking motion into low-dimensional space (a) Dimensionality reduction of motion data through PCA, MDS, and Isomap (b) Entire motion construction (c) Results of motion synthesis.

Parameterization-Based Motion Synthesis: Parameterization methods have been adopted by some researchers to represent human gestures. In motion synthesis, the new motions are generated by assigning parameter values. Rose et al. [240] provided an interesting technique which builds on verbs and adverbs. In this method, an unstructured motion data library is automatically processed, segmented, and classified into similar motion classes. Finally, motion synthesis is conducted by scattered data interpolation. Kovar and Gleicher [144] provide an automated method for identifying logically similar motions in a data set and use them to build a continuous and intuitively parameterized space of motions. To find logically similar motions that are numerically dissimilar, this method employs a novel distance metric to find "close" motions and then uses them as intermediaries to find more distant motions. Once a set of related motions has been extracted, they are automatically registered and blending techniques are applied to generate a continuous motion space. This algorithm extends previous work by explicitly constraining blend weights to reasonable values and having a runtime cost that is almost independent of the number of example motions. The scheme of this method is presented in Figure 1.11.

Figure 1.11 Visualization of the accessible locations for varied motions. In the left and right blocks, large red cubes show parameters of example motions; small gray cubes are sampled parameters.

Mukai and Kuriyama [204] proposed a common motion interpolation technique for realistic human animation, which is achieved by blending similar motion samples with weighting functions whose parameters are embedded in an abstract space. This method treats motion interpolations as statistical predictions of missing data in an arbitrarily definable parametric space. A practical technique is then introduced for statistically estimating the correlations between the dissimilarity of motions and the distance in the parametric space. Ahmed et al. [14] presented the employment of motion blending with time-warping for realistic parametric motion generation. This approach allows the animator to define the desired motion using its natural parameters, such as speed. Analysis has also been carried out to investigate the relationship between the walking speed and blending factor to remove the burden of trial and errors from the animator. As a result, a realistic walking motion with the speed specified by the user can be generated. The approaches proposed in Ref.[109] [302] integrated the control of the motion parameters in the motion graph techniques; thus, users can obtain motion data according to the input parameters. A similar idea can be found in Ref.[187] and [179].

Certain techniques [21, 94], based on machine learning techniques, concatenate disjointed segments of motion data to create novel motions. For instance, Arikan and Forsyth [21] adopted a support vector machine (SVM) to classify motion frames into behavior classes defined by the user, and Lee et al. [158] performed clustering of motion data to speed up motion synthesis. A totally different approach is taken by Lim and Thalmann [174]. An existing motion clip is interactively evolved into a new motion through the guidance of a user; no fitness function is required. In other words, the system produces candidate motion clips and the user specifies those he/she does and does not like. The genetic algorithm uses this feedback to produce the next generation of candidate motions. Through this technique, the user can easily modify the style of an existing animation (e.g., change the mood of a walking motion).

1.3.2   Physically based Computer Animation

Physically based computer animation is about simulating the physics of a system for graphical purposes. The techniques of physically based animation have been widely used in fluid simulations, including water animation, smoke animation, and explosion animation, as well as being successfully applied to character animation. Physically based methods have been used in other interesting fields, such as sound simulation and cloth animation. In this section, the research work of physically based animation is presented according to these three categories.

1.3.2.1   Physically Based Fluid Simulation   Pighin et al. [229] proposed a method for modeling incompressible fluid flows in which massless particles are advected through the fluid, and their paths are recorded. The entire fluid volume may then be reconstructed by interpolating these RBFs at a given time. Zheng et al. [360] proposed a fast dual-domain multiple boundary-integral solver, with linear complexity in the fluid domain's boundary. Enhancements are proposed for robust evaluation, noise elimination, acceleration, and parallelization. Wicke et al. [320] proposed a finite element simulation method that addresses the full range of material behavior, from purely elastic to highly plastic, for physical domains that are substantially reshaped by plastic flow, fracture, or large elastic deformations. By using this method, a dynamic meshing algorithm refines the drop while maintaining high-quality tetrahedra. At the narrowest part of the tendril, the mesher creates small, anisotropic tetrahedral where the strain gradient is anisotropic, so that a modest number is adequate. Work hardening causes the tendril to become brittle, whereupon it fractures.

Thurey et al. [292] presented a multiscale approach to mesh-based surface tension flows. In this approach, surface tension flows are simulated using a mesh-based surface representation. Lentine et al. [165] provided a novel algorithm for incompressible flow using only a coarse grid projection. This algorithm scales well to very large grids and large numbers of processors, allowing for high-fidelity simulations that would otherwise be intractable. Yu and Turk [344] proposed a novel surface reconstruction method for particle-based fluid simulators such as Smoothed Particle Hydrodynamics. In particle-based simulations, fluid surfaces are usually defined as a level set of an implicit function. Ando and Tsuruno [17] proposed a particle-based algorithm that preserves thin fluid sheets. This algorithm is effective in creating thin liquid animations and is capable of producing visually complex thin liquid animations. The scheme of this approach is presented in Figure 1.12.

Visualized Splash with Particles   →   Newly Inserted Particles with Pink Points   →   Results of Surface Generation

Figure 1.12   Water splash by the particle-based algorithm. The first and second diagrams: A visualized splash with particles. The pink points indicate newly inserted particles. The third diagram: A thin surface generated by anisotropic kernels.

Hong et al. [114] proposed a hybrid of Eulerian grid-based simulation and Lagrangian SPH for the realistic simulation of multiphase fluids, focusing on bubbles. Using this heuristic bubble model, they generated natural-looking computer generated bubbly water and formable objects, as well as both volumetric objects and thin shells. Zhao et al. [359] provided a framework to integrate turbulence to an existing/ongoing flow suitable for graphical controls. Compared to direct field addition, this framework avoids artificial and complex coupling by solving integration inside the NS solvers. Other techniques have been proposed for liquid simulation. Brochu et al. [251] provided a Eulerian liquid simulation framework based on the Voronoi diagram of a potentially unorganized collection of pressure, and they presented a simplified Voronoi Delaunay mesh velocity interpolation scheme and a direct extension of embedded free surfaces and solid boundaries to Voronoi meshes. Wojtan et al. [323] proposed a mesh-based surface tracking method for fluid animation that both preserves fine surface detail and robustly adjusts the topology of the surface in the presence of arbitrarily thin features such as sheets and strands. The interaction between objects and liquid has also been studied in fluid simulation. For example, Mihalef et al. [197] proposed a new Eulerian-Lagrangian method for physics-based simulation of fluid flow, which includes automatic generation of subscale spray and bubbles. The Marker Level Set method is used to provide a simple geometric criterion for free marker generation. Mosher et al. [202] proposed a novel solid/fluid coupling method that treats the coupled system in a fully implicit manner, making it stable for arbitrary time steps, large density ratios, and so on. The procedure is presented in Figure 1.13. Kim et al. [137] provided a novel wavelet method for the simulation of fluids at high spatial resolution. The algorithm enables large- and small-scale detail to be edited separately, allowing high-resolution detail to be added as a post-processing step.

Lenaerts et al. [163] proposed an SPH method for simulating the interesting fluid flowing through a porous material. Rigid and deformable objects are sampled by particles which represent local porosity and permeability distributions at a macroscopic scale. Figure 1.14 shows the simulation results.

Rigid Balls in a pool of water

Water splashes out of an cloth bag

Cloth Pulled Out of Water

Figure 1.13 Left: Many rigid balls with varying densities plunge into a pool of water. Center: Water splashes out of an elastic cloth bag. Right: Cloth pulled out of water.

Result of Fluid Flow Caused by Twisting a Wet Cloth

Result of Pouring Water against a Dry Cubic Sponge

Figure 1.14 Left: Result of fluid flow caused by twisting a wet cloth. Right: Result of pouring water against a dry cubic sponge.

Another popular application of fluid simulation is smoke animation. Robinson-Mosher et al. [239] proposed a novel method for obtaining more accurate tangential velocities for solid fluid coupling. This method works for both rigid and deformable objects as well as both volumetric objects and thin shells.

Narain et al. [208] proposed a novel technique for the animation of turbulent smoke by coupling a procedural turbulence model with a numerical fluid solver to introduce subgrid-scale flow detail. From the large-scale flow simulated by the solver, this models the production and behavior of turbulent energy using a physically motivated energy model, as shown in Figure 1.15.

Nielsen et al. [212] proposed a novel approach to guiding Eulerian-based smoke animations coupled simulations at different grid resolutions. They present a variational formulation that allows smoke animations to adopt low-frequency features from a lower resolution simulation (or nonphysical synthesis) while simultaneously developing higher frequencies. Lentine et al. [164] proposed a novel algorithm (shown in Figure 1.16) for mass and momentum conservation in incompressible flow and designed a new advection method using the basic building blocks used in semi-Lagrangian advection, which is known to work well for inviscid flows, coarse grids, and large time steps, a scenario common in computer graphics.

Nielsen and Christensen [211] proposed an improved mathematical model for Eulerian-based simulations which is better suited to dynamic, time-dependent guid-

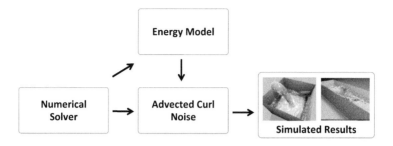

Figure 1.15   The framework of producing turbulent energy using a physically motivated energy model.

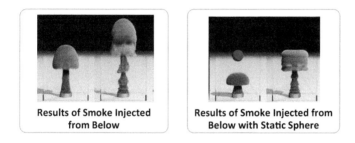

Figure 1.16   Left: Results of smoke injected from below. Right: Results of smoke injected from below with static sphere.

ance of smoke animations through a novel variational coupling of low-and high-resolution simulations. The procedure is shown in Figure 1.17.

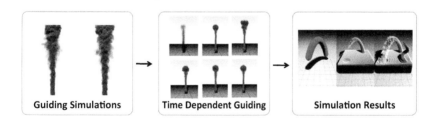

Figure 1.17   The framework of guiding simulations with a user-created flow.

Apart from water and smoke simulation, the flow effects of explosion have been explored in recent researches. Kwatra et al. [147] proposed a novel approach incorporating the ability to handle both the initial states of an explosion (including shock waves) along with the long time behavior of rolling plumes and other incompressible flow effects (as shown in Figure 1.18). In addition, Kawada and Kanai [135] provided another novel method to procedurally model explosion phenomena by considering physical properties along control paths specified by the user. The intention of the user can be taken into account by this method, and at the same time explosion flows with complex behaviors can be realized by considering the propagations of the pressure and density flow, the fuel combustion and the detonation state to represent the drastic pressure change.

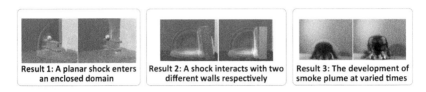

Result 1: A planar shock enters an enclosed domain   Result 2: A shock interacts with two different walls respectively   Result 3: The development of smoke plume at varied times

Figure 1.18 Left: A planar shock enters an enclosed domain. Middle: A shock interacts with two different walls respectively. Right: The development of smoke plume at varied times.

1.3.2.2 Physically Based Character Animation Over the decades, physically based techniques have been widely used in character animation. A typical example is NeuroAnimator [97], in which an artificial neural network performs function approximation of a physics system. James and Fatahalian [124] proposed a technique for the animation of deformable objects, as shown in Figure 1.19. This technique takes a tabulated approach to function approximation. The state is represented as the shape of an object, and then n distinct paths through the state space are sampled and stored without modification.

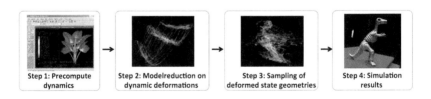

Step 1: Precompute dynamics   Step 2: Modelreduction on dynamic deformations   Step 3: Sampling of deformed state geometries   Step 4: Simulation results

Figure 1.19 Accelerated physically based animation through precomputation.

In motion synthesis and reuse, the physical property provides some specific and useful constraints. Though some physical properties can be used as spatial constraints, more properties are neglected to improve the algorithm's performance. One typical example is that Newton's laws are always neglected. Nevertheless, these properties are important in motion synthesis; for example, Popovic and Witkin [232] proposed a system of physically based motion transformation which preserves the essential physical properties of the motion. By using the spacetime constraints dynamics formulation, this algorithm maintains the realism of the original motion sequence without sacrificing full user control of the editing process. Recently, some researchers have proposed dynamic-based realistic motion synthesis methods; for example, based on motion capture data, Zordan et al. [367] introduced a novel technique for incorporating unexpected impacts into a motion-capture-driven animation system through the combination of a physical simulation which responds to contact forces and a specialized search routine. Using an actuated dynamic model, this system generates a physics-based response while connecting motion capture segments. This method allows characters to respond to unexpected changes in the environment based on the specific dynamic effects of a given contact while also taking advantage of the realistic movement made available through motion capture. To solve the problem of synthesizing the movements of a responsive virtual character in the event of unexpected perturbations, Ye and Liu [334] devised a fully automatic method which learns a nonlinear probabilistic model of dynamic responses from very few perturbed walking sequences. This model is able to synthesize responses and recovery motions under new perturbations different from those in the training examples. When perturbations occur, a physics-based method is adopted to initiate motion transitions to the most probable response example based on the dynamic states of the character. The effect of the proposed approach is shown in Figure 1.20.

Figure 1.20   The framework of perturbations of motion in different cases. The directions are indicated by the arrows, and the motion of the body is modified by the perturbations.

More related methods have been put forward. Ye and Liu [333] proposed a technique to enhance a kinematically controlled virtual character with a generic class of dynamic responses to small perturbations. This method re-parameterizes the motion degrees of freedom based on joint actuations in the input motion and can create physically responsive motion based on kinematic pose control without explicitly computing the joint actuations (as shown in Figure 1.21). Muico et al. [203] proposed algorithms that construct composite controllers to track multiple trajectories in parallel instead of sequentially switching from one control to another. The composite controllers can blend or transition between different path controllers at arbitrary times according to the current system state. Kwon and Hodgins [149] provided a balancing control algorithm based on a simplified dynamic model: an inverted pendulum on a cart. At runtime, the controller plans a desired motion at every frame based on the current estimate of the pendulum state and a predicted pendulum trajectory. Lee et al. [161] proposed a dynamic controller to physically simulate underactuated three-dimensional full-body biped locomotion. The data-driven controller takes motion capture reference data to reproduce realistic human locomotion through real-time physically based simulation. Lasa et al. [154] presented an approach to the control of physics-based characters based on high-level features of movement, such as center of mass, angular momentum, and end-effectors. More similar ideas of using the physical properties in motion synthesis can be found in Ref.[177, 9, 178, 252, 162, 148, 310, 123, 182, 122].

Figure 1.21   The framework of controlling virtual character with a generic class of dynamic responses to small perturbations.

1.3.2.3 Other Physically-Based Animation Systems   Physically based methods have also been implemented in other interesting research fields. For instance, Cordier and Magnenat-Thalmann [73] proposed a technique in precomputing cloth animation. In this technique, cloth is simulated offline and analyzed with respect to the underlying humanoid. Volino et al. [298] proposed a simple approach to non-linear tensile stiffness for accurate cloth simulation (as shown in Figure 1.22). This approach proposes a new simulation model that accurately reproduces the nonlinear tensile behavior of cloth materials which remains accurate and robust for very large deformations, while offering a very simple and streamlined computation process suitable for a high-performance simulation system. Kaldor et al. [132] presented a method for approximating penalty-based contact forces in yarn-yarn collisions by computing the exact contact response at one time step, then using a rotated linear force model to approximate forces in nearby deformed configurations. Aguiar et al. [12] proposed a technique for learning clothing models that enables the simultaneous animation of thousands of detailed garments in real time. This surprisingly simple conditional model learns and preserves the key dynamic properties of cloth motion along with folding details. Ozgen et al. [216] proposed a particle-based cloth model where half-derivative viscoelastic elements are included for describing both the internal and external dynamics of the cloth. These elements model the cloth responses to fluid stresses and are also able to emulate the memory-laden behavior of particles in a viscous fluid. The results are shown in Figure 1.23.

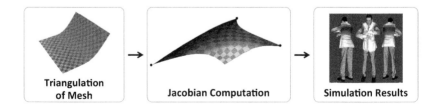

Figure 1.22   The accurate simulation of nonlinear anisotropic cloth materials is required for garment prototyping applications.

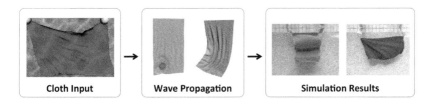

| Cloth Input | Wave Propagation | Simulation Results |

Figure 1.23   The cloth model based on fractional derivatives is able to achieve realistic underwater deformation behavior.

Fire synthesis is another interesting application of physically based simulation. Chadwick and James [64] proposed a practical method for synthesizing plausible fire sounds that are synchronized with physically based fire animations (as shown in Figure 1.24).

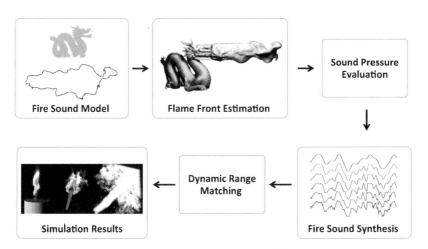

Figure 1.24   The framework of fire sound synthesis which produces the familiar sound of roaring flames synchronized with an underlying low-frequency physically based flame simulation.

1.3.3 Computer-Assisted Cartoon Animation

Cartoon animation is a popular and successful media form in contemporary life. Its creation is usually high-cost and labor-intensive, especially in traditional 2D cartoon production which includes many steps, e.g., keyframing, inbetweening, and painting. On the other hand, given the relatively long history of animation, there is a large-scale "cartoon library" that consists of various animation materials including character design, story board, scenes, and episodes, which is useful for animators and cartoon enthusiasts for effectively creating new animations by reusing and synthesizing.

Many attempts have been made in computer-aided animation, video-based cartoon generation and data driven-based cartoon synthesis to face these opportunities and challenges [67, 143, 131, 105, 195]. The following content examines these three aspects.

1.3.3.1 Computer-Aided Cartoon Animation

In a traditional computer-aided cartoon animation system, high-quality auto-inbetweening and auto-coloring is achieved by constructing accurate correspondences between keyframe objects, with which inbetween frames can be generated by interpolating corresponding objects and colors can thus be propagated. Early work on correspondence construction-based inbetweening was proposed in Ref.[82], where a manual correspondence setting for a vectorization process which digitizes traditional animation production to build a "paperless" system was mentioned. Subsequently, Kort [143] provided an interactive cartoon system for automatic inbetweening with a possible solution for the "undetectable" parts noticed in Ref. [82]. Whited et al. [319] proposed the "BetweenIT" system for the user-guided automation of tight inbetweening. They designed a set of user-guided semi-automatic techniques that fit well with current practice and minimize the number of required artist gestures. The performance of this system is shown in Figure 1.25. Baxter et al. [29] proposed a set of algorithms for the compatible embedding of 2D shapes. Such embeddings offer a convenient way to interpolate shapes with complicated structures and detailed features. This system has the advantages of less user input with faster and more robust implementation, which make it ideal for interactive use in practical applications.

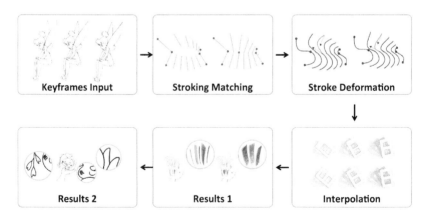

Figure 1.25   The framework for the user-guided automation of tight inbetweening.

Apart from these traditional interpolation-based systems, other computer-aided systems with novel ideas have been proposed for complicated cartoon animation production. Rivers et al. [237] proposed a method to bring cartoon objects and characters into the third dimension by giving them the ability to rotate and be viewed from any angle. Figure 1.26 shows how 2D vector art drawings of a cartoon from different views can be used to generate a novel structure, the 2.5D cartoon model, which can be used to simulate 3D rotations and generate plausible renderings of the cartoon from any view.

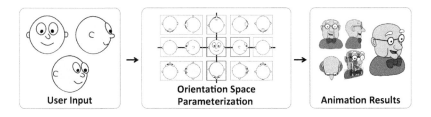

Figure 1.26   The framework of a 2.5D cartoon.(a) Taking the vector art drawings of a cartoon from different views. (b) Parameterizing orientation space with different views. (c) Generating a 2.5D cartoon automatically, which associates each stroke with a 3D position.

In recent years, Sykora and his colleagues have proposed a group of novel techniques [276, 275, 277] to enhance automatic 2D cartoon generation. In automatic depth generation, they proposed a novel interactive approach to cartoon pop-up that enables artists to quickly annotate their hand-made drawings and animations with additional depth information [276]. The scheme of this method is shown in Figure 1.27. In automatic coloring, they provided a novel color-by-example technique [275] which combines image segmentation, patch-based sampling, and probabilistic reasoning. This method is able to automate colorization when new color information is applied on the already designed black-and-white cartoon. The results are shown in Figure 1.28. A "LazyBrush" [277] is provided by their research group. "LazyBrush" is a new interactive tool which is used for painting hand-made cartoon drawings, based on an optimization framework that tries to mimic the behavior of an ideal painting tool as proposed by professional illustrators. In the field of automatic cartoon character generation, the researchers presented a new approach [274] to deformable image registration based on an approach analogous to the dynamic simulation of deformable objects. They adopted a novel geometrically motivated iterative scheme in which point movements are decoupled from shape consistency. By combining locally optimal block matching with as-rigid-as-possible shape regularization, this algorithm allows users to register images undergoing large free-form deformations and appearance variations.

Barnes et al. [28] proposed a novel interface for creating cutout style animations by manipulating paper puppets. The system relies on easy to use components for creating puppets, combined with a natural interface for controlling them. This system is presented in Figure 1.29.

Some researchers are focusing on the effects of light, shade, and smoke. McGuire and Fein [193] proposed an algorithm for rendering animated smoke particle systems in a cartoon style which includes outlines and cel-shading. They combine the renderer with a fast simulator that generates the phenomenology of real smoke but has artistically controllable parameters. Together they produce real-time interactive smoke animations at over 30 fps. Selle et al. [249] proposed a technique for rendering

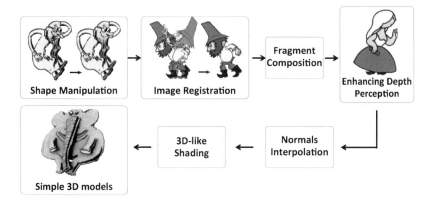

Figure 1.27   Examples of a pop-ups cartoon generating system.

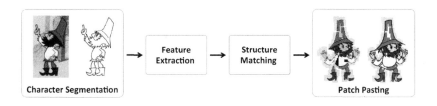

Figure 1.28   The framework of automatic colorization applied on the already designed black and white cartoon.

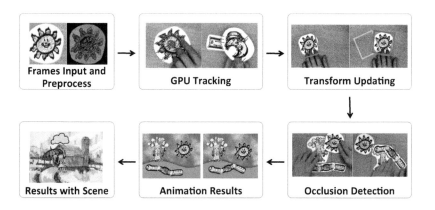

Figure 1.29   The framework of manipulating cutout paper puppets tracked in real time to control an animation.

stylized smoke. The underlying dynamics of the smoke are generated with a standard Navier-Stokes fluid simulator and output in the form of advected marker particles.

The results are shown in Figure 1.30. Anjyo [19] proposed a direct manipulation method that allows users to create and edit stylized highlights and cartoon-shaded areas in realtime, essentially with only click-and-drag operations. This method provides intuitive click-and drag operations for translating and deforming the shaded areas, including rotation, directional scaling, splitting, and squaring of highlights, all without tedious parameter tuning. The results can be found in Figure 1.31.

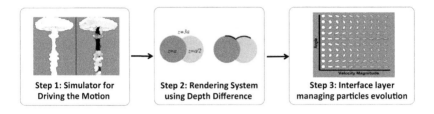

Figure 1.30   The framework of rendering stylized smoke.

Figure 1.31   Direct manipulation of stylized shading.

1.3.3.2 *Video-Based Cartoon Generation*

The computer-aided systems discussed above are designed to reduce the time cost of cartoon production; however, many skillful interactions are required due to the lack of effective cartoon representation. The quality of the obtained animation mainly relies on traditional manual production methods; therefore, these systems are specifically designed for professionals rather than nonprofessional users who produce cartoons for different purposes, such as fun and education. These drawbacks prompt researchers to provide novel systems which will allow users to quickly and efficiently generate cartoons from existing videos.

Liang et al. [173] proposed a prototype system for generating 3D cartoons from broadcast soccer video. This system takes advantage of computer vision and computer graphics techniques to provide users with a new experience which cannot be obtained from the original video. Collomosse et al. [72] proposed a novel NPR framework for synthesizing nonphotorealistic animations from video sequences. The spatio-temporal approach adopted by the framework enables the users to smoothly vary attributes, such as region or stroke color over time, and to create improved motion estimates of objects in the video. The generated results are presented in Figure 1.32.

Wang et al. [311] proposed a system for transforming an input video into a highly abstracted, spatio-temporally coherent cartoon animation with a range of styles.

Figure 1.32 Some of the available artistic effects. Top, left to right: Cartoon flat and gradient shaded animations from the BOUNCE sequence. Mixed reality effect where original footage has been selectively matted in to a sketchy line animation. Bottom, left to right: Water color wash effect and cartoon flat shaded bears with sketchy and thick stroke outlines.

In this system, the user simply outlines objects on keyframes. A mean-shift-guided interpolation algorithm is then employed to create three dimensional semantic regions by interpolation between the keyframes while maintaining smooth trajectories along the time dimension. A variety of rendering styles is shown in Figure 1.33.

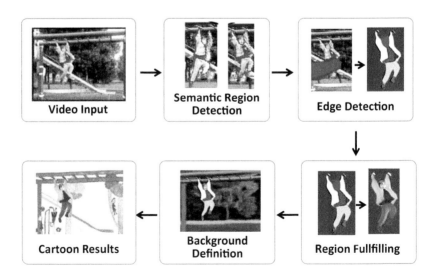

Figure 1.33 Examples created by Video Tooning with different styles.

Hays et al. [106] proposed a technique for transforming images and videos into painterly animations with different artistic styles. They determine and apply motion information from different user-specified sources to static and moving images. These properties that encode the spatio-temporal variations are then used to render (or paint) effects of selected styles to generate images and videos with a painted look. Painterly animations are generated using a mesh of brush stroke objects with dynamic spatio-temporal properties. The rendering results are shown in Figure 1.34.

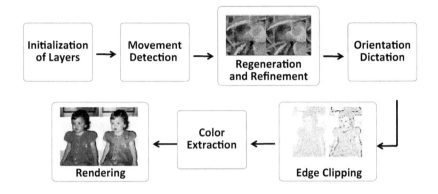

Figure 1.34   The framework of transforming images and videos into painterly animations with different artistic styles.

Lin et al. [175] provided an interactive system that stylizes an input video into a painterly animation. The system consists of two phases. The first is a Video Parsing phase that extracts and labels semantic objects with different material properties (skin, hair, cloth, and so on) in the video, and then establishes robust correspondence between frames for discriminative image features inside each object. The second Painterly Rendering phase performs the stylization based on video semantics and feature correspondence. This system can efficiently generate oil painting animations from the video clips. Similarly, Agarwala [11] proposed an interactive system that allows children and others untrained in cel animation to create two-dimensional cartoons from video streams and images. A cartoon is created in a dialogue with the system. After recording video material, the user sketches contours directly onto the first frame of the video. These sketches initialize a set of spline-based active contours which are relaxed to best fit the image and other aesthetic constraints. Small gaps are closed, and the user can choose colors for the cartoon. The system then uses motion estimation techniques to track these contours through the image sequence. The user remains in the process to edit the cartoon as it progresses. Some results are shown in Figure 1.35.

1.3.3.3 *Data-Driven-Based Cartoon Synthesis*   Data driven approaches have been widely used in cartoon animation; for instance, motion data are applied to drive the cartoon characters to move. Bregler et al. [53] proposed a new technique that captures the motion style of cartoons and retargets the same style to a different domain.

Figure 1.35 Creating cartoon images of toys. (a) The original photographs. (b) The user's tracing. (c) The finished, colored cartoons.

This is done by tracking affine motion and key-shape-based interpolation weights. Figure 1.36 shows how the motion extracted from the original character is retargeted to a new character. Li et al. [172] proposed a system to animate cartoon faces from speech with emotions. This system consists of two components: emotion-driven cartoon animation and speech-driven cartoon animation.

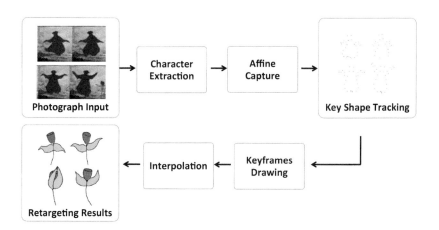

Figure 1.36 Motion of walking cartoon character retargeted to 3D model.

Another group of data-driven approaches in cartoon animation is to reuse the existing cartoon frames [342, 347] to synthesize novel animations. De Juan and Bodenheimer [131] proposed a Cartoon Clip Synthesis system which creates novel cartoon clips from existing cartoon data. This method combines sequences of similar-looking cartoon data into a user-directed sequence. Starting with a small amount of cartoon data, a nonlinear dimensionality reduction method is employed to discover a lower-dimensional structure of the data. The user selects a start and end frame and the system traverses this lower-dimensional manifold to re-sequence the data into a new animation. The performance is presented in Figure 1.37. Haevre et al. [103] proposed a novel method that facilitates the creation of endless animations or video loops for smaller-scale productions. This approach benefits from several ideas and techniques from cartoon textures, computer-assisted animation, and motion graphs. It combines the re-sequencing of existing material with the automatic generation of new data. Furthermore, the animator can interfere with the animation process at any arbitrary moment.

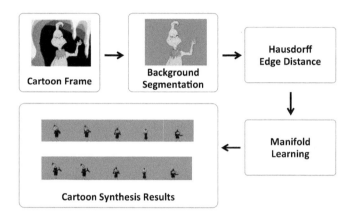

Figure 1.37   The framework of cartoon synthesis using "Cartoon Texture."

The method of cartoon texture performs well for simple cartoon characters, but for characters with complex colors and motion patterns, it fails to generate smooth clips because the edges can encode neither the color information nor the motion pattern. Therefore, Yu et al. [345] provided an efficient technique which combines both the motion difference and edge difference in similarity estimation. This model is controlled by a weight parameter.

In the linear combination method [345], it is not easy for users to determine the weights. In this case, Yu and his colleagues proposed a semi-supervised multiview subspace learning algorithm (semi-MSL) [339] to automatically combine multiple features in cartoon synthesis by using alternative optimization. In this approach, multiple features including color histogram, Hausdorff edge feature and skeleton feature, are adopted to represent cartoon characters. Retrieval-based cartoon synthesis is adopted which requires users to provide an initial character to start the retrieval. The final cartoon synthesis is conducted as an iteration process in which a group of similar cartoon characters is obtained to form new sequences. The results of cartoon synthesis are shown in Figure 1.38. The details of this approach will be introduced in the following chapters.

Cartoon character retrieval is critical for cartoonists to effectively and efficiently make cartoons by reusing existing cartoon data. To successfully achieve these tasks, it is essential to extract visual features to comprehensively represent cartoon characters and accurately estimate dissimilarity between cartoon characters. However, due to the semantic gap, the cartoon retrieval by using these visual features still cannot achieve excellent performance. Since the labeling information has been proven effective to reduce the semantic gap, Yu et al. [337] introduce a labeling procedure called Interactive Cartoon Labeling (ICL). The labeling information actually reflects userâ^s retrieval purpose. A dimension reduction tool, termed sparse transfer learning (SPA-TL) [294], is adopted to effectively and efficiently encode userâ^s search intention. In particular, SPA-TL exploits two pieces of knowledge data, i.e., the labeling knowledge contained in labeled data and the data distribution knowledge contained in all samples (labeled and unlabeled). Experimental evaluations in cartoon synthesis suggest the effectiveness of the visual features and SPA-TL. The framework is presented in Figure 1.39.

Figure 1.38   The result of retrieval-based cartoon synthesis.

1.3.4   Crowd Animation

In simulation, it is critical to create an interactive, complex, and realistic virtual world in which the user can have an immersive experience during their navigation through the world. As the size and complexity of environments in the virtual world increase, it becomes more necessary to populate them with people, and this is the reason why rendering crowds [37, 331, 76, 77, 24] in realtime is crucial. Generally, crowd animation is composed of three important areas: the realism of group behavior [291], the realism of individual behavior [157] and the integration of both. In the following section, recent developments in this field is reviewed according to these three categories.

1.3.4.1   Realism of Group Behavior   Group behavioral realism is mainly targeted for simple 2D visualizations because most of the attention is concentrated on simulating the behavior of the group. The concept is to create virtual characters

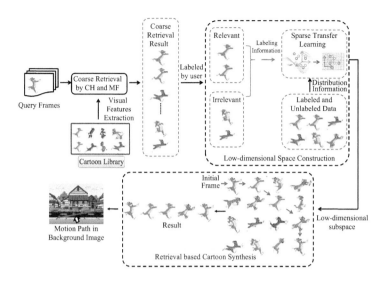

Figure 1.39   The framework of interactive cartoon reusing by sparse transfer learning (SPA-TL).

that are autonomous agents and thus self-animating. A character makes its decisions through a behavioral model: an executable model defining the character's thought process. Collision avoidance and path finding are mainly considered in this research field.

Ondrej et al. [214] proposed a novel vision-based approach of collision avoidance between walkers that fits the requirements of interactive crowd simulation. In imitation of humans, and based on cognitive science results, they detect future collisions as well as their dangerousness from visual stimuli. The simulation results are presented in Figure 1.40. Similarly, Guy et al. [101] proposed a robust algorithm for collision avoidance among multiple agents. This approach extends the notion of velocity obstacles from robotics and formulates the conditions for collision free navigation as a quadratic optimization problem. A discrete optimization method is used efficiently to compute the motion of each agent. It can robustly handle dense scenarios with tens or hundreds of thousands of heterogeneous agents in a few milliseconds. Some simulation results are presented in Figure 1.41. In addition, Lamarche and Donikian [152] provided a real-time crowd model based on continuum dynamics. In this model, a dynamic potential field simultaneously integrates global navigation with moving obstacles such as other people, efficiently solving the motion of large crowds without the need for explicit collision avoidance. Patil et al. [225] proposed a novel approach to direct and control virtual crowds using navigation fields. This method guides one or more agents toward desired goals based on guidance fields. A similar idea can be found in [256]. Paris et al. [219] proposed a method for solving interactions between pedestrians and avoiding inter-collisions. This approach is agent-based and predictive: Each agent perceives surrounding agents and extrapolates their trajectory in order to react to potential collisions. Similar works can be found in Ref. [100, 150, 278].

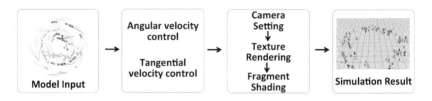

Figure 1.40   Emergent self-organized patterns appear in real crowds of walkers. This simulation displays similar effects by proposing an optic flow-based approach for steering walkers inspired by cognitive science work on human locomotion.

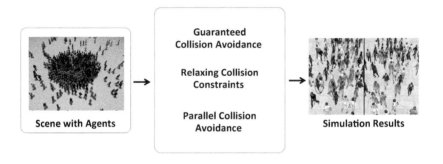

Figure 1.41   Dense Circle Scenario: 1000 agents are arranged uniformly around a circle and move towards their antipodal position. This simulation runs at over 1000 FPS on an Intel 3.14 GHz quad core, and over 8000 FPS on 32 Larrabee cores.

Apart from collision avoidance, path finding is another important issue in achieving behavioral realism in crowd simulation. Lamarche et al. [152] proposed a suitable topological structuring of the geometric environment to allow fast path finding as well as an efficient reactive navigation algorithm for virtual humans evolving inside a crowd. Putting together the high complexity of a realistic environment such as a city, a large number of virtual humans and the real-time constraint requires optimization of each aspect of the animation process. The objective of this work is to reproduce this crucial human activity inside virtual environments. The results of path finding in an indoor and outdoor scene are presented in Figure 1.42. Sung et al. [273] integrated the motion capture data into the crowd simulation offering a highly efficient motion synthesis algorithm that is well suited to animating large numbers of characters. Given constraints that require characters to be in specific poses, positions, and orientations in specified time intervals, this algorithm synthesizes motions that exactly satisfy these constraints. To provide a good initial guess for the search, they adopt a fast path planner based on probabilistic roadmaps to navigate characters through complex environments. Similarly, Lai et al. [151] proposed Group Motion Graphs, a data-driven animation technique for groups of discrete agents, such as flocks, herds or small crowds. Similar works can be found in Ref.[270].

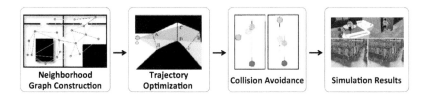

Figure 1.42   The framework of path finding for indoor and outdoor navigation.

Another interesting crowd simulation method imitates real human crowds by video tracking. Lee et al. [160] proposed a novel approach for simulating a crowd of virtual humans by recording the motion of a human crowd from an aerial view with a camcorder. Their method extract the two-dimensional moving trajectories of each individual in the crowd, and learns an agent model from observed trajectories. The agent model decides each agent's actions based on features of the environment and the motion of nearby agents in the crowd. Figure 1.43 shows the simulation results. Zhao et al. [358] proposed a model-based approach to interpret the image observations by multiple partially occluded human hypotheses in a Bayesian framework. Wang et al. [314] proposed a novel unsupervised learning framework to model activities and interactions in crowded and complicated scenes. In this framework, hierarchical Bayesian models are used to connect three elements in visual surveillance: low-level visual features, simple "atomic" activities, and interactions. A crowd synthesis method [129] has also been proposed to blend existing crowd data for the generation of a new crowd animation. The new animation includes an arbitrary number of agents, extends for an arbitrary duration, and yields a natural looking mixture of the input crowd data. Figure 1.44 illustrates the simulation results.

Additionally, Guy et al. [102] proposed a totally novel technique to generate heterogeneous crowd behaviors using personality trait theory. This formulation is based on adopting results of a user study to derive a mapping from crowd simulation parameters to the perceived behaviors of agents in computer-generated crowd simulations. The simulation results are shown in Figure 1.45.

1.3.4.2   *Realism of Individual Behavior*   Creating realistic motion for animated characters in crowds is an important problem in achieving individual realism. The use of motion capture data for animating virtual characters has become a popular technique in recent years. By capturing the movement of a real human and replaying this movement on a virtual character, the resulting motion exhibits a high degree of realism. Lau and Kuffner [157] presented a behavior planning approach to automatically generate realistic motions for animated characters in a crowd. First, the motion clips are organized into a finite-state machine (FSM) of behaviors. Each state of the FSM includes a collection of motions representing a high-level behavior. Given this behavior FSM and a pre-defined environment, this algorithm searches the FSM and

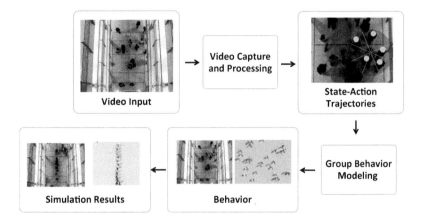

Figure 1.43   Simulation results of learning group behavior from crowd videos.

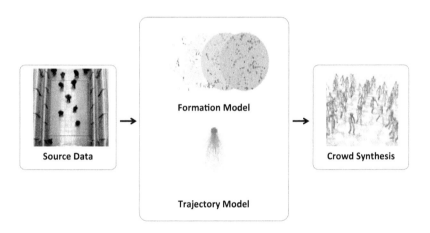

Figure 1.44   Morphable crowd models synthesize virtual crowds of any size and any length from input crowd data. The synthesized crowds can be interpolated to produce a continuous span of intervening crowd styles.

plans for a sequence of behaviors that allows the character to reach a user-specified goal. The simulation results are shown in Figure 1.46. Lerner et al. [167] proposed a data-driven approach for fitting behaviors to simulated pedestrian crowds. This method annotates agent trajectories, generated by any crowd simulator, with action-tags. The aggregate effect of animating the agents according to the tagged trajectories enhances the impression that the agents are interacting with one another and with the environment. Kim et al. [136] proposed a novel motion editing technique that allows the user to manipulate synchronized multiple character motions interactively. This method formulates the interaction among multiple characters as a collection of

Figure 1.45   Left: Pass-through Scenario. Middle: Hallway Scenario. Right: Narrowing Passage Scenario.

linear constraints and enforces the constraints, while the user directly manipulates the motion of characters in both spatial and temporal domains. The synthesized multiple character motions are presented in Figure 1.47.

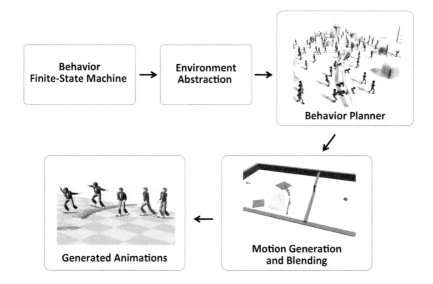

Figure 1.46   The framework of planning behaviors for animated characters navigating in a complex dynamic environment.

In addition to motion capture, the information from video tracking can be used to directly drive the characters. Lerner et al. [166] proposed a novel example-based crowd simulation technique. By learning from real-world examples contained in videos, the autonomous agents in this system display complex natural behaviors that are often missing in crowd simulations. Examples are created from tracked video segments of real pedestrian crowds. During a simulation, autonomous agents search for examples that closely match the situation that they are facing. Trajectories taken

Figure 1.47 The characters carry boxes in relay. The user interactively manipulates the synchronized multicharacter motion to shape a spiral.

by real people in similar situations are copied to the simulated agents, resulting in seemingly natural behaviors. The simulation results are shown in Figure 1.48.

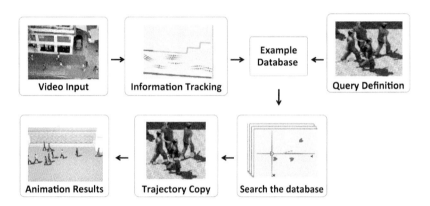

Figure 1.48 Framework of example-based crowd simulation technique. The top row depicts the construction of the database, which takes place during preprocessing: the input video is manually tracked, generating a set of trajectories which are encoded as examples and stored in the database. At runtime (bottom row) the trajectories of the agents are synthesized individually by encoding their surroundings (forming a query) and searching the database for a similar example. The trajectory from the example is copied to the simulated agent.

Sung et al. [272] presented a new approach to controlling the behavior of agents in a crowd. This method is scalable in the sense that increasingly complex crowd behaviors can be created without a corresponding increase in the complexity of the agents. Users can dynamically specify which crowd behaviors happen in various parts of an environment. Ennis et al. [80] investigated the importance of matching audio to body motion for virtual conversing characters. Yeh et al. [335] introduced the concept of composite agents to effectively model complex agent interactions for agent-based crowd simulation. Each composite agent consists of a basic agent that is associated with one or more proxy agents. This formulation allows an agent to exercise influence over other agents greater than that implied by its physical properties.

When simulating crowds, it is inevitable that the models and motions of many virtual characters will be replicated. Therefore, the perceptual impact of this trade-off should be studied. McDonnell et al. [191] proposed an algorithm to consider the ways in which an impression of variety can be created and the perceptual consequences of certain design choices. They established that replicated models can be masked by color variation, random orientation, and motion. Conversely, the perception of cloned motions remains unaffected by the model on which they are displayed. Other factors that influence the ability to detect clones were examined, such as proximity, model type and characteristic motion. The results are shown in Figure 1.49. The authors also investigated which body parts of virtual characters are most looked at in scenes containing duplicate characters or clones [192].

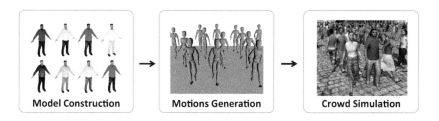

Figure 1.49   Examples of a crowd used in the Appearance Variation Experiment with the maximum number of clones.

1.3.4.3 Integration of Group Realism and Individual Realism   Some research works focus on achieving both group behavior realism and individual behavior realism; for instance, large dense crowds show aggregate behavior with reduced individual freedom of movement. Narain et al. [207] presented a novel, scalable approach for simulating such crowds, using dual representation both as discrete agents and as a single continuous system. In the continuous setting, they introduce a novel variational constraint called unilateral incompressibility to model the large-scale behavior of the crowd and accelerate inter-agent collision avoidance in dense scenarios. This method makes it possible to simulate very large, dense crowds composed of up to a hundred thousand agents at near-interactive rates on desktop computers. The simulation results are presented in Figure 1.50. Shao and Terzopoulos [250] proposed another sophisticated human animation system that combines perceptual, behavioral, and cognitive control components, whose major contribution is a comprehensive model of pedestrians as highly-capable individuals. They address the difficult open problem of emulating the rich complexity of real pedestrians in urban environments. In their approach, the comprehensive model features innovations in these components, as well as in their combination, yielding results of unprecedented fidelity and complexity for fully autonomous multi-human simulation in a large urban environment. The experimental results are presented in Figure 1.51. Pelechano et al. [227] proposed a novel system-HiDAC which focuses on the problem of simulating the local motion and global pathfinding behaviors of crowds moving in a natural manner within dynamically changing virtual environments. By applying a combination of psychological and geometrical rules with a social and physical forces model,HiDAC

exhibits a wide variety of emergent behaviors from agent line formation to pushing behavior and its consequences.

Figure 1.50   Some examples of large, dense crowds simulated with this technique.

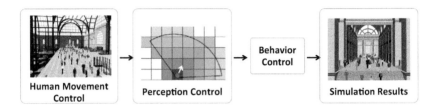

Figure 1.51   A large-scale simulation of a virtual train station populated by self-animated virtual humans.

Recent advances in local methods have significantly improved the collision avoidance behavior of virtual characters. However, existing methods fail to take into account that in real-life pedestrians tend to walk in small groups, consisting mainly of pairs or triples of individuals. Karamouzas and Overmars [133] proposed a novel approach to simulate the walking behavior of such small groups. This model describes how group members interact with each other, with other groups and individuals. In their approach, both the individual and group behavior are considered in crowd simulation. The results are shown in Figure 1.52.

(a)   (b)   (c)   (d)

Figure 1.52   Example test-case scenarios. (a) A group has to adapt its formation to pass through a doorway; (b) Group interactions in a confined environment; (c) A faster group overtakes a slower moving group; (d) A group of three agents walking through a narrow corridor.

1.3.5   Facial Animation

Recent interest in facial modeling and animation is spurred by the increasingly frequent appearance of virtual characters in film and video, inexpensive desktop processing power, and the potential for a new 3D immersive communication metaphor for human-computer interaction. According to the processed information and rendering effects, facial animation can be separated into 2D face synthesis and 3D face synthesis [176]. We review recent research developments in face animation from these two aspects.

1.3.5.1   2D Face Synthesis   According to the 2D face animation application, a variety of techniques including the statistical method, linear regression, support vector regressor and data-driven method have been applied in 2D face synthesis. The specific 2D face applications are natural face synthesis and cartoon face synthesis. Abboud and Davoine [8] presented a statistical-based method for extracting appearance parameters from a natural image or video sequence for natural face synthesis, which allows reproduction of natural-looking, expressive synthetic faces. This technique was used to perform face synthesis and tracking in video sequences as well as facial expression recognition [342, 264] and control. Leyvand et al. [170] proposed a digital face beautification method based on the optimization of a beauty function modeled by a support vector regressor. Given a new face, this method extracts a set of distances between a variety of facial feature locations which define a point in a high-dimensional "face space". The face space is then searched for a nearby point with a higher predicted attractiveness rating. Once such a point is found, the corresponding facial distances are embedded in the plane and serve as a target to define a 2D warp field which maps the original facial features to their adjusted locations. The simulation results are shown in Figure 1.53.

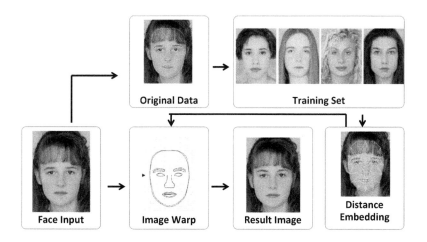

Figure 1.53   The framework of digital face beautification method.

Many systems have been proposed for cartoon face synthesis. Caricature Zone [1] is a cartoon face making system, which has stored many components of human face, such as hair, cheek, etc. Through this system, the user can select various cartoon style components to construct the specified human. UDrawFace Pro [5] adopts one human face and the user provides some interaction; the system then adopts edge detection to extract the facial features and create the cartoon face. Hsu and Jain [118] proposed semantic face graphs derived from a subset of vertices of a 3Dface model to construct cartoon faces for face matching. The cartoon faces are generated in a coarse-to-fine fashion; face detection results are used to coarsely align semantic face graphs with detected faces and interacting snakes are used to finely align face graphs with sensed face images. Chen et al. [66] presented a novel cartoon system called PicToon, which can generate a personalized cartoon face from an input Picture. PicToon is convenient to use and requires little user interaction. It consists of three major components: an image-based Cartoon Generator, an interactive Cartoon Editor for exaggeration, and a speech-driven Cartoon Animator. The framework of this method is shown in Figure 1.54.

Wang et al. [315] propose a novel face photo-sketch synthesis and recognition method using a multiscale Markov Random Fields(MRF) model. This system has three components: (1) given a face photo, synthesizing a sketch drawing; (2) given a face sketch drawing, synthesizing a photo; (3) searching for face photos in the database based on a query sketch drawn by an artist. It has useful applications for both digital entertainment and law enforcement. It is assumed that faces to be studied are in a frontal pose, with normal lighting and neutral expression, and have no occlusions. To synthesize sketch/photo images, the face region is divided into overlapping patches for learning. The size of the patches decides the scale of local face structures to be learned. From a training set which contains photo-sketch pairs, the joint photo-sketch model is learnt at multiple scales using a multiscale MRF model. By transforming a face photo to a sketch (or transforming a sketch to a photo), the difference between photos and sketches is significantly reduced, thus allowing effective matching between the two in face sketch recognition. After the photo-sketch transformation, in principle, most of the proposed face photo recognition approaches can be applied to face sketch recognition in a straightforward way. The synthesized results are presented in Figure 1.55.

Gao et al. [85] propose an automatic sketch photo synthesis and retrieval algorithm based on sparse representation. The proposed sketch-photo synthesis method (SNS-SRE) works at patch level and is composed of two steps: sparse neighbor selection (SNS) for an initial estimate of the pseudo-image (pseudo-sketch or pseudo-photo) and sparse-representation-based enhancement (SRE) for further improving the quality of the synthesized image. SNS can find closely related neighbors adaptively and then generate an initial estimate for the pseudo-image. In SRE, a coupled sparse representation model is first constructed to learn the mapping between sketch patches and photo patches, and a patch-derivative-based sparse representation method is subsequently applied to enhance the quality of the synthesized photos and sketches. Finally, four retrieval modes, namely sketch-based, photo-based, pseudo-sketch-based, and pseudo-photo-based retrieval, are proposed, and a retrieval algorithm is developed by using sparse representation. The framework of synthesis is presented in Figure 1.56.

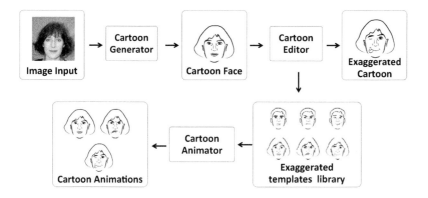

Figure 1.54   Framework of the PicToon System.

A closely related task in facial animation is speech animation. Some notable techniques are designed around machine learning. The goal is to learn how to properly animate a face so that realistic animations can be produced automatically for arbitrary speech. Ideally, the use of real-world examples should result in highly realistic animation. Realism is critical because human observers can easily detect incorrect speech animation. Some of the techniques in this area also propose integrated image-based rendering schemes. Bregler et al. [52] proposed a novel technique which can modify the movie sequence to synchronize the actor's lip motions to the new soundtrack. It uses computer-vision techniques to track points on the speaker's mouth in the training footage, and morphing techniques to combine these mouth gestures into the final video sequence. The new video combines the dynamics of the original actor's articulations with the mannerisms and setting dictated by the background footage. Ezzat et al. [81] provided a novel speech-driven method. It first records a human subject using a video camera as he/she utters a predetermined speech corpus. After processing the corpus automatically, a visual speech module is learned from the data that is capable of synthesizing the human subject's mouth uttering entirely novel utterances that were not recorded in the original video. The synthesized utterance is re-composited onto a background sequence which contains natural head and eye movement. At runtime, the input to the system can be either real audio sequences or synthetic audio produced by a text-to-speech system, as long as they have been phonetically aligned. Voice puppetry [48] is a fully automatic technique for creating novel speech animation from an example. Computer vision is utilized to track the facial features of a human demonstrator who reads a predefined script. This motion data are then learned using a hidden Markov model or HMM which represents the probabilities of transitions between different facial poses and velocities. Cao and colleagues [59] have also presented a method for speech motion editing through automatically discovered parameters. This is made possible through

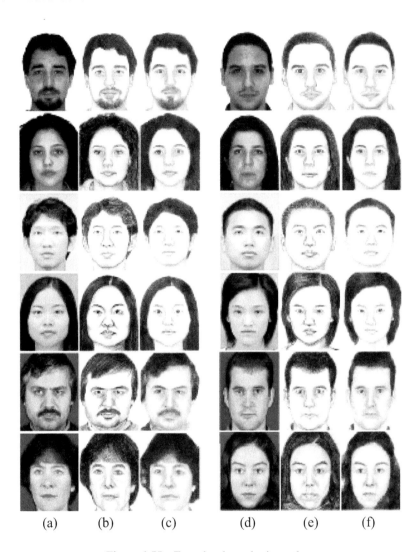

    (a)   (b)   (c)   (d)   (e)   (f)

Figure 1.55 Face sketch synthesis results.

manifold learning. Independent component analysis or ICA (a popular technique in machine learning and statistics [190]) is used to create parameters for the regression of speech motion.

Motion capture data can also be applied to drive the human face. Zhang et al. [348] proposed a geometry-driven facial expression synthesis system. Based on the point positions of a facial expression, this system automatically synthesizes a corresponding expression image that includes photorealistic and natural looking expression details. A technique is developed to infer the missing feature point motions from the tracked

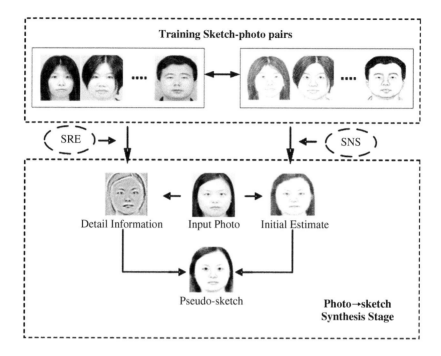

Figure 1.56 Framework of the proposed SNS-SRE image synthesis algorithm.

subset by using an example-based approach. The details of the technique are shown in Figure 1.57.

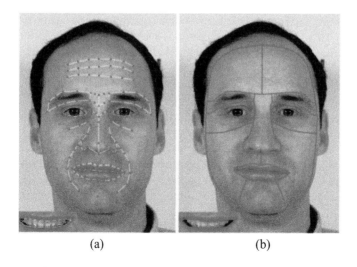

(a)   (b)

Figure 1.57 (a) Feature points; (b) Face region subdivision.

1.3.5.2 3D face synthesis   Pighin et al. [230] presented a new technique for creating photorealistic textured 3D facial models from photographs of a human subject, and for creating smooth transitions between different facial expressions by morphing between these different models. In this method, a scattered data interpolation technique is used to deform a generic face mesh to fit the particular geometry of the subject's face. Similarly, interpolation methods have been applied in [224, 20]. The results of interpolation is presented in Figure 1.58. The Pose Space Deformation(PSD) method presented by Lewis et al.[169] provides a general framework for example-based interpolation which can be used for blendshape facial animations. In their work, the deformation of a surface (face) is treated as a function of a set of abstract parameters, and a new surface is generated by scattered data interpolations.

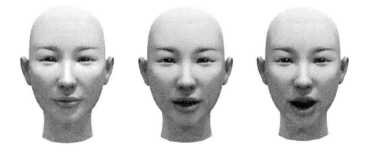

Figure 1.58   Linear Interpolation is performed on blend shapes. Left: Neutral pose. Middle: Interpolated shape. Right: "A" mouth shape.

Sifakis et al. [258] proposed an anatomically accurate face model controlled by muscle activations and kinematic bone degrees of freedom. The tissues are endowed with a highly nonlinear constitutive model including controllable anisotropic muscle activations based on fiber directions. A viable solution is proposed to automatically determine muscle activations which track a sparse set of surface landmarks. The scheme of this method is shown in Figure 1.59. Tao et al. [283] proposed a decoupled probabilistic algorithm calledBayesian tensor analysis (BTA). Theoretically, BTA can automatically and suitably determine dimensionality for different modalities of tensor data. With BTA, a collection of 3D faces can be well modeled. Empirical studies on expression retargeting also justify the advantages of BTA. The representation of the tensor face is shown in Figure 1.60.

Data-driven methods have also been widely applied in 3D face synthesis. King and Parent [138] proposed a facial model designed primarily to support animated speech. This facial model takes facial geometry as the input and transforms it into a parametric deformable model. According to this approach, the facial and coarticulation models must first be interactively initialized. The system then automatically creates accurate real-time animated speech from the input text. It is capable of cheaply producing tremendous amounts of animated speech with very low resource requirements. The results are shown in Figure 1.61. Deng and Neumann [75] proposed a novel data-driven animation system for expressive facial animation synthesis

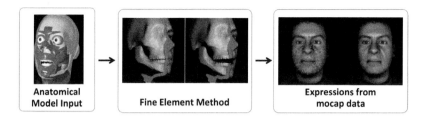

Figure 1.59 Facial expression created by the action of 32 transversely isotropic muscles and simulated on a quasistatic finite element tetrahedral mesh. The original markers are colored red, and the marker positions resulting from the simulation are depicted in green.

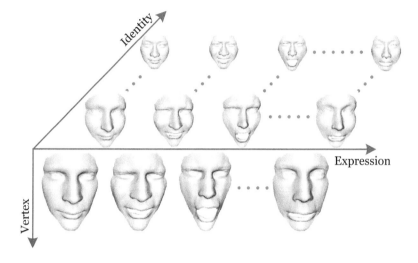

Figure 1.60 A collection of 3D facial data with different identities and different expressions.

and editing. Given novel phoneme-aligned speech input and its emotion modifiers (specifications), this system automatically generates expressive facial animation by concatenating captured motion data while animators establish constraints and goals. Ju and Lee [130] proposed a technique for generating subtle expressive facial gestures (facial expressions and head motion) semi-automatically from motion capture data. This approach is based on Markov random fields that are simulated in two levels. In the lower level, the coordinated movements of facial features are captured, parameterized, and transferred to synthetic faces using basis shapes. The results are shown in Figure 1.62. To achieve real-time motion retargeting, Weise et al. [318] proposed a complete integrated system for live facial puppetry that enables high-resolution real-time facial expression tracking with transfer to another person's face. The system utilizes a real-time structured light scanner that provides dense 3D data and texture. The motion retargeting result is shown in Figure 1.63.

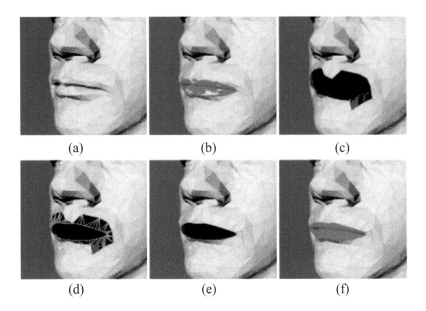

(a) (b) (c)

(d) (e) (f)

Figure 1.61 The grafting process. (a) The geometry inputting. (b) Lip model fitting. (c) Overlapping triangles removing. (d) The boundary of the lip model and the boundary of the removed triangles are retriangulated. (e) Adding new triangles. (f) The lip model geometry is added to the input geometry.

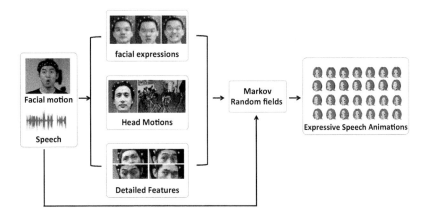

Figure 1.62 Expressive facial expressions and head motions are captured, parameterized, and transferred to the synthetic face.

Lau et al. [156] proposed an intuitive and easy-to-use system for interactively posing 3D facial expressions. The user can model and edit facial expressions by drawing freeform strokes, by specifying distances between facial points, by incre-

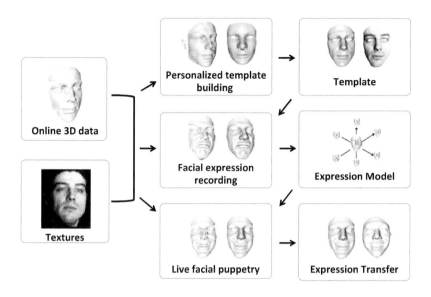

Figure 1.63   Accurate 3D facial expressions can be animated and transferred in real-time from a tracked actor to a different face.

mentally editing curves on the face, or by directly dragging facial points in 2D screen space. This system is shown in Figure 1.64. Na and Jung [206] proposed a novel technique for retargeting captured facial animation to new facial models. Dense motion data are used to express fine motions such as wrinkles. A normal mesh, which is a special multiresolution mesh, is then used to represent the source and target models. A normal mesh is defined by the base mesh and the sequence of its normal offsets. The retargeting consists of two steps: base mesh and detail mesh retargeting. For base mesh retargeting, an example-based technique is used to take advantage of the intuition of the user in specifying the similarity between the source and target expressions. In detail mesh retargeting, the variations of normal offsets in the source mesh are hierarchically computed and transferred to the target mesh.

Reconstruction of a 3D face model from a single 2D face image is fundamentally important for face recognition and animation because the 3D face model is invariant to changes of viewpoint, illumination, background clutter, and occlusions. Given a coupled training set that contains pairs of 2D faces and the corresponding 3D faces, Song et al. [263] train a novel coupled radial basis function network (C-RBF) to recover the 3D face model from a single 2D face image. The C-RBF network explores: (1) The intrinsic representations of 3D face models and those of 2D face images; (2) mappings between a 3D face model and its intrinsic representation; and (3) mappings between a 2D face image and its intrinsic representation. Since a particular face can be reconstructed by its nearest neighbors, it can be assumed that the linear combination coefficients for a particular 2D face image reconstruction are identical to those for the corresponding 3D face model reconstruction. Therefore, a

3D face model can be reconstructed by using a single 2D face image based on the C-RBF network. The whole framework is presented in Figure 1.65.

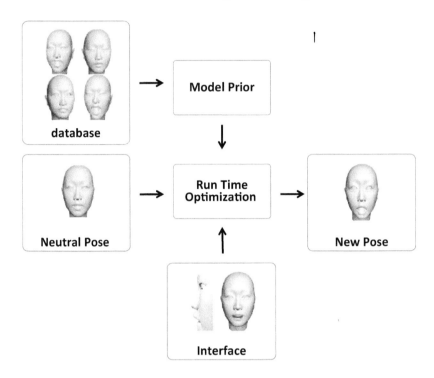

Figure 1.64   The face poser system allows intuitive modeling and editing of 3D facial expressions in real time.

1.4 CHAPTER SUMMARY

Many computer animation techniques are both data and computationally intensive. In this chapter, we have introduced how some machine learning methods or concepts are utilized to help alleviate these bottlenecks in animation techniques. However, machine learning has not as yet been used widely throughout the field of computer animation. We discussed in this chapter how animation research can leverage the machine learning literature to underpin, validate, and develop their proposed methods. A close relationship between computer animation and learning techniques is proposed, which will result in the development of new and enhanced animation techniques. In the following chapters, we shall introduce the emerging machine learning techniques and their applications in computer animation fields.

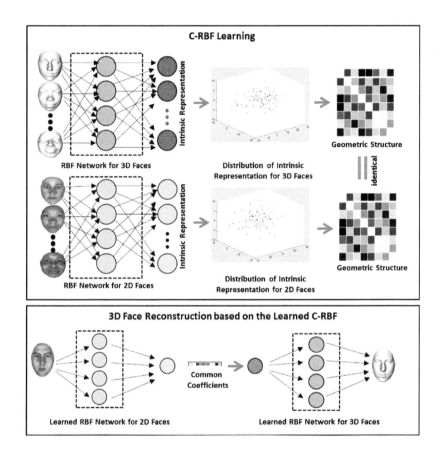

Figure 1.65 Framework of the C-RBF network.

CHAPTER 2

MODERN MACHINE LEARNING TECHNIQUES

Machine learning techniques have been widely used in computer animation and its related fields. It can be observed that animation has thus far benefited great from machine learning applications. In realistic motion synthesis [240, 144], a group of techniques have been proposed to create a generative model of motion through machine learning theory. The motion clips representing a class of motion (e.g., walking, waving, etc.) are collected by users. These clips are then manually placed in an n-dimensional parameter space determined by the user. The technique of scattered data interpolation is adopted to synthesize the novel motions. In computer-assisted cartoon animation, the prerequisite for achieving automatic character generation is the construction of accurate correspondences between keyframes. To efficiently solve the correspondence construction problem for complicated characters, semi-supervised learning [345] is adopted to improve the accuracy of building rates. In example-based cartoon synthesis, the manifold learning-based methods [131, 345] are proposed to synthesize novel cartoons from the existing frames. Additionally, graph-based transductive learning methods [60, 340] have been applied in cartoon synthesis. To automatically combine multiple features in cartoon synthesis by using alternative optimization, multiview subspace learning (MSL) [324] and multiview distance metric learning (MDML) are proposed. In these applications, many modern

Modern Machine Learning Techniques and Their Applications in Cartoon Animation Research,
First Edition. By Jun Yu and Dacheng Tao

machine learning techniques are proposed and include:patch alignment framework; spectral clustering, graph cut and convex relaxation; ensemble manifold learning; multiple kernel learning; multiview subspace learning [325], multiview distance metric learning and multi-task learning. The technical details of these methods will be introduced in this chapter and the application of these machine learning techniques to cartoon animation will be briefly elaborated.

To better present the technical details of these methods, important notations used are unified and explained below. Capital letter $\mathbf{X} = [\mathbf{x}_1, \ldots, \mathbf{x}_N] \in \mathbf{R}^{d \times N}$ represents the data matrix including all the data in the high dimensional space $\mathbf{R}^m$, and $\mathbf{Y} = [\mathbf{y}_1, \ldots, \mathbf{y}_N] \in \mathbf{R}^{d \times N}$ represents the corresponding low-dimensional space $\mathbf{R}^d$. Lower case letter $\mathbf{x}_i$ represents the vector of ith sample in $\mathbf{X}$, and $\mathbf{y}_i$ represents the corresponding low-dimensional of $\mathbf{x}_i$. In linear transformation, the projection matrix $\mathbf{U}$ is adopted to project the data from the original space onto the low-dimensional space through $\mathbf{Y} = \mathbf{U}^{\mathbf{T}}\mathbf{X}$. $\mathbf{W} \in \mathbf{R}^{N \times N}$ represents the weight matrix, which indicates the similarity between data samples. The number of nearest neighbors for each data sample $\mathbf{x}_i$ is k. For the semi-supervised learning algorithm, $\mathbf{N}_l$ indicates the number of the labeled data and $\mathbf{N}_u$ is the number of the unlabeled data. To introduce the multiview learning algorithm, we present some specific notations. Superscript (i), e.g. $\mathbf{X}^{(i)}$ and $\mathbf{x}^{(i)}$, represents data from the ith view. Therefore, the multiview data set can be represented as N objects and m representations, i.e., a set of matrices $\mathbf{X} = \{\mathbf{X}^{(i)} \in \mathbf{R}^{m_i \times N}\}$, in which $\mathbf{X}^{(i)}$ is the feature matrix for the ith view representation. For convenience, Table 2.1 lists these important notations used in the rest of the paper.

Table 2.1 Important Notations Used in Methods

Notation	Description	Notation	Description
$\mathbf{X}$	data set in a high-dimensional space	m	dimension of original data
$\mathbf{Y}$	dimension-reduced data set	$\mathbf{R}^d$	reduced low-dimensional space
N	size of the data set $\mathbf{X}$	$\mathbf{R}^m$	m-dimensional Euclidean space
$\mathbf{U}$	projection matrix	$\mathbf{L}_i$	representation of patch optimization
k	number of nearest neighbor	$\mathbf{X}_i$	local patch of data $\mathbf{x}_i$
$\mathbf{Y}_i$	low-dimensional representation for $\mathbf{X}_i$	$\mathbf{tr}(\cdot)$	trace operator
$\mathbf{S}_i$	selection matrix	$\mathbf{L}$	graph laplacian matrix
$\mathbf{I}_d$	$d \times d$ identity matrix	$\mathbf{W}$	weight matrix
t	controlling parameter in Gaussian kernel	N_l	number of the labeled data
N_u	number of the unlabeled data	$\mathbf{L_n}$	normalized graph laplacian matrix
$\mathbf{X}^{(i)}$	data from the ith view		

This chapter introduces the following multiple modern machine learning techniques: patch alignment framework; spectral clustering, graph cut and convex relaxation; ensemble manifold learning; multiple kernel learning; multiview subspace learning and multiview distance metric learning and multi-task learning. Section 2.1 introduces a novel framework called patch alignment framework which unifies all existing manifold learning. For spectral clustering, graph cut and convex relaxation, Section 2.2 presents a group of state-of-the-art techniques in this area. Sections 2.3, 2.4, 2.5, 2.6, and 2.7 introduce ensemble manifold learning, multiple-kernel learning, multiview subspace learning, multiview distance metric learning and multi-task learning respectively.

2.1 A UNIFIED FRAMEWORK FOR MANIFOLD LEARNING

Spectral-analysis-based dimensionality reduction algorithms are important and have been popularly applied in data mining and computer vision applications. To date, many algorithms have been developed, e.g., Principal Component Analysis (PCA) [116], Locally Linear Embedding (LLE) [241], Laplacian Eigenmaps (LE) [31], and Local Tangent Space Alignment (LTSA) [353]. All of these algorithms have been designed intuitively and pragmatically, i.e., on the basis of the experience and knowledge of experts for their own purposes. Therefore, it will be more informative to provide a systematic framework for understanding the common properties and intrinsic differences in different algorithms. This section introduces a framework, called "patch alignment," which consists of two stages: part optimization and whole alignment. The framework reveals that: (i) algorithms are intrinsically different in the patch optimization stage; and (ii) all algorithms share an almost-identical whole alignment stage. As an application of this framework, a new dimensionality reduction algorithm, termed Discriminative Locality Alignment (DLA), is proposed by imposing discriminative information in the part optimization stage.

2.1.1 Framework Introduction

Consider a dataset $\mathbf{X}$, which consists of N measurements $\mathbf{x}_i (1 \leq i \leq N)$ in a high-dimensional space $\mathbf{R}^m$. That is $\mathbf{X} = [\mathbf{x}_1, \ldots, \mathbf{x}_N] \in \mathbf{R}^{m \times N}$. The objective of a dimensionality reduction algorithm is to compute the corresponding low-dimensional representations $\mathbf{Y} = [\mathbf{y}_1, \ldots, \mathbf{y}_N] \in \mathbf{R}^{d \times N}$, where $d < m$, of $\mathbf{X}$. For the linear dimensionality reduction, it is necessary to find a projection matrix $\mathbf{U} \in \mathbf{R}^{m \times d}$, such that $\mathbf{Y} = \mathbf{U}^T \mathbf{X}$.

Initially, PAF builds N patches for each measurement in the dataset. Each patch consists of a measurement and its related ones, which depend on both the characteristics of the dataset and the objective of an algorithm. In PAF, local patches should be built based on a given measurement and its nearest neighbors to capture the local geometry (locality). Global patches are usually built for conventional linear algorithms, e.g., PCA and LDA, while local patches are usually formed in manifold learning-based algorithms, e.g., LLE and LE. With these built patches, optimization can be imposed on them based on an objective function, and the alignment trick can be utilized to form a global coordinate. The details of PAF are presented in the next two parts.

2.1.1.1 *Patch Optimization*   Considering a data $\mathbf{x}_i$ and its k related samples (e.g., nearest neighbors) $\mathbf{x}_{i_1}, \dots, \mathbf{x}_{i_K}$, the matrix $\mathbf{X}_i = [\mathbf{x}_i, \mathbf{x}_{i_1}, \dots, \mathbf{x}_{i_K}]$ is formed to denote the local patch. For $\mathbf{X}_i$, we have a patch mapping $f_i \colon \mathbf{X}_i \mapsto \mathbf{Y}_i$ and $\mathbf{Y}_i = [\mathbf{y}_i, \mathbf{y}_{i_1}, \dots, \mathbf{y}_{i_K}] \in \mathbf{R}^{d \times (k+1)}$. The patch optimization is defined as

$$\arg \min_{\mathbf{Y}_i} \mathbf{tr}(\mathbf{Y}_i \mathbf{L}_i \mathbf{Y}_i^{\mathbf{T}}) \tag{2.1}$$

where $\mathbf{tr}(\cdot)$ is the trace operator; $\mathbf{L}_i \in \mathbf{R}^{(k+1) \times k+1}$ encodes the objective function for the ith patch and $\mathbf{L}_i$ varies with the different algorithms.

2.1.1.2 *Whole Alignment*   For each patch $\mathbf{X}_i$, there is a low-dimensional representation $\mathbf{Y}_i$. All $\mathbf{Y}_i$s can be unified as a whole subspace by assuming that the coordinate for the ith patch $\mathbf{Y}_i = [\mathbf{y}_i, \mathbf{y}_{i_1}, \dots, \mathbf{y}_{i_k}]$ is selected from the global coordinate $\mathbf{Y} = [\mathbf{y}_1, \dots, \mathbf{y}_N]$, such that

$$\mathbf{Y}_i = \mathbf{Y} \mathbf{S}_i \tag{2.2}$$

where $\mathbf{S}_i \in \mathbf{R}^{N \times (k+1)}$ is the selection matrix and an entry is defined as: $(\mathbf{S}_i)_{pg} = 1$ if $p = F_i\{q\}$ and else $(\mathbf{S}_i)_{pg} = 0$. $F_i = i, i_1, \dots, i_k$ denotes the set of indices for ith patch which is built by the data $\mathbf{x}_i$ and its k related samples. Then, Eq. (2.1) can be rewritten as

$$\arg \min_{\mathbf{Y}} \mathbf{tr}(\mathbf{Y} \mathbf{S}_i \mathbf{L}_i \mathbf{S}_i^{\mathbf{T}} \mathbf{Y}^{\mathbf{T}}). \tag{2.3}$$

By summing over all the part optimizations described as Eq. (2.3), we can obtain the whole alignment as

$$\begin{aligned} & \arg \min_{\mathbf{Y}} \Sigma_{i=1}^{N} \mathbf{tr}(\mathbf{Y} \mathbf{S}_i \mathbf{L}_i \mathbf{S}_i^{\mathbf{T}} \mathbf{Y}^{\mathbf{T}}) \\ = & \arg \min_{\mathbf{Y}} \mathbf{tr}(\mathbf{Y} (\Sigma_{i=1}^{N} \mathbf{S}_i \mathbf{L}_i \mathbf{S}_i^{\mathbf{T}}) \mathbf{Y}^{\mathbf{T}}) \\ = & \arg \min_{\mathbf{Y}} \mathbf{tr}(\mathbf{Y} \mathbf{L} \mathbf{Y}^{\mathbf{T}}), \end{aligned} \tag{2.4}$$

where $\mathbf{L} = \Sigma_i^{N} \mathbf{S}_i \mathbf{L}_i \mathbf{S}_i^{\mathbf{T}} \in \mathbf{R}^{N \times N}$ is the graph Laplacian matrix. It is obtained based on an iterative procedure:

$$\mathbf{L}(F_i, F_i) \leftarrow \mathbf{L}(F_i, F_i) + \mathbf{L}_i, \tag{2.5}$$

for $i = 1, \dots, N$ with the initialization $\mathbf{L} = 0$. Note that $\mathbf{L}(F_i, F_i)$ is a submatrix constructed by selecting certain rows and columns from $\mathbf{L}$ according to the index set F_i.

To uniquely determine $\mathbf{Y}$, the constraint $\mathbf{Y}\mathbf{Y}^{\mathbf{T}} = \mathbf{I}_d$ is imposed on Eq. (2.4), where $\mathbf{I}_d$ is a identity matrix. The objective function is then defined as

$$\arg\min_{\mathbf{Y}} \mathbf{tr}(\mathbf{YLY^T}) \text{ s.t. } \mathbf{YY^T} = \mathbf{I}_d. \tag{2.6}$$

For linearization, we can consider $\mathbf{Y} = \mathbf{U^T X}$ and Eq. (2.6) is deformed as

$$\arg\min_{\mathbf{U}} \mathbf{tr}(\mathbf{U^T XLX^T U}) \text{ s.t. } \mathbf{U^T XX^T U} = \mathbf{I}_d. \tag{2.7}$$

In addition, we can impose $\mathbf{U^T U} = \mathbf{I}_d$ as another way to uniquely determine the projection matrix $\mathbf{U}$ such that $\mathbf{Y} = \mathbf{U^T X}$. Thus, the objective function can be written as

$$\arg\min_{\mathbf{U}} \mathbf{tr}(\mathbf{U^T XLX^T U}) \text{ s.t. } \mathbf{U^T U} = \mathbf{I}_d. \tag{2.8}$$

Equations (2.6), (2.7), and (2.8) are basic optimization problems which can be solved by using the Lagrangian multiplier method and their solutions can be obtained by conducting generalized or standard eigenvalue decomposition on $\mathbf{XLX^T}$, i.e., $\mathbf{L}\vec{\alpha} = \lambda\vec{\alpha}$, $\mathbf{XLX^T}\vec{\alpha} = \lambda\mathbf{XX^T}\vec{\alpha}$, and $\mathbf{XLX^T}\vec{\alpha} = \lambda\vec{\alpha}$, respectively. The optimal solution for Eq. (2.6), (2.7), or (2.8) is the d eigenvectors associated with d smallest eigenvalues.

2.1.2 Various Manifold Learning Algorithm Unifying

In this section, we introduce the unification of various manifold learning algorithms (e.g., LLE, LE and PCA) by PAF. The PAF identifies that these algorithms intrinsically differ in how to build patches and the corresponding optimizations on patches. All algorithms use an almost identical whole alignment procedure. Therefore, for each algorithm, we mainly illustrate how to build patch $\mathbf{X}_i$ and the patch optimization $\mathbf{L}_i$.

LLE represents the local geometry by using the linear coefficients which reconstruct a given measurement $\mathbf{x}_i$ by its k nearest neighbors $\mathbf{x}_{i_1}, \ldots, \mathbf{x}_{i_k}$. Therefore, the patch is $\mathbf{X}_i = [\mathbf{x}_i, \mathbf{x}_{i_1}, \ldots, \mathbf{x}_{i_k}]$ and $\mathbf{x}_i$ can be linearly reconstructed from $\mathbf{x}_{i_1}, \ldots, \mathbf{x}_{i_k}$ as

$$\mathbf{x}_i = (\mathbf{c}_i)_1 \mathbf{x}_{i_1} + (\mathbf{c}_i)_2 \mathbf{x}_{i_2} + \cdots + (\mathbf{c}_i)_k \mathbf{x}_{i_k} + \varepsilon_i, \tag{2.9}$$

where $\mathbf{c}_i$ is a k-dimensional vector to encode reconstruction coefficients and ε_i is the reconstruction error. Minimizing the error yields

$$\arg\min_{\mathbf{c_i}} \|\varepsilon_i\|^2 = \arg\min_{\mathbf{c_i}} \|\mathbf{x}_i - \sum_{j=1}^{k}(\mathbf{c}_i)_j \mathbf{x}_{i_j}\|^2. \tag{2.10}$$

With the sum-to-one constraint $\sum_{j=1}^{k}(\mathbf{c}_i)_j = 1$, $\mathbf{c}_i$ can be computed in a closed form as

$$(\mathbf{c}_i)_j = \sum_{i=1}^{k} \mathbf{G}_{jt}^{-1} / \sum_{p=1}^{k}\sum_{q=1}^{k} \mathbf{G}_{pq}^{-1}, \tag{2.11}$$

where $\mathbf{G}_{jt} = (\mathbf{x}_i - \mathbf{x}_{i_j})^{\mathbf{T}}(\mathbf{x}_i - \mathbf{x}_{i_t})$ is called the local Gram matrix. In LLE, it is assumed that $\mathbf{c}_i$ reconstructs both $\mathbf{x}_i$ from $\mathbf{x}_{i_1}, \ldots, \mathbf{x}_{i_k}$ in the high-dimensional space and $\mathbf{y}_i$ from $\mathbf{y}_{i_1}, \ldots, \mathbf{y}_{i_k}$ in the low-dimensional subspace. Based on this point, the cost function can be reformulated as

$$
\begin{aligned}
\arg\min_{\mathbf{Y}_i} \|\varepsilon_i\|^2 &= \arg\min_{\mathbf{Y}_i} \left\| \mathbf{y}_i - \sum_{j=1}^{k} (\mathbf{c}_i)_j \mathbf{y}_{i_j} \right\|^2 \\
&= \arg\min_{\mathbf{Y}_i} \mathrm{tr}(\mathbf{Y}_i \begin{bmatrix} -1 \\ \mathbf{c}_i \end{bmatrix} [\, -1 \quad \mathbf{c}_i^{\mathbf{T}} \,] \mathbf{Y}_i^{\mathbf{T}}) \\
&= \arg\min_{\mathbf{Y}_i} \mathrm{tr}(\mathbf{Y}_i \mathbf{L}_i \mathbf{Y}_i^{\mathbf{T}}),
\end{aligned}
\tag{2.12}
$$

where, $\mathbf{L}_i = \begin{bmatrix} -1 \\ \mathbf{c}_i \end{bmatrix} [\, -1 \quad \mathbf{c}_i^{\mathbf{T}} \,] = \begin{bmatrix} 1 & -\mathbf{c}_i^{\mathbf{T}} \\ -\mathbf{c}_i & \mathbf{c}_i \mathbf{c}_i^{\mathbf{T}} \end{bmatrix}$. With $\mathbf{L}_i$, 2.12, and 2.6, we can obtain the low-dimensional representations under the proposed framework.

LE preserves the local geometry based on manipulations on an undirected weighted graph, which indicates the neighbor relations of pairwise samples. The objective function of LE is

$$
\arg\min_{\mathbf{Y}} \sum_{i=1}^{N} \sum_{j=1}^{N} \|\mathbf{y}_i - \mathbf{y}_j\|^2 \mathbf{W}(i,j),
\tag{2.13}
$$

where $\mathbf{W} \in \mathbf{R}^{N \times N}$ is the matrix weighted by the Gaussian kernels: $\mathbf{W}(i,j) = \exp(-\|\mathbf{x}_i - \mathbf{x}_j\|^2/t)$ if $\mathbf{x}_i$ is one of the k nearest neighbors of $\mathbf{x}_i$ or $\mathbf{x}_j$ is one of the k nearest neighbors of $\mathbf{x}_i$, otherwise 0, and t is a controlling parameter. To unify LE into the proposed framework, we rewrite Eq. (2.13) as

$$
\arg\min_{\mathbf{y}_i} \sum_{i=1}^{N} \sum_{j=1}^{l} \|\mathbf{y}_i - \mathbf{y}_{i_j}\|^2 (\mathbf{w}_i)_j,
\tag{2.14}
$$

where $\mathbf{y}_{i_j}, j = 1, \ldots, l$, are l connected points of a given data $\mathbf{y}_i$ in the graph and $\mathbf{w}_i$ is the l-dimensional vector weighted by $(\mathbf{w}_i)_j = \exp(-\|\mathbf{x}_i - \mathbf{x}_{i_j}\|^2/t)$. Therefore, Eq. (2.14) can be reformulated to

$$
\begin{aligned}
\arg\min_{\mathbf{y}_i} \sum_{i=1}^{N} \mathrm{tr} &\left(\begin{bmatrix} (\mathbf{y}_i - \mathbf{y}_{i_1})^{\mathbf{T}} \\ \vdots \\ (\mathbf{y}_i - \mathbf{y}_{i_l})^{\mathbf{T}} \end{bmatrix} [\, \mathbf{y}_i - \mathbf{y}_{i_1}, \quad \ldots, \quad \mathbf{y}_i - \mathbf{y}_{i_l} \,] \mathrm{diag}(\mathbf{w}_i) \right) \\
&= \arg\min_{\mathbf{Y}_i} \sum_{i=1}^{N} \mathrm{tr}(\mathbf{Y}_i \begin{bmatrix} -\mathbf{e}_l^{\mathbf{T}} \\ \mathbf{I}_l \end{bmatrix} \mathrm{diag}(\mathbf{w}_i)[\, -\mathbf{e}_l \quad \mathbf{I}_l \,] \mathbf{Y}_i^{\mathbf{T}}) \\
&= \arg\min_{\mathbf{Y}_i} \sum_{i=1}^{N} \mathrm{tr}(\mathbf{Y}_i \mathbf{L}_i \mathbf{Y}_i^{\mathbf{T}}),
\end{aligned}
$$

$$
\tag{2.15}
$$

which serves as the whole alignment for all measurements. PCA maximizes the trace of total scatter matrix in the projected subspace, that is

$$
\arg\max \mathrm{tr}(\mathbf{S}_T) = \arg\max_{\mathbf{y}_i} \mathrm{tr}(\sum_{i=1}^{N} (\mathbf{y}_i - \mathbf{y}^m)(\mathbf{y}_i - \mathbf{y}^m)^{\mathbf{T}}),
\tag{2.16}
$$

where $\mathbf{y}^m$ is the centroid of all measurements. To unify PCA into the proposed framework, we rewrite Eq. (2.16) as

$$\arg\max_{\mathbf{y}_i} \sum_{i=1}^{N} \mathbf{tr}(\frac{1}{N^2}(\sum_{j=1}^{N-1}(\mathbf{y}_i - \mathbf{y}_{i_j}))(\sum_{j=1}^{N-1}(\mathbf{y}_i - \mathbf{y}_{i_j}))^{\mathbf{T}}), \qquad (2.17)$$

where $\mathbf{y}_{i_j}$, $j = 1, \ldots, N - 1$, are the remaining measurements for $\mathbf{y}_i$. Equation (2.17) reduces to

$$\arg\max_{\mathbf{y}_i} \sum_{i=1}^{N} \mathbf{tr}(\frac{1}{N^2}(\mathbf{Y}_i[\begin{smallmatrix} N-1 \\ -\mathbf{e}_{N-1} \end{smallmatrix}])(\mathbf{Y}_i[\begin{smallmatrix} N-1 \\ -\mathbf{e}_{N-1} \end{smallmatrix}])^{\mathbf{T}})$$
$$= \arg\max_{\mathbf{y}_i} \sum_{i=1}^{N} \mathbf{tr}(\mathbf{Y}_i \mathbf{L}_i \mathbf{Y}_i^{\mathbf{T}}). \qquad (2.18)$$

In the above section, we discussed the unification of LLE, LE, and PCA under the patch alignment framework. Other manifold learning methods (e.g. ISOMAP [287], LDA [83], LTSA [353], etc.) can also be unfied by PAF. The details of these methods are listed in Table 2.2.

Table 2.2   Summary of Manifold Learning Algorithms

Algorithms	$\mathbf{X}_i$	$\mathbf{L}_i$
LLE/ NPE/ ONPP	Given data and its neighbors	$\begin{bmatrix} 1 & -\mathbf{c}^{\mathbf{T}} \\ -\mathbf{c} & \mathbf{c}\mathbf{c}^{\mathbf{T}} \end{bmatrix}$
ISOMAP	Given data and the remaining ones	$(1/N) \cdot \tau(\mathbf{D}_G^i)$
LE/LPP	Given data and its connected ones	$\begin{bmatrix} \sum_{j=1}^{l}(\mathbf{w}_i)_j & -\mathbf{w}_i^{\mathbf{T}} \\ -\mathbf{w}_i & \mathrm{diag}(\mathbf{w}_i) \end{bmatrix}$
LTSA/LLTSA	Given data and its neighbors	$R_{k+1} - \mathbf{V}_i\mathbf{V}_i^{\mathbf{T}}$
HLLE	Given data and its neighbors	$\mathbf{H}_i\mathbf{H}_i^{\mathbf{T}}$

2.1.3 Discriminative Locality Alignment

In this section, a new manifold learning algorithm termed Discriminative Locality Alignment(DLA) is developed as an application of the PAF. In DLA, the discriminative information, i.e., labels of measurements, is imposed on the part optimization stage and the whole alignment stage constructs the global coordinate in the projected low-dimensional subspace.

In patch optimization, for a given data $\mathbf{x}_i$, according to the label information, the other data can be separated into two groups: measurements in the same class with $\mathbf{x}_i$ and measurements from different classes with $\mathbf{x}_i$. k_1 nearest neighbors

$\mathbf{x}_{i^1}, \ldots, \mathbf{x}_{i^{k_1}}$ can be selected with respect to $\mathbf{x}_i$. In addition, k_2 nearest neighbors $\mathbf{x}_{i_1}, \ldots, \mathbf{x}_{i_{k_2}}$ can be selected with respect to $\mathbf{x}_i$. Thus, the local patch for $\mathbf{x}_i$ can be constructed by putting $\mathbf{x}_i$, $\mathbf{x}_{i^1}, \ldots, \mathbf{x}_{i^{k_1}}$, and $\mathbf{x}_{i_1}, \ldots, \mathbf{x}_{i_{k_2}}$ together: $\mathbf{X}_i = [\mathbf{x}_i, \mathbf{x}_{i^1}, \ldots, \mathbf{x}_{i^{k_1}}, \mathbf{x}_{i_1}, \ldots, \mathbf{x}_{i_{k_2}}]$. In each patch, the corresponding output in the low-dimensional space is denoted by $\mathbf{Y}_i = [\mathbf{y}_i, \mathbf{y}_{i^1}, \ldots, \mathbf{y}_{i^{k_1}}, \mathbf{y}_{i_1}, \ldots, \mathbf{y}_{i_{k_2}}]$. In the low-dimensional space, we expect that distances between the given measurement and the neighbor measurements of a same class are as small as possible, while distances between the given measurement and the Neighbor Measurements of Different Classes are as large as possible.

For each patch in the low-dimensional subspace, it is expected that distances between $\mathbf{y}_i$ and the neighbor measurements of a same class are as small as possible, so the following can be obtained:

$$\arg\min_{\mathbf{y}_i} \sum_{j=1}^{k_1} \|\mathbf{y}_i - \mathbf{y}_{i^j}\|^2. \tag{2.19}$$

Meanwhile, it can be expected that distances between $\mathbf{y}_i$ and the Neighbor Measurements of Different Classes are as large as possible, so we have

$$\arg\max_{\mathbf{y}_i} \sum_{p=1}^{k_2} \|\mathbf{y}_i - \mathbf{y}_{i_p}\|^2. \tag{2.20}$$

Thus, the part discriminator can be formulated as

$$\arg\min_{\mathbf{y}_i}\left(\sum_{j=1}^{k_1} \|\mathbf{y}_i - \mathbf{y}_{i^j}\|^2 - \beta \sum_{p=1}^{k_2} \|\mathbf{y}_i - \mathbf{y}_{i_p}\|^2\right), \tag{2.21}$$

where β is a scaling factor in [0,1] to unify different measures of the within-class distance and the between-class distance. To define the coefficients vector

$$\vec{\omega}_i = [\overbrace{1, \ldots, 1}^{k1}, \overbrace{-\beta, \ldots, -\beta}^{k2}]^{\mathrm{T}}, \tag{2.22}$$

Eq. (2.21) reduces to

$$\arg\min_{\mathbf{y}_i}\left(\sum_{j=1}^{k_1} \|\mathbf{y}_i - \mathbf{y}_{i^j}\|^2 (\mathbf{w}_i)_j + \sum_{p=1}^{k_2} \|\mathbf{y}_i - \mathbf{y}_{i_p}\|^2 (\mathbf{w}_i)_{p+k_i}\right)$$

$$= \arg\min_{\mathbf{y}_i}\left(\sum_{j=1}^{k_1+k_2} \|\mathbf{y}_{F_i(1)} - \mathbf{y}_{F_i(j+1)}\|^2 (\mathbf{w}_i)_j\right) \tag{2.23}$$

$$= \arg\min_{\mathbf{y}_i} \mathbf{tr}\left(\mathbf{Y}_i \begin{bmatrix} -\mathbf{e}_{k_1+k_2}^{\mathrm{T}} \\ \mathbf{I}_{k_1+k_2} \end{bmatrix} \mathrm{diag}(\mathbf{w}_i)[\begin{array}{cc} -\mathbf{e}_{k_1+k_2} & \mathbf{I}_{k_1+k_2} \end{array}]\mathbf{Y}_i^{\mathrm{T}}\right)$$

$$= \arg\min_{\mathbf{y}_i} \mathbf{tr}(\mathbf{Y}_i \mathbf{L}_i \mathbf{Y}_i^{\mathrm{T}}),$$

where

$$\mathbf{L}_i = \left[\begin{array}{cc} \sum_{j=1}^{k_1+k_2} (\mathbf{w}_i)_j & -\mathbf{w}_i^{\mathbf{T}} \\ -\mathbf{w}_i & \mathrm{diag}(\mathbf{w}_i) \end{array} \right], \tag{2.24}$$

$F_i = \{i, i^1, \ldots, i^{k_1}, i_1, \ldots, i_{k_2}\}$ is the set of indices for measurements on the patch; $\mathbf{e}_{k_1+k_2} = [1, \ldots, 1]^{\mathbf{T}} \in \mathbf{R}^{k_1+k_2}$; and $\mathbf{I}_{k_1+k_2}$ is a $(k_1 + k_2) \times (k_1 + k_2)$ identity matrix.

With the constructed patch optimization $\mathbf{L}_i$, the graph Laplacian matrix $\mathbf{L}$ can be built to achieve the whole alignment by Eq. (2.5). To obtain the linear and orthogonal projection matrix $\mathbf{U}$ with d columns, the objective function is designed as Eq. (2.8) and the problem is converted to a standard eigenvalue problem.

2.1.4 Discussions

When discovered by the proposed PAF, all algorithms have an almost identical whole alignment stage and their intrinsic differences are how to build patches and the associated optimization. Based on this point of view, we make the following observations, which are helpful for understanding existing manifold learning algorithms, and for guiding us to design new algorithms with specific properties.

Observation 1: Patches in manifold learning algorithms consider the local geometry of measurements, while conventional linear algorithms do not. LLE builds each patch by a measurement and its nearest neighbors. Each patch of LE consists of two parts: (i) a measurement $\mathbf{x}_i$ and its nearest neighbors and (ii) measurements which deem $\mathbf{x}_i$ as their nearest neighbors. Each patch in PCA is built by all measurements in a dataset.

Observation 2: Different types of geometry are preserved in patches. LLE preserves reconstruction coefficients, which are obtained in the original high-dimensional space for patch representation, in the low-dimensional subspace. LE preserves the nearby relations of a patch. Of the manifold learning algorithms, LE has less computational cost than others because it only minimizes the sum of distances on local patches. PCA preserves the global geometry by minimizing or maximizing scatters of each patch.

Observation 3: According to PAF, the new properties can be added into the local patch construction. For example, in DCA, the discriminative information is added to build the new patch. Thus, a novel manifold learning algorithm can be created. More applications of PAF will be introduced in the following chapters.

2.2 SPECTRAL CLUSTERING AND GRAPH CUT

This section introduces recent research developments in the fields of spectral clustering and graph cut.Spectral clustering has become one of the most popular modern clustering algorithms. It is simple to implement [69] and can be solved efficiently by standard linear algebra software. It often outperforms traditional clustering algorithms such as k-means. Initially, spectral clustering appears slightly mysterious, and it is not obvious to see why it works and what it really does. The goal of Section 2.2.1

is to provide some those questions. We will present the most common spectral clustering algorithms, and derive those algorithms from scratch, using several different approaches. The advantages and disadvantages of the different spectral clustering algorithms are discussed. Subsequently, we elaborate on spectral clustering from the graph cut point of view and provide details of both the connection between NCut and normalized spectral clustering, and the connection between RatioCut and unnormalized spectral clustering.

2.2.1 Spectral Clustering

Clustering is one of the most widely used techniques for data analysis, with applications ranging from statistics, computer science and biology to social sciences or psychology. In these research fields, researchers attempt to obtain a first impression of their data by trying to identify groups of "similar behavior." Compared to the "traditional algorithms" such as k-means, spectral clustering has many fundamental advantages, and the results obtained from spectral clustering often outperform traditional approaches. This section provides a detailed introduction to spectral clustering. We derive spectral clustering from scratch and present different points of view as to why spectral clustering works. However, we do not attempt to give a concise review of all the literature on spectral clustering, which is impossible due to the overwhelming amount of literature on this subject. The first Subsection 3.2.1.1 is a step-by-step introduction to the mathematical objects used by spectral clustering algorithm. The next Subsection 3.2.1.2 is devoted to explaining why spectral clustering works. The reasons are given from the viewpoints of graph partition, random walk perspective and perturbation theory. In Subsection 3.2.1.3, some practical issues related to spectral clustering are presented.

2.2.1.1 Basic Notations   Given a data set $\mathbf{X} = [\mathbf{x}_1, \dots, \mathbf{x}_N] \in \mathbf{R}^{m \times N}$ and some notion of similarity $\mathbf{W}_{ij} > 0$ between all pairs of data points $\mathbf{x}_i$ and $\mathbf{x}_j$, the intuitive purpose of clustering is to separate the data points into different classes. The data in the same class are similar and data in a different class are dissimilar to one another. Therefore, a natural way of representing the distance among data is in the form of similarity graph $\mathbf{G} = (\mathbf{V}, \mathbf{E})$. Here, each vertex $\mathbf{v}_i$ in the graph represents a data point $\mathbf{x}_i$. When the similarity $\mathbf{W}_{ij}$ between the corresponding data points $\mathbf{x}_i$ and $\mathbf{x}_j$ is positive or larger than a certain threshold, the two vertices are connected in the similarity graph; also, the edge is weighted by $\mathbf{W}_{ij}$. Therefore, the clustering problem can be reformulated by using the similarity graph: A partition of the graph can be found such that the edges between different classes have very low weights (which means the data points in different classes are dissimilar from one another) and the edges within a group have high weights (which means that points within the same classes are similar to one another). Hence, we first introduce some basic graph notation and discuss the kind of graphs we will study.

Let $\mathbf{G} = (\mathbf{V}, \mathbf{E})$ be an undirected graph with vertex set $\mathbf{V} = \{\mathbf{v}_1, \dots, \mathbf{v}_N\}$. It is assumed that the graph $\mathbf{G}$ is weighted, and each edge between two vertices $\mathbf{v}_i$ and $\mathbf{v}_j$ has a weight $\mathbf{w}_{ij} \geq 0$. The matrix $\mathbf{W}$ is adopted as the weighted adjacency matrix of the graph. If $\mathbf{w}_{ij} = 0$, it means that the vertices $\mathbf{v}_i$ and $\mathbf{v}_j$ are not connected by an edge. Since $\mathbf{G}$ is undirected, we require $\mathbf{w}_{ij} = \mathbf{w}_{ji}$. The degree of a vertex $\mathbf{v}_i \in \mathbf{V}$ is defined as: $d_i = \sum_{j=1}^{n} \mathbf{w}_{ij}$. Therefore, the degree matrix $\mathbf{D}$ can be defined as the diagonal matrix with the degrees $d_1, \ldots, d_N$ on the diagonal. A subset of vertices $\mathbf{C} \subset \mathbf{V}$ can be denoted as the complement $\mathbf{V}/\mathbf{C}$ by $\overline{\mathbf{C}}$.

Several popular constructions have been proposed to transform a given set of data points $\mathbf{x}_1, \ldots, \mathbf{x}_N$ with pairwise similarities $\mathbf{w}_{ij}$ into a graph. The goal of constructing the similarity graphs is to model the local neighborhood relationships between data points. There are several ways to construct the graph:

- The fully connected graph: we simply connect all points with positive similarity with each other. Here, all edges are weighted by $\mathbf{w}_{ij}$. Since the graph should represent the local neighborhood relationships, the construction is only useful if the similarity function itself models local neighborhoods. One popular similarity function is the Gaussian similarity function $\mathbf{W}(\mathbf{x}_i, \mathbf{x}_j) = \exp(-\|\mathbf{x}_i - \mathbf{x}_j\|^2/t)$, in which the parameter t controls the width of the neighborhoods.

- The k-nearest neighbor graphs: the goal of constructing this graph is to connect vertex $\mathbf{v}_i$ with vertex $\mathbf{v}_j$ if $\mathbf{v}_j$ is among the k-nearest neighbors of $\mathbf{v}_i$. However, this definition leads to a directed graph, as the neighborhood relationship is not symmetric. To make this graph undirected, we can simply ignore the directions of the edges; that is, we connect $\mathbf{v}_i$ and $\mathbf{v}_j$ with an undirected edge if $\mathbf{v}_i$ is among the k-nearest neighbors of $\mathbf{v}_j$ or if $\mathbf{v}_j$ is among the k-nearest neighbors of $\mathbf{v}_i$. The resulting graph is what is usually called the k-nearest neighbor graph.

- The ε-neighborhood graph: This graph is constructed by connecting all points whose pairwise distances are smaller than ε. Since the distances between all connected points are roughly of the same scale (at most ε), weighting the edges will not incorporate more information about the data into the graph. Hence, the ε-neighborhood graph is usually considered as an unweighted graph.

The graphs mentioned above are widely used in spectral clustering.

2.2.1.2 *The properties of Graph Laplacian*   The main tools for spectral clustering arc graph Laplacian matrices. A research field has been dedicated to the study of these matrices and is known as spectral graph theory [70]. In this subsection, we introduce several graph Laplacians and emphasize their most important characteristics. Different variants of graph Laplacians will be carefully distinguished. It should be noted that in the literature there is no unique convention as to precisely which matrix is called "graph Laplacian"; authors simply call their matrices "graph Laplacian."

In the following we can assume that $\mathbf{G}$ is an undirected, weighted graph with weight matrix $\mathbf{W}$, in which $\mathbf{w}_{ij} = \mathbf{w}_{ji} \geq 0$. When using the eigenvectors of a matrix, we will not necessarily assume that they are normalized. Eigenvalues will always be ordered increasingly. Therefore, "the first d eigenvectors" refers to the eigenvectors corresponding to the d smallest eigenvalues. In the following, we will introduce the details of two kinds of graph Laplacian: unnormalized graph Laplacian and normalized graph Laplacian.

The unnormalized graph Laplacian matrix is defined as

$$\mathbf{L} = \mathbf{D} - \mathbf{W}. \tag{2.25}$$

An overview of many of its properties can be found in Ref. [200]. The following properties summarize the most critical characteristics for spectral clustering. The graph Laplacian matrix of $\mathbf{L}$ satisfies the following properties:

1. For every vector $\mathbf{f} \in \mathbf{R}^n$, we have

$$\mathbf{f}^{\mathbf{T}}\mathbf{L}\mathbf{f} = \frac{1}{2} \sum_{i,j=1}^{n} \mathbf{w}_{ij}(\mathbf{f}_i - \mathbf{f}_j)^2. \tag{2.26}$$

2. The matrix $\mathbf{L}$ is symmetric and positive semidefinite.

3. The matrix $\mathbf{L}$ has n non-negative, real-valued eigenvalues $0 = \lambda_1 \leq \lambda_2 \leq \dots \leq \lambda_n$.

The proof for constructing the matrix $\mathbf{L}$ is shown in Eq. (2.27):

$$
\begin{aligned}
&\mathbf{f}^{\mathbf{T}}\mathbf{L}\mathbf{f} \\
&= \mathbf{f}^{\mathbf{T}}\mathbf{D}\mathbf{f} - \mathbf{f}^{\mathbf{T}}\mathbf{W}\mathbf{f} \\
&= \sum_{i=1}^{n} d_i \mathbf{f}_i^2 - \sum_{i,j=1}^{n} \mathbf{f}_i \mathbf{f}_j \mathbf{W}_{ij}.
\end{aligned}
\tag{2.27}
$$

The unnormalized graph Laplacian is independent of the diagonal elements of the weight matrix $\mathbf{W}$. Each weight matrix which coincides with $\mathbf{W}$ on all off-diagonal positions leads to the same unnormalized graph Laplacian $\mathbf{L}$. The unnormalized graph Laplacian and its eigenvalues and eigenvectors can be used to describe many properties of graphs.

Two kinds of matrices are called normalized graph Laplacians in the literature. Both are closely related to each other and are defined as:

$$
\begin{aligned}
\mathbf{L}_{sym} &:= \mathbf{D}^{-1/2}\mathbf{L}\mathbf{D}^{-1/2} = \mathbf{I} - \mathbf{D}^{-1/2}\mathbf{W}\mathbf{D}^{-1/2}, \\
\mathbf{L}_{rw} &:= \mathbf{D}^{-1}\mathbf{L} = \mathbf{I} - \mathbf{D}^{-1}\mathbf{W}.
\end{aligned}
\tag{2.28}
$$

The first matrix $\mathbf{L}_{sym}$ is denoted as the symmetric matrix, and the second one $\mathbf{L}_{rw}$ is closely related to a random walk. The properties of $\mathbf{L}_{sym}$ and $\mathbf{L}_{rw}$ are summarized as follows:

1. For every $\mathbf{f} \in \mathbf{R}^n$

$$\mathbf{f}^{\mathbf{T}}\mathbf{L}_{sym}\mathbf{f} = \frac{1}{2} \sum_{i,j=1}^{n} \mathbf{w}_{ij}\left(\frac{\mathbf{f}_i}{\sqrt{d_i}} - \frac{\mathbf{f}_j}{\sqrt{d_j}}\right)^2. \tag{2.29}$$

2. λ is an eigenvalue of $\mathbf{L}_{rw}$ with eigenvector $\mathbf{u}$ if and only if λ is an eigenvalue of $\mathbf{L}_{sym}$ with eigenvector $\mathbf{D}^{1/2}\mathbf{u}$.

3. λ is an eigenvalue of $\mathbf{L}_{rw}$ with eigenvector $\mathbf{u}$ if and only if λ and $\mathbf{u}$ solve the generalized eigenproblem $\mathbf{Lu} = \lambda\mathbf{Du}$.

4. $\mathbf{L}_{sym}$ and $\mathbf{L}_{rw}$ are positive semi-definite and have n non-negative real-valued eigenvalues $0 = \lambda_1 \leq \ldots \leq \lambda_n$.

The proof for Eq. (2.29) is similar to the proof shown in Eq. (2.27).

2.2.1.3 Algorithm for Spectral Clustering

In this subsection, we introduce three popular spectral clustering algorithms. We assume that our data consists of N "points" $\mathbf{X} = \{\mathbf{x}_1, \ldots, \mathbf{x}_N\}$. Their pairwise similarities $\mathbf{W}_{ij} = \mathbf{W}(\mathbf{x}_i, \mathbf{x}_j)$ are measured by the similarity function which is symmetric and non-negative. Hence, the corresponding similarity matrix is denoted as $\mathbf{W} = (\mathbf{W}_{ij})_{i,j=1,\ldots,N}$. The unnormalized spectral clustering is proposed in LE. The details of the algorithm are listed below:

step 1 Construct a similarity graph by one of the methods described in Section 2.2.1.1. Let $\mathbf{W}$ be its weighted matrix.

step 2 Compute the unnormalized Laplacian $\mathbf{L}$.

step 3 Compute the first d eigenvectors $\mathbf{u}_1, \ldots, \mathbf{u}_d$ of $\mathbf{L}$.

step 4 Let $\mathbf{U} \in \mathbf{R}^{N \times d}$ be the matrix containing the vectors $\mathbf{u}_1, \ldots, \mathbf{u}_d$ as columns.

step 5 For $i = 1, \ldots, N$, let $\mathbf{y}_i \in \mathbf{R}^d$ be the vector corresponding to the ith row of $\mathbf{U}$.

step 6 Cluster the points $(\mathbf{y}_i)_{i=1,\ldots,N}$ in $\mathbf{R}^d$ with k-means algorithm into clusters $C_1, \ldots, C_d$.

output: Clusters $A_1, \ldots, A_d$ with $A_i = \{j | \mathbf{y}_j \in C_i\}$.

Besides unnormalized spectral clustering, there are two different versions of normalized spectral clustering, which are introduced by Refs. [251] and [210]. We present the normalized spectral clustering used in Ref.[251]:

step 1 Construct a similarity graph by one of the methods described in Section 2.2.1.1. Let $\mathbf{W}$ be its weighted adjacency matrix.

step 2 Compute the unnormalized Laplacian $\mathbf{L}$.

step 3 Compute the first d eigenvectors $\mathbf{u}_1, \ldots, \mathbf{u}_k$ of the generalized eigenproblem $\mathbf{Lu} = \lambda\mathbf{Du}$.

step 4 Let $\mathbf{U} \in \mathbf{R}^{N \times d}$ be the matrix containing the vectors $\mathbf{u}_1, \ldots, \mathbf{u}_d$ as columns.

step 5 For $i = 1, \ldots, N$, let $\mathbf{y}_i \in \mathbf{R}^d$ be the vector corresponding to the ith row of $\mathbf{U}$.

step 6 Cluster the points $(\mathbf{y}_i)_{i=1,\ldots,N}$ in $\mathbf{R}^d$ with k-means algorithm into clusters $C_1, \ldots, C_d$.

output Clusters $A_1, \ldots, A_d$ with $A_i = \{j | \mathbf{y}_j \in C_i\}$.

Note that the above algorithm uses the generalized eigenvectors of $\mathbf{L}$, which corresponds to the eigenvectors of the matrix $\mathbf{L}_{rw}$. Hence, the algorithm works with eigenvectors of the normalized Laplacian $\mathbf{L}_{rw}$, and is called normalized spectral clustering. The next algorithm also uses a normalized Laplacian, but this time the matrix $\mathbf{L}_{sym}$ instead of $\mathbf{L}_{rw}$. We can see that this algorithm needs to introduce an additional row normalization step which is not needed in the other algorithms. The details of this algorithm are:

step 1 Construct a similarity graph by one of the methods described in Section 2.2.1.1. Let $\mathbf{W}$ be its weighted adjacency matrix.

step 2 Compute the unnormalized Laplacian $\mathbf{L}$.

step 3 Compute the first d eigenvectors $\mathbf{u}_1, \ldots, \mathbf{u}_k$ of $\mathbf{L}_{sym}$.

step 4 Let $\mathbf{U} \in \mathbf{R}^{N \times d}$ be the matrix containing the vectors $\mathbf{u}_1, \ldots, \mathbf{u}_k$ as columns.

step 5 Form the matrix $\mathbf{T} \in \mathbf{R}^{N \times d}$ from $\mathbf{U}$ by normalizing the rows to norm 1, that is set $t_{ij} = u_{ij} / (\sum_k u_{ik}^2)^{1/2}$.

step 6 For $i = 1, \ldots, N$, let $\mathbf{y}_i \in \mathbf{R}^d$ be the vector corresponding to the ith row of $\mathbf{T}$.

step 7 Cluster the points $(\mathbf{y}_i)_{i=1,\ldots,N}$ with k-means algorithm into clusters $C_1, \ldots, C_d$.

output Clusters $A_1, \ldots, A_d$ with $A_i = \{j | \mathbf{y}_j \in C_i\}$.

The three algorithms stated above look rather similar, apart from the fact that they use three different graph Laplacians. In these three algorithms, the main trick is to change the representation of the original data points $\mathbf{x}_i$ to new representations $\mathbf{y}_i$. Due to the properties of graph Laplacians, this change of representation is useful.

2.2.2 Graph Cut Approximation

The purpose of clustering is to partition data points in different groups according to their similarities. For data points given in the form of a similarity graph, this problem can be restated as follows: we want to find a partition of the graph such that the edges between different groups have a very low weight (data points in different clusters are dissimilar from one another), and the edges within a group have high weight (data points within the same cluster are similar to one another). In this section we will elaborate that spectral clustering can be derived as the approximation of graph cut methods.

Given a similarity graph with adjacency matrix $\mathbf{W}$, the simplest and most direct way to construct a partition of the graph is to solve the mincut problem. To define it, $\mathbf{W}(P, Q) := \sum_{i \in P, j \in Q} \mathbf{w}_{ij}$ and $\overline{C}$ represents the complement of C. To give a number d for subsets, the mincut approach simply consists in choosing a partition $C_1, \ldots, C_d$ which minimizes

$$\text{cut}(C_1, \ldots, C_d) = \arg \min_{C_1, \ldots, C_d} \sum_{i=1}^{d} \frac{1}{2} \mathbf{W}(C_i, \overline{C}_i). \tag{2.30}$$

Here the factor 1/2 is adopted to avoid counting each edge twice in the cut. In particular, for $d = 2$, mincut [268] is relatively easy and can be solved efficiently. However, mincut often does not lead to satisfactory partitions. The problem is that in many cases, the mincut solution simply separates one individual vertex from the rest of the graph. Of course, this is not what we want to achieve in clustering because clusters should be groups of points with appropriate size. One way to achieve this is to explicitly request that the sets $C_1, \ldots, C_d$ are "reasonably large." The two most common objective functions to encode this are RatioCut [104] and the normalized cut Ncut [251]. In RatioCut, the size of a subset C of a graph is measured by its number of vertices $|C|$, while in Ncut the size is measured by the weights of its edges $\text{vol}(C)$. The definitions of RationCut and Ncut are formulated as

$$\text{RatioCut}(C_1, \ldots, C_d) = \arg \min_{C_1, \ldots, C_d} \sum_{i=1}^{d} \frac{1}{2} \frac{\mathbf{W}(C_i, \overline{C}_i)}{|C_i|} = \sum_{i=1}^{d} \frac{\text{cut}(C_i, \overline{C}_i)}{|C_i|}, \tag{2.31}$$

$$\text{Ncut}(C_1, \ldots, C_d) = \arg \min_{C_1, \ldots, C_d} \sum_{i=1}^{d} \frac{1}{2} \frac{\mathbf{W}(C_i, \overline{C}_i)}{\text{vol}(C_i)} = \sum_{i=1}^{d} \frac{\text{cut}(C_i, \overline{C}_i)}{|\text{vol}(C_i)|}. \tag{2.32}$$

We observe that the objective functions in Equation (2.32) and Equation (2.33) take a small value if the clusters C_i are not too small. In particular, the minimum of the function $\sum_{i=1}^{d}(1/|C_i|)$ is achieved if all $|C_i|$ coincide, and the minimum of $\sum_{i=1}^{d}(1/|\text{vol}(C_i)|)$ is achieved if all $\text{vol}(C_i)$ coincide. Therefore, both objective functions try to achieve a balance among clusters, which is measured by the number of vertices or edge weights. However, adding balancing conditions causes the simple mincut problem to become NP hard. Detailed discussion of this can be found in Ref.[299]. Spectral clustering is a way to solve relaxed versions of those problems. We will see that relaxing Ncut leads to normalized spectral clustering, while relaxing RatioCut leads to unnormalized spectral clustering.

2.2.2.1 Approximating RatioCut with 2 Classes
We start with the case of RatioCut for 2 classes, because the relaxation is easy to understand. In this case, the objective function can be formulated as

$$\min_{C \subset V} \text{RatioCut}(C, \overline{C}). \tag{2.33}$$

To give a subset $C \subset \mathbf{V}$, it can be defined as the vector $\mathbf{y} = (\mathbf{y}_1, \ldots, \mathbf{y}_d)^{\mathbf{T}}$ with entries

$$\mathbf{y}_i = \begin{cases} \sqrt{|\overline{C}|/|C|} & \text{if } v_i \in C \\ -\sqrt{|C|/|\overline{C}|} & \text{if } v_i \in \overline{C}. \end{cases} \tag{2.34}$$

Hence, by using the unnormalized graph Laplacian, the RatioCut objective function can be reformulated as

$$
\begin{aligned}
\mathbf{y}^{\mathbf{T}}\mathbf{L}\mathbf{y} &= \frac{1}{2} \sum_{i,j=1}^{d} \mathbf{w}_{ij}(\mathbf{y}_i - \mathbf{y}_j)^2 \\
&= \frac{1}{2} \sum_{i \in C, j \in \overline{C}} \mathbf{W}_{ij}(\sqrt{|\overline{C}|/|C|} + \sqrt{|C|/|\overline{C}|})^2 \\
&\quad + \frac{1}{2} \sum_{i \in \overline{C}, j \in C} \mathbf{W}_{ij}(-\sqrt{|\overline{C}|/|C|} - \sqrt{|C|/|\overline{C}|})^2 \\
&= \text{cut}(C, \overline{C})(|\overline{C}|/|C| + |C|/|\overline{C}| + 2) \\
&= \text{cut}(C, \overline{C})((|C| + |\overline{C}|)/|C| + (\|C\| + |\overline{C}|)/|\overline{C}|) \\
&= |V| \cdot \text{RatioCut}(C, \overline{C}).
\end{aligned} \tag{2.35}
$$

We also have

$$
\begin{aligned}
\sum_{i=1}^{d} \mathbf{y}_i &= \sum_{i \in C} \sqrt{|\overline{C}|/|C|} - \sum_{i \in \overline{C}} \sqrt{|C|/|\overline{C}|} \\
&= |C|\sqrt{\|\overline{C}\|/|C|} - |\overline{C}|\sqrt{\|C\|/|\overline{C}|} = 0.
\end{aligned} \tag{2.36}
$$

In other words, the vector $\mathbf{y}$ defined in Eq. (2.34) is orthogonal to the constant one vector $\mathbf{p}$. Therefore, the vector $\mathbf{y}$ satisfies

$$\|\mathbf{y}\|^2 = \sum_{i=1}^{d} \mathbf{y}_i^2 = |C|\frac{|\overline{C}|}{|C|} + |\overline{C}|\frac{|C|}{|\overline{C}|} = |\overline{C}| + |C| = d. \tag{2.37}$$

Based on the above derivation, the problem of minimizing the objective function in Eq. (2.33) can be equivalently rewritten as

$$\min_{C \subset V} \mathbf{y}^{\mathbf{T}}\mathbf{L}\mathbf{y} \text{ s.t. } \mathbf{y} \perp \mathbf{p}, \tag{2.38}$$

in which $\mathbf{y}_i$ is defined in Eq. (2.34), and $\|\mathbf{y}\| = \sqrt{n}$. Clearly, Eq. (2.38) is a discrete optimization problem as the entries of the solution vector y are only permitted to take two particular values. Of course, this is still a NP hard problem. The most evident relaxation method in this setting is to remove the discreteness condition and allow $\mathbf{y}_i$ to take arbitrary values in $\mathbf{R}$. This will cause the relaxed optimization problem.

$$\min_{\mathbf{y} \in \mathbf{R}^d} \mathbf{y}^\mathbf{T} \mathbf{L} \mathbf{y} \text{ s.t. } \mathbf{y} \perp \mathbf{p}. \tag{2.39}$$

According to the Rayleigh-Ritz theorem [184], the solution of this problem is given by the vector $\mathbf{y}$ which is the eigenvector corresponding to the second smallest eigenvalue of $\mathbf{L}$. Therefore, we can approximate a minimizer of RatioCut by the second eigenvector of $\mathbf{L}$. To obtain a partition of the graph, we need to re-transform the real-valued solution vector (y) of the relaxed problem into a discrete indicator vector. This can easily be achieved by using the sign of (y) as an indicator function. It means

$$\begin{cases} v_i \in C & \text{if } \mathbf{y}_i \geq 0 \\ v_i \in \overline{C} & \text{if } \mathbf{y}_i < 0. \end{cases} \tag{2.40}$$

2.2.2.2 *Approximating RatioCut with d Classes*   The relaxation of the RatioCut minimization problem in the case of a general value d follows a similar principle to the one above. To separate $\mathbf{V}$ into d sets $C_1, \ldots, C_d$, the indicator vectors $\mathbf{y}_j = (\mathbf{y}_{1,j}, \ldots, \mathbf{y}_{N,j})$ can be constructed by

$$\mathbf{y}_{ij} = \begin{cases} 1/\sqrt{|C_j|} & \text{if } v_i \in C_j, \\ 0 & \text{otherwise,} \end{cases} \tag{2.41}$$

where $i = 1, \ldots, N$; and $j = 1, \ldots, d$. Hence, we define the matrix $\mathbf{Y} \in \mathbf{R}^{N \times d}$ as the matrix, which contains those d indicator vectors as columns. It can be observed that the columns in $\mathbf{Y}$ are orthonormal to each other, that is, $\mathbf{Y}^\mathbf{T} \mathbf{Y} = \mathbf{I}$. Similar to the calculation in Eq. (2.32) in the last subsection, we can obtain that

$$\mathbf{y}_i^\mathbf{T} \mathbf{L} \mathbf{y}_i = (\mathbf{Y}^\mathbf{T} \mathbf{L} \mathbf{Y})_{ii} = \frac{\mathrm{cut}(C_i, \overline{C_i})}{|C_i|}. \tag{2.42}$$

To combine those facts, we get

$$\begin{aligned} \mathrm{RatioCut}(C_1, \ldots, C_d) &= \sum_{i=1}^d \mathbf{y}_i^\mathbf{T} \mathbf{L} \mathbf{y}_i \\ &= \sum_{i=1}^d (\mathbf{Y}^\mathbf{T} \mathbf{L} \mathbf{Y})_{ii} = \mathrm{tr}(\mathbf{Y}^\mathbf{T} \mathbf{L} \mathbf{Y}), \end{aligned} \tag{2.43}$$

where $\mathrm{tr}(\cdot)$ denotes the trace of a matrix. Therefore, the problem of minimizing $\mathrm{RatioCut}(C_1, \ldots, C_d)$ can be rewritten as

$$\min_{C_1, \ldots, C_d} \mathrm{tr}(\mathbf{Y}^\mathbf{T} \mathbf{L} \mathbf{Y}) \text{ s.t.} \mathbf{Y}^\mathbf{T} \mathbf{Y} = \mathbf{I}. \tag{2.44}$$

In this case, we can relax the problem by allowing the entries of the matrix $\mathbf{L}$ to take arbitrary real values. This leads to the general unnormalized spectral clustering algorithm, as presented in Section 2.2.1.

2.2.2.3 Approximating NCut

Similar to the techniques used in RatioCut, it can be used to derive normalized spectral clustering as a relaxation of minimizing Ncut. In the case $d = 2$ we define the cluster indicator vector by

$$\mathbf{y}_i = \begin{cases} \sqrt{\mathrm{vol}(\overline{C})/\mathrm{vol}C} & \text{if } v_i \in C, \\ -\sqrt{\mathrm{vol}(C)/\mathrm{vol}\overline{C}} & \text{if } v_i \in \overline{C}. \end{cases} \tag{2.45}$$

The problem of minimizing Ncut can be reformulated as

$$\min_{C} \mathbf{y}^{\mathbf{T}}\mathbf{L}\mathbf{y} \text{ s.t.} \mathbf{D}\mathbf{y} \perp 1, \mathbf{y}^{\mathbf{T}}\mathbf{D}\mathbf{y} = \mathrm{vol}(\mathbf{V}). \tag{2.46}$$

This problem can be relaxed by allowing $\mathbf{y}$ to take arbitrary real values

$$\min_{\mathbf{y} \in \mathbf{R}^d} \mathbf{y}^{\mathbf{T}}\mathbf{L}\mathbf{y} \text{ s.t.} \mathbf{D}\mathbf{y} \perp 1, \mathbf{y}^{\mathbf{T}}\mathbf{D}\mathbf{y} = \mathrm{vol}(\mathbf{V}). \tag{2.47}$$

To substitute $\mathbf{g} := \mathbf{D}^{1/2}\mathbf{y}$, the problem can be reformulated as

$$\min_{\mathbf{g} \in \mathbf{R}^N} \mathbf{g}^{\mathbf{T}}\mathbf{D}^{-1/2}\mathbf{L}\mathbf{D}^{-1/2}\mathbf{g} \text{ s.t.} \mathbf{g} \perp \mathbf{D}^{1/2}1, \|\mathbf{g}\|^2 = \mathrm{vol}(\mathbf{V}), \tag{2.48}$$

where $\mathbf{D}^{-1/2}\mathbf{L}\mathbf{D}^{-1/2} = \mathbf{L}_{sym}$, $\mathbf{D}^{1/2}1$ is the first eigenvector of $\mathbf{L}_{sym}$, and $\mathrm{vol}(\mathbf{V})$ is a constant. The solution $\mathbf{g}$ of Eq. (2.48) is given by the second eigenvector of $\mathbf{L}_{sym}$. Re-substituting $\mathbf{y} = \mathbf{D}^{-1/2}\mathbf{g}$, $\mathbf{y}$ can be obtained by the second eigenvector of $\mathbf{L}_{rw}$, or equivalently the generalized eigenvector of $\mathbf{L}\mathbf{u} = \lambda\mathbf{D}\mathbf{u}$. In the case of finding $d > 2$ clusters, the indicator vector $\mathbf{y}_j = (\mathbf{y}_{1,j}, \ldots, \mathbf{y}_{N,j})$ can be defined as

$$\mathbf{y}_{ij} = \begin{cases} 1/\sqrt{\mathrm{vol}(C_j)} & \text{if } v_i \in C_j \\ 0 & \text{otherwise,} \end{cases} \tag{2.49}$$

in which $i = 1, \ldots, N$; $j = 1, \ldots, d$. The matrix $\mathbf{Y}$ can be defined as containing those d indicator vectors as columns. It can be observed that $\mathbf{Y}^{\mathbf{T}}\mathbf{Y} = \mathbf{I}$, $\mathbf{y}_i^{\mathbf{T}}\mathbf{D}\mathbf{y}_i$ and $\mathbf{y}_i^{\mathbf{T}}\mathbf{L}\mathbf{y}_i = \mathrm{cut}(C_i, \overline{C}_i)/\mathrm{vol}(C_i)$. The problem of minimizing Ncut can be written as

$$\min_{C_1,\ldots,C_d} \mathrm{tr}(\mathbf{Y}^{\mathbf{T}}\mathbf{L}\mathbf{Y}) \text{ s.t. } \mathbf{Y}^{\mathbf{T}}\mathbf{D}\mathbf{Y} = \mathbf{I}. \tag{2.50}$$

By relaxing the discreteness condition and substituting $\mathbf{T} = \mathbf{D}^{1/2}\mathbf{S}$, we obtain the relaxed problem

$$\min_{C_1,\ldots,C_d} \mathrm{tr}(\mathbf{T}^{\mathbf{T}}\mathbf{D}^{-1/2}\mathbf{L}\mathbf{D}^{-1/2}\mathbf{T}) \text{ s.t. } \mathbf{T}^{\mathbf{T}}\mathbf{T} = \mathbf{I}. \tag{2.51}$$

This is also a standard trace minimization problem that is solved by the matrix $\mathbf{T}$ which contains the first d eigenvectors of $\mathbf{L}_{sym}$ as columns. This yields the normalized spectral clustering algorithm.

2.3   ENSEMBLE MANIFOLD LEARNING

This section introduces an automatic approximation of the intrinsic manifold for general semi-supervised learning problems. Unfortunately, it is not trivial to define an optimization function to obtain optimal hyperparameters. Usually, pure cross-validation is considered but it does not necessarily scale up. A second problem derives from the suboptimality incurred by discrete grid search and overfitting problems. As a consequence, an ensemble manifold regularization(EMR) framework is presented in this section to approximate the intrinsic manifold by combining several initial guesses.

2.3.1   Motivation for EMR

The common motivation of the Semi-supervised Learning (SSL) algorithms [365] is trying to exploit the intrinsic geometry of the probability distribution of unlabeled samples by restricting the inductive or transductive prediction to comply with this geometry. The manifold regularization framework, one of the most representative works, assumes that the geometry of the intrinsic data probability distribution is supported on the low-dimensional manifold. To approximate the manifold, the Laplacian of the adjacency graph is computed in an unsupervised manner from the data points by using LE in the feature space.

Generally, there are no explicit rules to choose graph hyperparameters for intrinsic manifold estimation, because it is non-trivial to define an objective function to obtain these hyperparameters. Usually, cross-validation is utilized for parameter selection. However, this grid-search technique tries to select parameters from discrete states in the parameter space and lacks the ability to approximate the optimal solution. Moreover, performance measurements of the learned model, e.g., the classification accuracy, are weakly relevant to the difference between the approximated and intrinsic manifolds. Thus, automatic and data-driven manifold approximation is invaluable for the manifold regularization-based SSL.

To tackle the aforementioned problems, an ensemble manifold regularization (EMR) framework is introduced to combine the automatic intrinsic manifold approximation and the semi-supervised classifier learning. By providing a series of initial guesses of graph Laplacian, the framework learns to combine them to approximate the intrinsic manifold in a conditionally optimal way. EMR is fully automatic for learning the intrinsic manifold hyperparameters implicitly. It is conditionally optimal for intrinsic manifold approximation under a mild and reasonable assumption and is scalable for a large number of candidate manifold hyperparameters, from both time and space perspectives.

2.3.2   Overview of EMR

Consider the semi-supervised learning (SSL) setting, where the data set $\mathbf{X} = [\mathbf{x}_1, \ldots, \mathbf{x}_N] \in \mathbf{R}^m \times N$ is available. In this set, there are N_l labeled samples $\{(\mathbf{x}_i, \mathbf{y}_i)\}_{i=1}^{N_l}$ and N_u unlabeled samples $\{\mathbf{x}_i\}_{i=N_l+1}^{N_u+N_l}$, with $\mathbf{y}_i \in \mathbf{R}$ as the label of

$\mathbf{x}_i$, and $N_l + N_u = N$. Suppose the labeled samples are $(\mathbf{x}, \mathbf{y}) \in \mathbf{R}^m \times \mathbf{R}$ pairs drawn from a probability distribution P, and unlabeled samples are simply drawn according to the marginal distribution P_X of P. To utilize P_X induced by unlabeled samples for SSL, the well-known manifold regularization framework is proposed. It assumes that the support of P_X is a compact manifold, and incorporates an additional regularization term to minimize the function complexity along the manifold. The problem takes the following form:

$$\min_{\mathbf{f} \in H_K} \frac{1}{N_l} \sum_{i=1}^{N_l} V(\mathbf{f}, \mathbf{x}_i, \mathbf{y}_i) + \gamma_A \|\mathbf{f}\|_K^2 + \gamma_I \|\mathbf{f}\|_I^2, \qquad (2.52)$$

where H_K is the reproducing kernel hilbert space (RKHS); V is a general loss function, e.g., the least-square error, or the hinge loss; $\|\mathbf{f}\|_K^2$ penalizes the classifier complexities measured in an appropriately chosen RKHS and is similar to that in SVM; $\|\mathbf{f}\|_I^2$ is the smooth penalty term reflecting the smoothness along the manifold supporting P_X. Parameters γ_A and γ_I balance between the loss function and regularizations $\|\mathbf{f}\|_K^2$ and $\|\mathbf{f}_I^2\|$. The manifold regularization term $\|\mathbf{f}_I^2\|$ is the key to SSL and models the classifier smoothness along the manifold estimated from the unlabeled samples.

It turns out that in an appropriate coordinate system (exponential, which to the first order coincides with the local coordinate system given by a tangent plan in $\mathbf{R}^m$), $\|\mathbf{f}\|_I^2$ is approximated by the graph Laplacian $\mathbf{L}$ and the function prediction $\mathbf{f} = [\mathbf{f}(\mathbf{x}_1), \ldots, \mathbf{f}(\mathbf{x}_{N_l+N_u})]^T$, i.e., $\|\mathbf{f}\|_I^2 = \frac{1}{(N_u+N_l)^2} \mathbf{f}^T \mathbf{L} \mathbf{f}$. In the above setting, the graph Laplacian is defined as $\mathbf{L} = \mathbf{D} - \mathbf{W}$, or normalized graph Laplacian matrix $\mathbf{L}_n = \mathbf{D}^{-1/2}(\mathbf{D} - \mathbf{W})\mathbf{D}^{-1/2}$. The matrix $\mathbf{W} \in \mathbf{R}^{N_l+N_u} \times \mathbf{R}^{N_l+N_u}$ is the data adjacency graph, wherein each element $\mathbf{W}_{ij}$ is the edge weight between two samples $\mathbf{x}_i$ and $\mathbf{x}_j$. In the diagonal matrix $\mathbf{D} \in \mathbf{R}^{N_l+N_u} \times \mathbf{R}^{N_l+N_u}$, $\mathbf{D}_{ii} = \sum_{i=1}^{N_l+N_u} \mathbf{W}_{ij}$.

The construction of the graph Laplacian involves setting hyperparameters for creating the data adjacency graph, which is data-dependent and generally performed by experiences, cross-validation or both. Our framework is designed to automatically, effectively and efficiently approximate the optimal graph Laplacian.

It is nontrivial to directly obtain the optimal graph Laplacian hyperparameters according to Eq. (2.52). As a consequence, an alternative approach is proposed to learn the optimal hyperparameters implicitly, by assuming that the intrinsic manifold lies in the convex hull of a number of pre-given manifold candidates. Since the optimal graph Laplacian is the discrete approximation to the manifold, the above assumption is equivalent to constraining the search space of possible graph Laplacians, i.e.,

$$\mathbf{L} = \sum_{j=1}^{n} \mu_j \mathbf{L}_j, \ \text{s.t.} \sum_{j=1}^{n} \mu_j = 1, \mu_j \geq 0, \ j = 1, \ldots, n, \qquad (2.53)$$

where we define a set of candidate graph Laplacians $C = \{\mathbf{L}_1, \ldots, \mathbf{L}_n\}$ and denote the convex hull of set A as

$$\text{conv}A = \{\theta_1 \mathbf{x}_1 + \cdots + \theta_k \mathbf{x}_k | \theta_1 + \cdots + \theta_k = 1, \mathbf{x}_i \in A, \theta_i \geq 0, i = 1, \ldots, k\}. \qquad (2.54)$$

Therefore, we have $\mathbf{L} \in \text{conv}C$.

Under this constraint, the optimal graph Laplacian hyperparameter estimation is turned into the problem of learning the optimal linear combination of certain pre-given candidates. Because each candidate graph Laplacian represents a certain manifold of the given samples, the EMR framework can be understood geometrically as follows: First, compute all possible approximated manifolds, each of which corresponds to a "guess" at the intrinsic data distribution, and then learn to linearly combine them for an optimal composite. To minimize the classifier complexity over the composite manifold, a new manifold regularization term is proposed:

$$\|\mathbf{f}\|_I^2 = \frac{1}{(N_l + N_u)^2}\mathbf{f}^T\mathbf{L}\mathbf{f} = \frac{1}{(N_l + N_u)^2}\mathbf{f}^T\left(\sum_{j=1}^n \mu_j\mathbf{L}_j\right)\mathbf{f}$$

$$= \sum_{j=1}^n \mu_j\|\mathbf{f}\|_{I(j)}^2.$$

(2.55)

Then, we obtain the EMR framework as

$$\min_{\mathbf{f}\in H_K, \mu\in\mathbf{R}^m} \frac{1}{N_l}\sum_{i=1}^{N_l} V(\mathbf{f}, \mathbf{x}_i, \mathbf{y}_i) + \gamma_A\|\mathbf{f}\|_K^2 + \gamma_I\sum_{j=1}^n \mu_j\|\mathbf{f}\|_{I(j)}^2 + \gamma_R\|\mu\|_2^2,$$

$$\text{s.t. } \sum_{j=1}^n \mu_j = 1, \ \mu_j \geq 0, j = 1, \ldots, n,$$

(2.56)

where the regularization term $\|\mu\|_2^2$ is introduced to avoid the parameter overfitting to only one manifold; and $\gamma_R \in \mathbf{R}^+$ is the trade-off parameter to control the contribution of the regularization term $\|\mu\|_2^2$. Because Eq. (2.56) contains a weighted combination of multiple manifold regularization terms, we name the new regularization framework an ensemble manifold regularization (EMR). For a fixed μ, Eq. (2.56) degenerates to Eq. (2.53), with $\mathbf{L} = \sum_{j=1}^n \mu_j\mathbf{L}_j$ for $\|\mathbf{f}\|_I^2$. On the other hand, for a fixed $\mathbf{f}$, Eq. (2.56) is simplified to

$$\min_{\mu\in\mathbf{R}^m} \sum_{j=1}^n \mu_j s_j + \gamma_R\|\mu\|^2,$$

$$\text{s.t. } \sum_{j=1}^n \mu_j = 1, \mu_j \geq 0, \ j = 1, \ldots, n,$$

(2.57)

where $s_j = \frac{\gamma_I}{(N_l + N_u)^2}\mathbf{f}^T\mathbf{L}_j\mathbf{f}$. Under this condition, if $\gamma_R = 0$, the solution of Eq. (2.57) will be: $\mu_j = 1$ if $s_j = \min_{k=1,\ldots,n} s_k$ and $\mu_j = 0$ otherwise. Such a trivial case will assign all the weight to one manifold, which is extremely sparse and not desirable for learning a composite manifold. If $\gamma_R \to +\infty$, the solution tends to give identical weights to all the graph Laplacians.

Here, we present some theoretical analysis of EMR. Because the Laplacian matrix for each graph satisfies the semidefinite positive property, i.e., $\mathbf{L}_i \in S_{N_l+N_u}^+$, their convex combination satisfies $\mathbf{L} \in S^+_{N_l+N_u}$. Consequently, $\mathbf{L} \in \text{conv}C$ is a graph Laplacian. According to Ref. [33], the representer theorem follows for a fixed μ. For a $\mathbf{L} \in \text{conv}C$, the minimization in Eq. (2.56) w.r.t. $\mathbf{f}$ with a fixed μ, exists and has the representation

$$\mathbf{f}(x) = \sum_{i=1}^{N_l+N_u} \alpha_i K(\mathbf{x}_i, \mathbf{x}), \qquad (2.58)$$

which is an expansion in terms of the labeled and unlabeled examples.

Equation (2.58) presents us with the existence and general form of the solution of Eq. (2.56) under any fixed μ. However, EMR is motivated to learn both the SSL classifier $\mathbf{f}$ and the linear combination coefficients μ. Fortunately, we can adopt the alternating optimization technique to solve Eq. (2.56) in an iterative manner, i.e., first solving (2.56) w.r.t. $\mathbf{f}$ with a fixed μ, resulting in the solution represented by (2.58); then optimizing (2.56) w.r.t. μ, with $\mathbf{f}$ taking the value solved in the last iteration; and alternately iterating the above two steps, until the decrement of the objective function is zero. For any convex loss function $\mathbf{H}_K \times \mathbf{R}^m \times \mathbf{R}$, Eq. (2.56) is convex not only w.r.t. $\mathbf{f}$ for fixed μ but also w.r.t. μ for fixed $\mathbf{f}$. Consequently, the alternating optimization of Eq. (2.56), iteratively over parameters $\mathbf{f}$ and μ converges.

However, Eq. (2.56) is not convex w.r.t. $(\mathbf{f}, \mu)$ jointly. We can solve the problem based on two strategies: (a) set a large value for γ_R so that Eq. (2.56) is convex w.r.t. $(\mathbf{f}, \mu)$; (b) initialize $\mu = 1/n$. The later strategy initializes $\mathbf{L}$ as the mean of the graph Laplacians in the candidate set, which usually leads to a satisfied solution. In the following elaborations, the second strategy is adopted for all experiments and shows its effectiveness.

The theoretical analysis shown above presents the basic properties of the proposed EMR and ensures that the framework can be implemented into numerous algorithms for various machine learning applications, e.g., data classification and regression.

2.3.3 Applications of EMR

We consider the general-purpose classification task in this section, and we show how to implement the EMR framework based on the support vector machine (SVM).

In SVM, the hinge loss is adopted. For a fixed μ, the solution is given by Eq. (2.58). Substituting Eq. (2.58) into the framework of EMR, we can obtain the EMR-SVM:

$$\min_{\alpha \in R^{N_l+N_u}, \xi \in R^{N_l}, \mu \in R^n} \frac{1}{N_l} \sum_{i=1}^{N_l} \xi_i + \gamma_A \alpha^T \mathbf{K} \alpha$$

$$+ \frac{\gamma_I}{(N_I + N_u)^2} \sum_{j=1}^{n} \mu_j \alpha^T \mathbf{K} \mathbf{L}_j \mathbf{K} \alpha + \gamma_R \|\mu\|_2^2,$$

$$\text{s.t. } \mathbf{y}_i \left(\sum_{j=1}^{N_l+N_u} \alpha_i \mathbf{K}(\mathbf{x}_i, \mathbf{x}_j) + b \right) \geq 1 - \xi_i, i = 1, \dots, N_l, \qquad (2.59)$$

$$\xi_i \geq 0, i = 1, \dots, N_l,$$

$$\sum_{j=1}^{n} \mu_j = 1, \mu_j \geq 0, \ j = 1, \dots, n,$$

where $\mathbf{K} \in \mathbf{R}^{N_l+N_u}$ is the gram matrix and its entry is $\mathbf{K}_{ij} \in \mathbf{K}(\mathbf{x}_i, \mathbf{x}_j)$. To adopt the alternating optimization for obtaining the solution of Eq. (2.59), we need to obtain the solution of $\mathbf{f}$ (represented by α according to Eq. (2.58) with a fixed μ, as well as the solution μ of with a fixed $\mathbf{f}$.

For a fixed μ, we can introduce non-negative Lagrange multipliers β and ς for the inequality constraints in Eq. (2.59), which leads to

$$L(\alpha, \xi, b, \beta, \varsigma) = \frac{1}{2} \alpha^T (2\gamma_A \mathbf{K} + \frac{2\gamma_A}{(N_I + N_u)^2} \mathbf{K}(\sum_{j=1}^{n} \mu_j \mathbf{L}_j) \mathbf{K}) \alpha + \frac{1}{N_l} \sum_{i=1}^{N_l} \xi_i$$

$$- \sum_{i=1}^{N_l} \beta_i (\mathbf{y}_i (\sum_{j=1}^{N_l+N_u} \alpha_i \mathbf{K}(\mathbf{x}_i, \mathbf{x}_j) + b) - 1 + \xi_i) - \sum_{i=1}^{N_l} \varsigma \xi_i. \qquad (2.60)$$

By taking the partial derivative w.r.t. α, β, ς and requiring them to be zero, we can eliminate those variables by substituting their solutions back into Eq. (2.60) for the dual format:

$$\beta^* = \max_{\beta \in \mathbf{R}^{N_l}} \sum_{i=1}^{N_l} \beta_i - \frac{1}{2} \beta^T \mathbf{Q} \beta,$$

$$\text{s.t. } \sum_{i=1}^{N_l} \beta_i \mathbf{y}_i = 0, \ 0 \leq \beta_i \leq \frac{1}{N_l}, i = 1, \dots, N_l, \qquad (2.61)$$

where $\mathbf{Q} = \mathbf{Y} \mathbf{J} \mathbf{K} (2\gamma_A \mathbf{I}_{N_l+N_u} + \frac{2\gamma_I}{(N_l+N_u)^2} \sum_{j=1}^{n} \mu_j \mathbf{L}_j \mathbf{K})^{-1} \mathbf{J}^T \mathbf{Y}$, $\mathbf{Y} = diag(\mathbf{y}_1, \dots, \mathbf{y}_l)$, $\mathbf{I} \in \mathbf{R}^{N_l+N_u} \times \mathbf{R}^{N_l+N_u}$ denotes a identity matrix and $\mathbf{J} = [\ \mathbf{I}_{N_l} \quad 0\ ] \in \mathbf{R}^{N_l} \times \mathbf{R}^{N_l+N_u}$. The solution of Eq. (2.59) is given by

$$\alpha^* = (2\gamma_A \mathbf{I} + \frac{2\gamma_I}{(N_l + N_u)^2} \sum_{j=1}^{n} \mu_j \mathbf{L}_j \mathbf{K})^{-1} \mathbf{J}^T \mathbf{Y} \beta^*. \qquad (2.62)$$

The learning procedure combines different graph Laplacians into $\mathbf{Q}$, and the optimization of Eq. (2.61) is approximately independent of the number of graph Laplacians n. Therefore, with a fixed μ, we do not incorporate additional computational costs, except for some sparse matrix additions, which are negligible.

On the other hand, for learning μ with a fixed $\mathbf{f}$, Eq. (2.59) degenerates to Eq. (2.57), and we can adopt a coordinate descent algorithm. In each iteration, we select two elements for updating while the others are fixed. Suppose at an iteration, the ith and jth elements are selected. Due to the constraint $\sum_{j=1}^{n} \mu_j = 1$, the summation of μ_i and μ_j will not change after this iteration. Therefore, we have the solution of this iteration:

$$
\begin{aligned}
&\mu_i^* = 0, \mu_j^* = \mu_i + \mu_j, \text{ if } 2\gamma_R(\mu_i + \mu_j) + (s_j - s_i) \leq 0, \\
&\mu_i^* = \mu_i + \mu_j, \mu_j^* = 0, \text{ if } 2\gamma_R(\mu_i + \mu_j) + (s_i - s_j) \leq 0, \\
&\mu_i^* = \frac{2\gamma_R(\mu_i + \mu_j) + (s_j - s_i)}{4\gamma_R}, \ \mu_j^* = \mu_i + \mu_j - \mu_i^*, \text{else.}
\end{aligned}
\tag{2.63}
$$

We iteratively traverse all pairs of elements in μ and adopt the solution in Eq. (2.63), until the objective function in (2.57) does not decrease. Intuitively, the update criteria in (2.63) tends to assign larger value μ_j to smaller s_j. Because $s_j = \frac{\gamma_I}{(N_l+N_u)^2}\mathbf{f}^T\mathbf{L}_j\mathbf{f}$ measures the smoothness of the function $\mathbf{f}$ over the jth manifold approximated by the graph Laplacian $\mathbf{L}_j$, the algorithm will prefer the pre-given manifold that coincides with current iteration SSL classifier $\mathbf{f}$.

2.4   MULTIPLE KERNEL LEARNING

Kernel-based methods such as support vector machines (SVMs) have proven to be powerful for a wide range of different data analysis problems. They employ a so-called kernel function which intuitively calculates the similarity between data samples. Recent developments in the literature on SVMs and other kernel methods have shown the need to consider multiple kernels. This offers flexibility and reflects the fact that typical learning problems often include multiple, heterogeneous data sources. This so-called "multiple kernel learning" (MKL) problem can in principle be solved via cross-validation. Recently, some research works have focused on more efficient methods for multiple kernel learning [65, 36, 96, 215, 23, 153, 40]. Compared with other approaches, the central problem with kernel methods is that the resulting decision function (shown in Eq. (2.64) is hard to interpret. Thus, it is difficult to adopt in order to extract relevant knowledge about the problem at hand.

The solution of this problem can be achieved by considering the convex combination of multiple kernels. The optimized combination coefficients can then be used to understand which features of the examples are of importance for discrimination; if one is able to obtain an accurate classification by a sparse weighting, then one can quite easily interpret the resulting decision function. The present article additionally offers a more general and complete derivation of the main optimization problem. In related papers, non-sparse MKL has been applied, extended, and further analyzed by several researchers since its initial publication in Kloft et al. [140] and Cortes et al. [74]. Varma and Babu [297] also derive a projected gradient-based optimization method for l_2-norm MKL. Yu et al. [346] present a more general dual view of l_2-norm MKL and show the advantages of l_2-norm over an unweighted-sum kernel SVM on six bioinformatics data sets. Cortes et al. [63] provide generalization bounds for l_1-and $l_{p \leq 2}$-norm MKL. The details of these achievements will be elaborated in the following section.

2.4.1 A Unified Mulitple Kernel Learning Framework

According to Ref. [186], the proposed multiple kernel learning methods can be unified into one framework, which presents a regularized loss minimization formulation with additional norm constraints on the kernel mixing coefficients. Initially, the classical supervised learning setup is reviewed. Given a labeled sample $\{(\mathbf{x}_i, \mathbf{y}_i)\}$, in which the $\mathbf{x}_i$ lie in an input space $\mathbf{X}$ and $\mathbf{y}_i \in \mathbf{Y}$, the goal is to find a hypothesis $\mathbf{f} \in H$ that generalizes well on new and unseen data. The regularized risk minimization returns a minimized $\mathbf{f}^*$,

$$\mathbf{f}^* \in \arg \min_{\mathbf{f}} R_{emp}(\mathbf{f}) + \lambda \Omega(\mathbf{f}), \qquad (2.64)$$

where $R_{emp}(\mathbf{f} = (1/N)) \sum_{i=1}^{N} V(\mathbf{f}(\mathbf{x}_i), \mathbf{y})$ is the empirical risk of hypothesis $\mathbf{f}$ w.r.t. to a convex loss function $V : R \times \mathbf{Y} \to R$, $\Omega : H \to R$ is a regularizer, and $\lambda > 0$ is a trade-off parameter. The linear models of the form can be considered as

$$\mathbf{f}_{\mathbf{w}',b}(\mathbf{x}) = \langle \mathbf{w}', \psi(\mathbf{x}) \rangle + b, \qquad (2.65)$$

together with a mapping $\psi : \mathbf{X} \to H$ to a Hilbert space H. The regularization is constrained to be of the form $\Omega(\mathbf{f}) = \frac{1}{2} \|\mathbf{w}'\|_2^2$ which allows kernelization of the resulting models and algorithms. The kernel function $K(\mathbf{x}, \mathbf{x}^\mathbf{T}) = \langle \psi(\mathbf{x}), \psi(\mathbf{x}^\mathbf{T}) \rangle_H$ is adopted to compute inner products in H. When learning with multiple kernels, M different feature mappings $\psi_m : \mathbf{X} \to H_m$, $m = 1, \ldots, M$, are provided and each gives rise to a reproducing kernel K_m of H_m. Here, convex approaches to multiple kernel learning consider linear kernel mixtures $K_\theta = \sum \theta_m H_m, \theta_m \geq 0$. Therefore, the elementary model for multiple kernel learning can be formulated as

$$\mathbf{f}_{\mathbf{w}',b,\theta}(\mathbf{x}) = \sum_{m=1}^{M} \sqrt{\theta_m} \langle \mathbf{w}'_m, \psi_m(\mathbf{x}) \rangle_{H_m} + b = \langle \mathbf{w}', \psi_\theta(\mathbf{x}) \rangle_H + b, \qquad (2.66)$$

where the parameter vector $\mathbf{w}'$ and the composite feature map ψ_θ have a block structure. The aim of multiple kernel learning can be assumed to be minimizing the loss on the training data w.r.t to optimal kernel mixture $\sum \theta_m K_m$ in addition to regularizing θ to avoid overfitting. Thus, the optimization problem can be formulated as [186]

$$\inf_{\mathbf{w}',b,\theta:\theta \geq 0} \frac{1}{N} \sum_{i=1}^{N} V \left(\sum_{m=l}^{M} \sqrt{\theta_m} \langle \mathbf{w}'_m, \psi_m(\mathbf{x}_i) \rangle_{H_m} + b, \mathbf{y}_i \right) + \frac{\lambda}{2} \sum_{m=1}^{M} \|\mathbf{w}'_m\|_{H_m}^2 + \mu \Omega[\theta].$$

$$(2.67)$$

In Ref. [186], the convex regularizers of the form $\Omega[\theta] = \|\theta\|^2$ are used, and $\|\cdot\|^2$ is an arbitrary norm in R^m, which allows for non-sparse solutions and the incorporation of prior knowledge. The product $\sqrt{\theta_m}\mathbf{w}'_m$ causes the nonconvexity in the loss term of Eq. (2.67). This problem can be resolved by substituting $\mathbf{w}_m \leftarrow \sqrt{\theta_m}\mathbf{w}'_m$. In addition, the regularization parameter and the sample size can be decoupled by introducing $C = \frac{1}{N\lambda}$. Thus the unified optimization framework can be rewritten as

$$\inf_{\mathbf{w}',b,\theta:\theta\geq 0} C\sum_{i=1}^{N} V\Big(\sum_{m=1}^{M}\langle \mathbf{w}_m, \psi_m(\mathbf{x})_i\rangle_{H_m} + b, \mathbf{y}_i\Big) + \frac{1}{2}\sum_{m=1}^{M}\frac{\|\mathbf{w}'_m\|^2_{H_m}}{\theta_m} + \mu\|\theta\|^2,$$

(2.68)

where we use the convention that $\frac{t}{0} = 0$ if $t = 0$ and ∞ otherwise. In general, Eq. (2.68) can be written as

$$\inf_{\mathbf{w},b,\theta:\theta\geq 0} C\sum_{i=1}^{N} V\Big(\sum_{m=1}^{M}\langle \mathbf{w}_m, \psi_m(\mathbf{x})_i\rangle_{H_m} + b, \mathbf{y}_i\Big) + \frac{1}{2}\sum_{m=1}^{M}\frac{\|\mathbf{w}_m\|^2_{H_m}}{\theta_m},$$

(2.69)

$$\text{s.t.}\|\theta\|^2 \leq 1.$$

The optimization problem (2.69) can be rewritten by expanding the decision values into slack variable as follows

$$\inf_{\mathbf{w},b,t,\theta} C\sum_{i=1}^{N} V(\mathbf{t}_i, \mathbf{y}_i) + \frac{1}{2}\sum_{m=1}^{M}\frac{\|\mathbf{w}_m\|^2_{H_m}}{\theta_m},$$

$$\text{s.t.}\forall i : \sum_{m=1}^{M}\langle \mathbf{w}_m, \psi_m(\mathbf{x})_i\rangle_{H_m} + b = \mathbf{t}_i; \|\theta\|^2 \leq 1; \theta \geq 0,$$

(2.70)

where $\|\cdot\|$ is an arbitrary norm in $\mathbf{R}^m$ and $\|\cdot\|_{H_m}$ denotes the Hilbertian norm of $\mathbf{H}_m$. Subsequently, we can apply Lagrange's theorem to re-incorporate the constraints into the objective by introducing Lagragian multipliers $\alpha \in \mathbf{R}^n$, $\beta \in \mathbf{R}_+$, and $\gamma \in \mathbf{R}_M$. Then, the problem becomes

$$\sup_{\alpha,\beta,\gamma,\beta\geq 0,\gamma\geq 0} \inf_{\mathbf{w},b,t,\theta} C\sum_{i=1}^{N} V(\mathbf{t}_i, \mathbf{y}_i) + \frac{1}{2}\sum_{m=1}^{M}\frac{\|\mathbf{w}_m\|^2_{H_m}}{\theta_m}$$

$$-\sum_{i=1}^{N}\alpha_i\Big(\sum_{m=1}^{M}\langle \mathbf{w}_m, \psi_m(\mathbf{x})_i\rangle_{H_m} + b - \mathbf{t}_i\Big) + \beta\left(\frac{1}{2}\|\theta\|^2 - \frac{1}{2}\right) - \gamma^{\mathbf{T}}\theta.$$

(2.71)

To set the objective function's first partial derivatives with respect to $\mathbf{w}$ and b to 0 reveals the optimal conditions

$$\mathbf{1}^{\mathbf{T}}\alpha = 0,$$

$$\mathbf{w}_m = \theta_m\sum_{i=1}^{N}\alpha_i\psi_m(\mathbf{x}_i), \quad \forall m = 1,\ldots,M.$$

(2.72)

To substitute these two terms into the objective function in Eq. (2.71), it becomes

$$\sup_{\alpha,\gamma,1^{\mathbf{T}}\alpha=0,\gamma\geq0} -C\sum_{i=1}^{N} V^*(-\frac{\alpha_i}{C}, \mathbf{y}_i) - \left\|\left(\frac{1}{2}\alpha^{\mathbf{T}}K_m\alpha + \gamma_m\right)_{m=1}^{M}\right\|_*, \quad (2.73)$$

where $\|\cdot\|_*$ denotes the dual norm. In the following parts, some existing multiple kernel learning methods are introduced and they are unified into this framework.

2.4.2 SVM with Multiple Unweighted-Sum Kernels

The support vector machine with an unweighted-sum kernel can be recovered as a special case of Eq. (2.73). Here, the regularized risk minimization problem can be considered to be the hinge loss function $V(t,y) = \max(0, 1 - ty)$ and the regularizer $\|\theta\|_\infty$. The dual loss of the hinge loss is noted as $V^*(t,y) = \frac{t}{y}$ if $-1 \leq \frac{t}{y} \leq 0$ and ∞ otherwise. For each i the term $V^*(-\frac{\alpha_i}{C}, \mathbf{y}_i)$ of the generalized dual, that is, the optimization problem in Eq. (2.73) translates to $-\frac{\alpha_i}{C\mathbf{y}_i}$, provided that $0 \leq \frac{\alpha_i}{\mathbf{y}_i} \leq C$. Thus, Eq. (2.73) can be rewritten as

$$\max_{\alpha,\gamma,\gamma\geq0} 1^{\mathbf{T}}\alpha - \|(\frac{1}{2}\alpha^{\mathbf{T}}\mathbf{Y}\mathbf{K}_m\mathbf{Y}\alpha + \gamma_m)_{m=1}^{M}\|_*,$$
$$\text{s.t. } \mathbf{y}^{\mathbf{T}}\alpha = 0 \text{ and } 0 \leq \alpha \leq C1, \quad (2.74)$$

where the $Y = \text{diag}(y)$ is denoted. The primal l_∞-norm penalty $\|\theta\|_\infty$ is dual to $\|\theta\|_1$. Thus this leads to the dual

$$\max_{\alpha} 1^{\mathbf{T}}\alpha - \sum_{m=1}^{M} \alpha^{\mathbf{T}}\mathbf{Y}\mathbf{K}_m\mathbf{Y}\alpha,$$
$$\text{s.t. } \mathbf{y}^{\mathbf{T}}\alpha = 0 \text{ and } 0 \leq \alpha \leq C1, \quad (2.75)$$

which is precisely an SVM with an unweighted-sum kernel.

2.4.3 QCQP Multiple Kernel Learning

A common approach in multiple kernel learning is to employ regularizers of the form $\Omega(\theta) = \|\theta\|_1$, which is called l_1-norm regularizers for sparisity-inducing regularizers. The obtained kernel mixtures usually have a considerably large fraction of zero entries. This sparse MKL introduce by Lanckriet et al. [153] is a special case of the framework. Based on the definition of l_p-norm, the right-hand side of optimization problem (73) translates to $\max_{m\in\{1,...,M\}} \alpha^{\mathbf{T}}\mathbf{Y}\mathbf{K}_m\mathbf{Y}\alpha$. The object function becomes

$$\sup_{\alpha,\xi} 1^{\mathbf{T}}\alpha - \xi,$$
$$\text{s.t. } \forall m : \frac{1}{2}\alpha^{\mathbf{T}}\mathbf{Y}\mathbf{K}_m\mathbf{Y}\alpha \leq \xi; \mathbf{y}^{\mathbf{T}}\alpha = 0; 0 \leq \alpha \leq C1, \quad (2.76)$$

which is the original QCQP formulation of MKL, presented in Ref. [153].

2.5   MULTIVIEW SUBSPACE LEARNING

In computer vision and multimedia search, it is common to use multiple features from different views to represent an object. For example, to successfully characterize a natural scene image, it is essential to find a set of visual features [262, 265, 330] to represent its color, texture and shape information and encode each feature into a vector. The traditional subspace learning algorithm cannot deal with the datum directly, so these vectors have to be concatenated as a new vector. This concatenation is not physically meaningful because each feature has a specific statistical property. Therefore, in this section, we introduce a novel subspace learning algorithm which can encode different features in different ways to achieve a physically meaningful embedding.

2.5.1   Approach Overview

In this section, we present a novel multiview subspace learning algorithm calledPA-MSL which finds a low-dimensional and sufficiently smooth embedding simultaneously over all views. Some important notations are provided at the beginning of this chapter. The PA-MSL is proposed based on patch alignment framework which has been clearly explained in Section 2.1. Initially, PA-MSL builds a patch for a sample on a single-view. Based on the patches from different views, the part optimization can be performed to obtain the optimal low-dimensional embedding for each view. All low-dimensional subspaces from different patches are then unified as a whole by global coordinate alignment. Finally, the solution of PA-MSL is derived by using the alternating optimization. Given the ith view $\mathbf{X}^{(i)} = [\mathbf{x}_1^{(i)}, \ldots, \mathbf{x}_N^{(i)}] \in \mathbf{R}^{m_i \times N}$, consider an arbitrary point $\mathbf{x}_j^{(i)}$ and its k related points in the same view (e.g. nearest neighbors) $\mathbf{x}_{j_1}^{(i)}, \ldots, \mathbf{x}_{j_k}^{(i)}$; the patch of $\mathbf{x}_j^{(i)}$ is defined as $\mathbf{X}_j^{(i)} = [\mathbf{x}_j^{(i)}, \mathbf{x}_{j_1}^{(i)}, \ldots, \mathbf{x}_{j_k}^{(i)}] \in \mathbf{R}^{m_i \times (k+1)}$. For $\mathbf{x}_j^{(i)}$, there exists a mapping $\mathbf{X}_j^{(i)} \rightarrow \mathbf{Y}_j^{(i)}$, in which $\mathbf{Y}_j^{(i)} = [\mathbf{y}_j^{(i)}, \mathbf{y}_{j_1}^{(i)}, \ldots, \mathbf{y}_{j_k}^{(i)}] \in \mathbf{R}^{d \times (k+1)}$.

2.5.2   Techinique Details

To preserve the locality in the projected low-dimensional space, the part optimization for the ith patch on the ith view is

$$\arg \min_{\mathbf{Y}_j^{(i)}} \sum_{n=1}^{k} (\mathbf{w}_j^{(i)})_n \|\mathbf{y}_j^{(i)} - \mathbf{y}_{j_n}^{(i)}\|^2, \tag{2.77}$$

in which $\mathbf{w}_j^{(i)}$ is calculated by

$$(\mathbf{w}_j^{(i)})_n = \exp(-\|\mathbf{x}_j^{(i)} - \mathbf{x}_{j_n}^{(i)}\|^2 / t). \tag{2.78}$$

According to Eq. (2.78), Eq. (2.77) can be reformulated as

$$\arg\min_{\mathbf{Y}_j^{(i)}} \mathbf{tr} \begin{bmatrix} (\mathbf{y}_j^{(i)} - \mathbf{y}_{j_1}^{(i)})^{\mathbf{T}} \\ \cdots \\ \mathbf{y}_j^{(i)} - \mathbf{y}_{j_k}^{(i)})^{\mathbf{T}} \end{bmatrix} \times [\ \mathbf{y}_j^{(i)} - \mathbf{y}_{j_1}^{(i)}, \quad \cdots, \quad \mathbf{y}_j^{(i)} - \mathbf{y}_{j_k}^{(i)}\ ] \mathrm{diag}(\mathbf{w}_j^{(i)})$$

$$= \arg\min_{\mathbf{Y}_j^{(i)}} \mathbf{tr}(\mathbf{Y}_j^{(i)} \begin{bmatrix} -\mathbf{e}_k^{\mathbf{T}} \\ \mathbf{I}_k \end{bmatrix} \mathrm{diag}(\mathbf{w}_j^{(i)}) \times [\ -\mathbf{e}_k \quad \mathbf{I}_k\ ](\mathbf{Y}_j^{(i)})^{\mathbf{T}})$$

$$= \arg\min_{\mathbf{Y}_j^{(i)}}(\mathbf{Y}_j^{(i)} \mathbf{L}_j^{(i)} (\mathbf{Y}_j^{(i)})^{\mathbf{T}}),$$

$$(2.79)$$

in which $\mathbf{e}_k = [1, \ldots, 1]^{\mathbf{T}}$, $\mathbf{I}_k$ is a $k \times k$ identity matrix, and $\mathbf{tr}(\cdot)$ is the trace operator. $\mathbf{L}_j^{(i)} \in \mathbf{R}^{(k+1) \times (k+1)}$ represents the objective function for jth patch on the ith view. The $\mathbf{L}_j^{(i)}$ can be represented as

$$\mathbf{L}_j^{(i)} = [\ \begin{matrix} -\mathbf{e}_k^{\mathbf{T}} \\ \mathbf{I}_k \end{matrix}\ ] \mathrm{diag}(\mathbf{w}_j^{(i)})[\ -\mathbf{e}_k \quad \mathbf{I}_k\ ]$$

$$= \begin{bmatrix} \sum_{n=1}^{k}(\mathbf{w}_j^{(i)})_n & -(\mathbf{w}_j^{(i)})^{\mathbf{T}} \\ -\mathbf{w}_j^{(i)} & \mathrm{diag}(\mathbf{w}_j^{(i)}) \end{bmatrix}. \qquad (2.80)$$

Hence, the part optimization for $\mathbf{X}_j^{(i)}$ in ith view is

$$\arg\min_{\mathbf{Y}_j^{(i)}} \mathbf{tr}(\mathbf{Y}_j^{(i)} \mathbf{L}_j^{(i)} (\mathbf{Y}_j^{(i)})^{\mathbf{T}}). \qquad (2.81)$$

According to the locality information encoded in $\mathbf{L}_j^{(i)}$, Eq. (2.81) constructs a sufficiently smooth low-dimensional embedding $\mathbf{Y}_j^i$ by preserving the intrinsic structure of the jth patch on the ith view.

On account of the complementary characteristics of multiple views, different views make different contributions to the low-dimensional subspace. To successfully investigate the complementary characteristics of different views, a set of non-negative weights $\beta = [\beta_1, \ldots, \beta_z]$ can be imposed on local patch optimization of different views. The larger β_i means the more important role the view $\mathbf{X}_j^{(i)}$ plays in learning to obtain the low-dimensional subspace $\mathbf{Y}_j^{(i)}$. To sum over all views, the multiview local patch optimization for the jth patch is

$$\arg\min_{\mathbf{Y}=\{\mathbf{Y}_j^{(i)}\}_{i=1}^z, \beta} \sum_{i=1}^{z} \beta_i \mathbf{tr}(\mathbf{Y}_j^{(i)} \mathbf{L}_j^{(i)} (\mathbf{Y}_j^{(i)})^{\mathbf{T}}). \qquad (2.82)$$

For each patch $\mathbf{X}_j^{(i)}$, there is a low-dimensional subspace $\mathbf{Y}_j^{(i)}$. These $\mathbf{Y}_j^{(i)}$s can be unified as a whole by assuming that the coordinate for $\mathbf{Y}_j^{(i)} = [\mathbf{Y}_j^{(i)}, \mathbf{Y}_{j_1}^{(i)}, \ldots, \mathbf{Y}_{j_k}^{(i)}]$

is selected from the global coordinate $\mathbf{Y} = [\mathbf{y}_1, \ldots, \mathbf{y}_N]$, i.e., $\mathbf{Y}_j^{(i)} = \mathbf{Y}\mathbf{S}_j^{(i)}$, which has been introduced by Eq. (2.2). This means that low-dimensional subspace in different views is globally consistent. Hence, Eq. (2.82) can be equivalently rewritten as

$$\arg\min_{\mathbf{Y},\beta} \sum_{i=1}^{z} \beta_i \mathbf{tr}(\mathbf{Y}\mathbf{S}_j^{(i)}\mathbf{L}_j^{(i)}(\mathbf{S}_j^{(i)})^{\mathbf{T}}\mathbf{Y}^{\mathbf{T}}). \qquad (2.83)$$

To sum over all local patch optimizations defined in Eq. (2.83), the global alignment is given by

$$\begin{aligned}
&\arg\min_{\mathbf{Y},\beta} \sum_{j=1}^{N}\sum_{i=1}^{z} \beta_i \mathbf{tr}(\mathbf{Y}\mathbf{S}_j^{(i)}\mathbf{L}_j^{(i)}(\mathbf{S}_j^{(i)})^{\mathbf{T}}\mathbf{Y}^{\mathbf{T}}) \\
&= \arg\min_{\mathbf{Y},\beta} \sum_{i=1}^{z} \beta_i \mathbf{tr}(\mathbf{Y}\mathbf{L}^{(i)}\mathbf{Y}^{\mathbf{T}}),
\end{aligned} \qquad (2.84)$$

in which $\mathbf{L}^{(i)} \in \mathbf{R}^{N \times N}$ is the alignment matrix for the ith view, and is defined as

$$\mathbf{L}^{(i)} = \sum_{j=1}^{N} \mathbf{S}_j^{(i)}\mathbf{L}_j^{(i)}(\mathbf{S}_j^{(i)})^{\mathbf{T}}. \qquad (2.85)$$

If we put Eq. (2.80) into Eq. (2.85), we have

$$\mathbf{L}^{(i)} = \mathbf{D}^{(i)} - \mathbf{W}^{(i)}, \qquad (2.86)$$

in which $\mathbf{W}^{(i)} \in \mathbf{R}^{N \times N}$ and $[\mathbf{W}^{(i)}]_{pq} = \exp(-\|\mathbf{x}_p^{(i)} - \mathbf{x}_q^{(i)}\|^2/t)$ if $\mathbf{x}_p^{(i)}$ is among the k-nearest neighbors of $\mathbf{x}_q^{(i)}$ or vice versa; $[\mathbf{W}^{(i)}]_{pq} = 0$ otherwise. Besides, $\mathbf{D}^{(i)}$ is diagonal, and $[\mathbf{D}^{(i)}]_{jj} = \sum_n [\mathbf{W}^{(i)}]_{jn}$. Therefore, $\mathbf{L}^{(i)}$ is an unnormalized graph Laplacian matrix. In PA-MSL, the normalized graph Laplacian matrix is adopted by conducting the normalization on $\mathbf{L}^{(i)}$:

$$\begin{aligned}
\mathbf{L}_n^{(i)} &= (\mathbf{D}^{(i)})^{-1/2}\mathbf{L}^{(i)}(\mathbf{D}^{(i)})^{-1/2} \\
&= \mathbf{I} - (\mathbf{D}^{(i)})^{-1/2}\mathbf{W}^{(i)}(\mathbf{D}^{(i)})^{-1/2},
\end{aligned} \qquad (2.87)$$

in which $\mathbf{L}_n^{(i)}$ is symmetric and positive semidefinite. The constraint $\mathbf{Y}\mathbf{Y}^{\mathbf{T}} = \mathbf{I}$ is imposed on Eq. (2.9) to uniquely determine the low-dimensional subspace $\mathbf{Y}$:

$$\begin{aligned}
&\arg\min_{\mathbf{Y},\beta} \sum_{i=1}^{z} \beta_i \mathbf{tr}(\mathbf{Y}\mathbf{L}_n^{(i)}\mathbf{Y}^{\mathbf{T}}) \\
&\text{s.t.} \mathbf{Y}\mathbf{Y}^{\mathbf{T}} = \mathbf{I}; \sum_{i=1}^{z} \beta_i = 1, \; \beta_i \geq 0.
\end{aligned} \qquad (2.88)$$

The solution to β in Eq. (2.88) is $\beta_k = 1$ corresponding to minimize $\mathbf{tr}(\mathbf{Y}\mathbf{L}^{(i)}\mathbf{Y}^{\mathbf{T}})$ over different views, and $\beta_k = 0$ otherwise. This solution cannot meet our objective of exploring the complementary property of multiple views to obtain a better embedding than one based on a single view.

2.5.3 Alternative Optimization Used in PA-MSL

To solve the problem in PA-MSL, the alternating optimization [39] is iteratively adopted to obtain a local optimal solution. The alternating optimization iteratively updates $\mathbf{Y}$ and β in an alternating fashion. First, $\mathbf{Y}$ is fixed to update β. By using a Lagrange multiplier λ to take the constraint $\sum_{i=1}^{z} \beta_i = 1$ into consideration, the Lagrange function can be obtained:

$$L(\beta, \lambda) = \sum_{i=1}^{z} \beta_i^r \mathbf{tr}(\mathbf{Y}\mathbf{L}_n^{(i)}\mathbf{Y}^{\mathbf{T}}) - \lambda(\sum_{i=1}^{z} \beta_i - 1). \tag{2.89}$$

To set the derivative of $L(\beta, \lambda)$ with respect to β_i and λ to zero, we can obtain

$$\frac{\partial L(\beta, \lambda)}{\partial \beta_i} = r\beta_i^{r-1}\mathbf{tr}(\mathbf{Y}\mathbf{L}_n^{(i)}\mathbf{Y}^{\mathbf{T}}) - \lambda = 0, \quad i = 1, \ldots, z,$$

$$\frac{\partial L(\beta, \lambda)}{\partial \lambda} = \sum_{i=1}^{z} \beta_i - 1 = 0. \tag{2.90}$$

Hence, β_i can be obtained as

$$\beta_i = \frac{(1/\mathbf{tr}(\mathbf{Y}\mathbf{L}_n^{(i)}\mathbf{Y}^{\mathbf{T}}))^{1/(r-1)}}{\sum_{i=1}^{z}(1/\mathbf{tr}(\mathbf{Y}\mathbf{L}_n^{(i)}\mathbf{Y}^{\mathbf{T}}))^{1/(r-1)}}. \tag{2.91}$$

The alignment matrix $\mathbf{L}_n^{(i)}$ is positive semi-definite, so we have $\beta_i \geq 0$ naturally. When $\mathbf{Y}$ is fixed, Eq. (2.91) can offer the global optimal β. According to Eq. (2.91), the parameter r is used to control β. When $r \to \infty$, different β_i will be close to each other. When $r \to 1$, only $\beta_i = 1$ corresponds to the minimum $\mathbf{tr}(\mathbf{Y}\mathbf{L}_n^{(i)}\mathbf{Y}^{\mathbf{T}})$ over different views, and $\beta_i = 0$ otherwise. Therefore, the selection of r should be based on the complementary property of all views. Afterward, β can be fixed to update $\mathbf{Y}$. The optimization problem in Eq. (2.88) is equivalent to

$$\min_{\mathbf{Y}} \mathbf{tr}(\mathbf{Y}\mathbf{L}\mathbf{Y}^{\mathbf{T}}) \text{ s.t.} \mathbf{Y}\mathbf{Y}^{\mathbf{T}} = \mathbf{I}, \tag{2.92}$$

in which $\mathbf{L} = \sum_{i=1}^{z} \beta_i^r \mathbf{L}_n^{(i)}$. Since $\mathbf{L}_n^{(i)}$ is symmetric, $\mathbf{L}$ is symmetric. According to the aforementioned descriptions, the alternating optimization procedure can be formulated in Algorithm 1 to obtain a local optimal solution of PA-MSL. The details of this algorithm are presented below:

Input: A multiview datum $\mathbf{X} = \{\mathbf{X}^{(1)} \in \mathbf{R}^{m_i \times N}\}_{i=1}^{z}$, the dimension of the low-dimensional subspace $d(d < m_i, 1 \leq i \leq z)$, and $r > 1$.

Output: A spectral subspace $\mathbf{Y} \in \mathbf{R}^{d \times N}$.

Method:

step 1: Calculate $\mathbf{L}_n^{(i)}$ for each view according to the patch alignment.

step 2: Initialize $\beta = [1/z, \ldots, 1/z]$.

step 3: Repeat.

step 4: $\mathbf{Y} = \mathbf{U^T}$, where $\mathbf{U} = [\mathbf{u}_1, \ldots, \mathbf{u}_d]$ are the eigenvectors associated with the smallest d eigenvalues of the matrix $\mathbf{L}$ defined in Eq. (2.91).

step 5: $\beta_i = ((1/\mathbf{tr}(\mathbf{YL}^{(i)}\mathbf{Y^T}))^{1/(r-1)})/(\sum_{i=1}^z (1/\mathbf{tr}(\mathbf{YL}^{(i)}\mathbf{Y^T}))^{1/(r-1)})$.

step 6: Until convergence.

The algorithm converges because the objective function $\sum_{i=1}^z \beta_i^r \mathbf{tr}(\mathbf{YL}_n^{(i)}\mathbf{Y^T})$ reduces with the increasing of the iteration numbers. In particular, with fixed β, the optimal $\mathbf{Y}$ can reduce the value of the objective function, and with fixed $\mathbf{Y}$, the optimal β will also reduce the value of the objective function. The application of the PA-MSL in cartoon animation will be presented in Chapter 4.

2.6 MULTIVIEW DISTANCE METRIC LEARNING

Machine learning algorithms frequently suffer from the insufficiency of training data, the use of inappropriate distance metrics and the deficiency of single-view data. Semi-supervised learning, distance metric learning and multiview learning respectively are the methods that are intended to address these difficulties. To explore unlabeled data, semi-supervised learning is expected to construct more accurate models than those obtainable by purely supervised methods. In distance metric learning [42, 43], the goal is to build an optimal distance metric for the given learning task based on the pairwise relationships among the training samples. However, in traditional distance metric learning, it is assumed that the data are represented in a single vector. They can all be regarded as methods with a single modality and thus can hardly deal with data described with multiple modalities. In this section, we present a Multiview Distance Metric Learning (MDML) method which benefits from the simultaneous learning of labels and distance metrics from multiple modalities. Since the benefits of multiview learning have been introduced clearly in Section 2.5, we will present the advantages of simultaneous learning of labels and distance metrics.

2.6.1 Motivation for MDML

Semi-supervised learning aims to solve the problem of training data insufficiency. It tries to enhance classification accuracy by exploiting unlabeled data. In recent years, many different semi-supervised learning methods have been proposed. Many works attempt to develop semi-supervised methods based on the SVM model, such as Transductive SVM [126] and Semi-Supervised SVM [35]. Blum and Mitchell [46] propose a co-training method in which two classifiers are modeled and then let the classifiers label unlabeled samples for each other. Several other methods have been developed based on a graph in which the vertices are samples and the edges represent the pairwise similarities among samples; regularization schemes are then formulated based on the smoothness of labels on the graph. However, these methods also rely heavily on the adopted distance metric; thus, parameter tuning is also a problem.

Distance metric learning plays an important role in many machine learning and data mining tasks. It is often accomplished by exploring the pairwise constraints of labeled data. Many methods aim to construct a metric under which the sample pairs with equivalence constraints are closer than those with inequivalence constraints. Goldberger et al. [95] propose a Neighborhood Component Analysis (NCA) method that learns a Mahalanobis distance by directly maximizing the leave-one-out cross-validation accuracy of k-NN. Weinberger et al. [317] take margin into account and propose a Large Margin Nearest Neighbor(LMNN) method which enforces the k-nearest neighbors belonging to the same class while the samples of different classes are separated by a large margin. These methods will encounter the over-fitting problem when training samples are limited. Recently, several semi-supervised metric learning algorithms have been proposed which leverage unlabeled data in the metric construction. However, it is worth noting that semi-supervised metric learning is different from the MDML approach introduced in this section. The difference actually lies on the fact that MDML has used unlabeled data as labeled data by coupling metric and label learning.

2.6.2 Graph-Based Semi-supervised Learning

We first introduce the traditional graph-based semi-supervised learning, called Local and Global Consistency(LLGC) [361]. Consider a c-class classification problem, there are N_l labeled samples $(\mathbf{x}_1, \mathbf{y}_1), \ldots, (\mathbf{x}_{N_l}, \mathbf{y}_{N_l})(\mathbf{y} \in \{1, 2, 3, \ldots, c\}, \mathbf{x} \in \mathbf{R}^m)$ and N_u unlabeled samples $\mathbf{x}_{N_l+1}, \ldots, \mathbf{x}_{N_l+N_u}$. Let $N = N_l + N_u$ be the total number of samples, $\mathbf{W}$ is an $N \times N$ affinity matrix with $\mathbf{W}_{ij}$ indicating the dissimilarity measure between $\mathbf{x}_i$ and $\mathbf{x}_j$ and $\mathbf{W}_{ii}$ is set to 0.

Let $\mathbf{D}$ be a diagonal matrix with its (i, i)-element equals the sum of the ith row of $\mathbf{W}$. Let $\mathbf{Y}$ be an $N \times c$ label matrix where $\mathbf{Y}_{ij}$ is 1 if $\mathbf{x}_i$ is a labeled sample and belongs to class j, and 0 otherwise. Define an $N \times c$ matrix $\mathbf{F} = [\mathbf{F}_1^\mathrm{T}, \mathbf{F}_2^\mathrm{T}, \ldots, \mathbf{F}_N^\mathrm{T}]$, where $\mathbf{F}_{ij}$ is the confidence of $\mathbf{x}_i$ with the label $\mathbf{y}_j$. The classification rule is to assign each sample $\mathbf{x}_i$ a label according to $\mathbf{y}_i = \arg\max_{j \leq c} \mathbf{F}_{ij}$. LLGC can obtain the matrix $\mathbf{F}$ by minimizing the following objective function:

$$Q = \sum_{i,j=1}^{N} \mathbf{W}_{ij} \left\| \frac{\mathbf{F}_i}{\sqrt{\mathbf{D}_{ii}}} - \frac{\mathbf{F}_j}{\sqrt{\mathbf{D}_{jj}}} \right\|^2 + \mu \sum_{i=1}^{N} \|\mathbf{F}_i - \mathbf{Y}_i\|^2. \qquad (2.93)$$

There are two terms in Eq. (2.93); The first term implies the smoothness of the labels on the graph and the second term indicates the constraint of the training data.

2.6.3 Overview of MDML

Based on LLGC, the novel distance metric learning method is proposed to simultaneously learn the labels and distance metric. Initially, the Euclidean distance metric is replaced by a Mahalanobis distance metric, which turns to:

$$\mathbf{W}_{ij} = \exp(-\|\mathbf{A}(\mathbf{x}_i - \mathbf{x}_j)\|^2) = \exp(-(\mathbf{x}_i - \mathbf{x}_j)^{\mathbf{T}} \mathbf{A}^{\mathbf{T}} \mathbf{A}(\mathbf{x}_i - \mathbf{x}_j)). \quad (2.94)$$

Thus, distance metric $\mathbf{A}^{\mathbf{T}}\mathbf{A}$ and the labels $\mathbf{F}$ can be optimized smultaneously according to the minimization:

$$\arg \min_{\mathbf{A},\mathbf{F}} Q(\mathbf{F}, \mathbf{A}) = \arg \min_{\mathbf{A},\mathbf{F}} \sum_{i,j=1}^{N} \mathbf{W}_{ij}(\mathbf{A}) \| \frac{\mathbf{F}_i}{\sqrt{\mathbf{D}_{ii}}} - \frac{\mathbf{F}_j}{\sqrt{\mathbf{D}_{jj}}} \|^2 + \mu \sum_{i=1}^{N} \|\mathbf{F}_i - \mathbf{Y}_i\|^2.$$
$$(2.95)$$

Then, to obtain $\mathbf{F}$, $\mathbf{A}$ can be fixed to update $\mathbf{F}$ by setting the partial derivatives of Eq. (2.95) with respect to $\mathbf{F}$ as zero and obtaining

$$\mathbf{F} = \frac{\mu}{1+\mu}(\mathbf{I} - \frac{\mathbf{S}}{1+\mu})^{-1}\mathbf{Y}, \quad (2.96)$$

where $\mathbf{S} = \mathbf{D}^{-1/2}\mathbf{W}\mathbf{D}^{-1/2}$. Then, to obtain $\mathbf{A}$, $\mathbf{F}$ can be fixed to update $\mathbf{A}$ by setting the partial derivatives of Eq. (2.95) with respect to $\mathbf{A}$ as zero.

$$
\frac{\partial}{\partial \mathbf{A}} \left[\sum_{i,j=1}^{N} \mathbf{W}_{ij}(\frac{\mathbf{F}_i}{\sqrt{\mathbf{D}_{ii}}} - \frac{\mathbf{F}_j}{\sqrt{\mathbf{D}_{jj}}})^2 + \mu \sum_{j=1}^{N} \|\mathbf{F}_j - \mathbf{Y}_j\|^2 \right]
$$
$$
= \sum_{i,j=1}^{N} \frac{\partial}{\partial \mathbf{A}} \mathbf{W}_{ij} \left(\frac{\mathbf{F}_i}{\sqrt{\mathbf{D}_{ii}}} - \frac{\mathbf{F}_j}{\sqrt{\mathbf{D}_{jj}}} \right)^2 \quad (2.97)
$$
$$
= \sum_{i,j} \left\{ \frac{\partial \mathbf{W}_{ij}}{\partial \mathbf{A}} \|c_{ij}\|^2 - \mathbf{W}_{ij}(\frac{c_{ij}^{\mathbf{T}}\mathbf{F}_i}{\sqrt{\mathbf{D}_{ii}^3}} \frac{\partial \mathbf{D}_{ii}}{\partial \mathbf{A}} - \frac{c_{ij}^{\mathbf{T}}\mathbf{F}_j}{\sqrt{\mathbf{D}_{jj}^3}} \frac{\partial \mathbf{D}_{jj}}{\partial \mathbf{A}}) \right\},
$$

where

$$c_{ij} = \frac{\mathbf{F}_i}{\sqrt{\mathbf{D}_{ii}}} - \frac{\mathbf{F}_j}{\sqrt{\mathbf{D}_{jj}}}, \quad (2.98)$$

$$\frac{\partial \mathbf{W}_{ij}}{\partial \mathbf{A}} = -2\mathbf{W}_{ij}\mathbf{A}(\mathbf{x}_i - \mathbf{x}_j)^{\mathbf{T}}(\mathbf{x}_i - \mathbf{x}_j), \quad (2.99)$$

$$\frac{\partial \mathbf{D}_{ii}}{\partial \mathbf{A}} = \sum_{j=1}^{N} \frac{\partial \mathbf{W}_{ij}}{\partial \mathbf{A}}. \quad (2.100)$$

In this algorithm, $\mathbf{A}$ is updated by using the gradient descent method. In the gradient descent process, the step size is dynamically adapted to accelerate the process while guaranteeing its convergence. $\mathbf{A}_s$ is denoted as the values of $\mathbf{A}$ in the sth turn of the gradient descent process. If $Q(\mathbf{F}, \mathbf{A}_{s+1})$, i.e., the cost function obtained after gradient descent is reduced, then the step size is doubled; otherwise, the step size is decreased and $\mathbf{A}$ is not updated, i.e., $\mathbf{A}_{s+1} = \mathbf{A}_s$. The implementation of the gradient descent method is described below:

step 1: Set s to 0, ϑ_s to 1 and $\mathbf{A}_s$ as a diagonal matrix $\mathbf{I}/\sigma$. Fix $\mathbf{F}$ to update $\mathbf{A}_s$.

step 2: Let $\mathbf{A}_{s+1} = \mathbf{A}_s - \vartheta_s \frac{\partial Q}{\partial \mathbf{A}}|_{\mathbf{A}=\mathbf{A}_s}$.

step 3: If $Q(\mathbf{F}, \mathbf{A}_{s+1}) > Q(\mathbf{F}, \mathbf{A}_s)$,

Let $\mathbf{A}_{s+1} = \mathbf{A}_s - \vartheta_s \frac{\partial Q(\mathbf{F},\mathbf{A})}{\partial \mathbf{A}}|_{\mathbf{A}=\mathbf{A}_s}$ and $\vartheta_{s+1} = 2\vartheta_s$;

otherwise, $\mathbf{A}_{s+1} = \mathbf{A}_s$, $\vartheta_{s+1} = \vartheta_s/2$.

step 4: Let $s = s + 1$. If $s > S$, quit iteration and output the results, otherwise go to step 2.

Based on the gradient descent method, we come up with an iterative process that alternates a metric update step and a label update step. The implementation of the alternating optimization is described clearly in Section 2.5.

The above scheme can now be extended to multimodal feature sets for multimodal labels and distance metric learning. In the following equations, superscript (i), e.g., $\mathbf{X}^{(i)}$ and $\mathbf{x}^{(i)}$ represents the feature vector from the ith feature space. The graphs constructed from multimodal feature sets can be linearly combined through the weights α_i and by adding a regularizer to the weights. Thus, the objective function can be formulated as

$$Q(\mathbf{F}, \alpha, \mathbf{A}^{(1)}, \mathbf{A}^{(2)}, \ldots, \mathbf{A}^{(k)})$$

$$= \sum_{k=1}^{K} \sum_{i,j=1}^{n} \alpha_k \mathbf{W}_{ij}^{(k)} \left\| \frac{\mathbf{F}_i}{\sqrt{\mathbf{D}_{ii}^{(k)}}} - \frac{\mathbf{F}_j}{\sqrt{\mathbf{D}_{jj}^{(k)}}} \right\|^2 + \mu \sum_{i=1}^{n} \|\mathbf{F}_i - \mathbf{Y}_i\|^2 + \lambda \|\alpha\|^2,$$

$$\text{s.t.} \sum_{k=1}^{K} \alpha_k = 1,$$

$$(2.101)$$

where

$$\mathbf{W}_{ij}^{(k)} = \exp(-(\mathbf{x}_i - \mathbf{x}_j)^{\mathbf{T}} \mathbf{A}^{(k)\mathbf{T}} \mathbf{A}^{(k)} (\mathbf{x}_i - \mathbf{x}_j)), \qquad (2.102)$$

$$\mathbf{D}_{ii}^{(k)} = \sum_{j} \mathbf{W}_{ij}^{(k)}. \qquad (2.103)$$

Here, the alternating optimization can be adopted to solve the above problem. Each time, one set of variables can be updated (there are $k+2$ sets of variables in all). Then, $\mathbf{F}$ and $\mathbf{A}^{(1)}, \mathbf{A}^{(2)}, \ldots, \mathbf{A}^{(k)}$ is fixed to update α. By using a Lagrange multiplier η to take the constraint $\sum_{k=1}^{K} \alpha_k = 1$ into consideration, the objective function can be obtained:

$$L(\alpha, \eta) = \sum_{k=1}^{K} \sum_{i,j=1}^{n} \alpha_k \mathbf{W}_{ij}^{(k)} \left\| \frac{\mathbf{F}_i}{\sqrt{\mathbf{D}_{ii}^{(k)}}} - \frac{\mathbf{F}_j}{\sqrt{\mathbf{D}_{jj}^{(k)}}} \right\|^2$$

$$+ \mu \sum_{i=1}^{n} \|\mathbf{F}_i - \mathbf{Y}_i\|^2 + \lambda \|\alpha\|^2 - \eta \left(\sum_{k=1}^{K} \alpha_k - 1 \right). \qquad (2.104)$$

By setting the derivative of $L(\alpha, \eta)$ with respect to α and η, α_k can be obtained according to

$$
\alpha_k = \frac{2\lambda + \sum_{k=1}^{K} \sum_{i,j=1}^{n} \mathbf{W}_{ij}^{(k)} \| \frac{\mathbf{F}_i}{\sqrt{\mathbf{D}_{ii}}} - \frac{\mathbf{F}_j}{\sqrt{\mathbf{D}_{jj}}} \|^2 - K \sum_{i,j=1}^{n} \mathbf{W}_{ij}^{(k)} \| \frac{\mathbf{F}_i}{\sqrt{\mathbf{D}_{ii}}} - \frac{\mathbf{F}_j}{\sqrt{\mathbf{D}_{jj}}} \|^2}{2\lambda K}
$$

(2.105)

In MDML, the multimodal implementation of alternating optimization for $\mathbf{F}$, $\mathbf{A}^{(1)}$, $\mathbf{A}^{(2)}$, ... and α_k is presented as

step 1: Set t to 0. Set θ_t to 1 and $\mathbf{A}_t^{(1)}, \mathbf{A}_t^{(2)}, \ldots, \mathbf{A}_t^{(k)}$ as a diagonal matrix $\mathbf{I}/\sigma$. Construct the adjacency matrix $\mathbf{W}_t^{(1)}, \mathbf{W}_t^{(2)}, \ldots, \mathbf{W}_t^{(k)}$ with entries. Compute $\mathbf{D}_t^{(1)}, \mathbf{D}_t^{(2)}, \ldots, \mathbf{D}_t^{(k)}$ and $\mathbf{S}_t^{(1)}, \mathbf{S}_t^{(2)}, \ldots, \mathbf{S}_t^{(k)}$ accordingly.

step 2: Label Update. Compute the optimal $\mathbf{F}_t$ based on $\partial Q(\mathbf{F}_t, \alpha, \mathbf{A}_t^{(1)}, \mathbf{A}_t^{(2)}, \ldots, \mathbf{A}_t^{(k)})$ 0, which can be derived as: $\mathbf{F}_{t_1} = \frac{1}{1+\mu}(\mathbf{I} - \frac{\mu}{1+\mu} \sum_{k=1}^{K} \mathbf{S}_t^{(k)})^{-1}\mathbf{Y}$.

step 3: Distance metric update for each view. Initialize $k = 1$.

step 4: Update $\mathbf{A}_t^{(k)}$ with gradient descent method.

step 5: If $k < K$, update $k = k + 1$ and go to step 4, otherwise go to step 6.

step 6: Update the weights α_k.

step 7: After obtaining $\mathbf{A}_t^{(k)}$ and α_k, update the adjacency matrix $\mathbf{W}_t^{(k)}$. Then compute $\mathbf{D}_t^{(k)}$ and $\mathbf{S}_t^{(k)}$ accordingly.

step 8: Let $t = t + 1$. If $t > T$, quit iteration and output the results, otherwise go to step 2.

Since the value of the objective function keeps decreasing in the whole process and it is lower bounded by 0, the process is guaranteed to converge. In addition to simultaneously learning labels, distance metrics and feature weights, it is worth noting that another advantage of our proposed algorithm is that it avoid the radius parameters σ because the scaling of the distance metrics is automatically learned. In Chapter 4, the application of MDML in cartoon retrieval and synthesis will be introduced.

2.7 MULTI-TASK LEARNING

Semi-supervised learning algorithms generally adopt both labeled and unlabeled data to train a classifier; for example, Vapnik introduced the notion of transductive inference [296], which may be regarded as an approach to semi-supervised learning. Although some success has been reported, there has also been criticism pointing out that this method may not behave well under some circumstances [349]. Another popular semi-supervised learning method is co-training [46], which is related to the bootstrap method used in some NLP applications. However, it was pointed out by Pierce and Cardie [228] that this method may degrade classification performance when the assumptions of the method are not satisfied.

Another approach to semi-supervised learning is based on a different philosophy. The basic idea is to construct good functional structures using unlabeled data. Since it does not bootstrap labels, there is no label noise to potentially corrupt the learning procedure. An example of this approach is to use unlabeled data to create a data manifold (graph structure), on which proper smooth function classes can be defined [365, 361]. If such smooth functions can characterize the underlying classifier well, it is possible to improve classification performance. It is worth pointing out that smooth function classes based on graph structures do not necessarily have good predictive power. Therefore a more general approach, based on the same underlying principle, is to directly learn a good underlying smooth function class.

The multi-task learning framework [18] has been proposed to learn underlying predictive functional structures (smooth function classes) that can characterize good predictors. This problem is called structural learning. Our key idea is to learn such structures by considering multiple prediction problems simultaneously. Once important predictive structures on the predictor space are discovered, the information can be used to improve upon each individual prediction problem. In the following content, we will introduce the structural learning problem under the framework of standard machine learning. We will also introduce a specific multi-tasking learning algorithm for finding a common low-dimensional feature space shared by the multi-problems.

2.7.1   Introduction of Structural Learning

In the standard formulation of supervised learning, a predictor is explored to project an input vector $\mathbf{x} \in \mathbf{X}$ to the corresponding output $\mathbf{y} \in \mathbf{Y}$. Generally, the predictor is selected from a set H of functions based on a finite set of training examples $\{(\mathbf{x}_i, \mathbf{y}_i)\}$ which are independently generated according to unknown probability distribution D. The set H, called the hypothesis space, consists of functions from $\mathbf{X}$ to $\mathbf{Y}$ which can be used to predict the output in $\mathbf{Y}$ of an input datum in $\mathbf{X}$. The goal is to find a predictor f so that its error with respect to D is as small as possible. Based on the training data, a frequently used method for finding a predictor $\widehat{f} \in H$ is to minimize the empirical error on the training data:

$$\widehat{f} = \arg\min_{f \in H} \sum_{i=1}^{N} L(f(\mathbf{x}_i), \mathbf{y}_i). \qquad (2.106)$$

It is well-known that with a fixed number of training data, the smaller the hypothesis space H, the easier it is to learn the best predictor in H. The error caused by learning the best predictor from a finite sample is called the estimation error. However, the smaller the hypothesis space H, the less accurate the best predictor in H becomes. The error caused by using a restricted H is often referred to as the approximation error. In supervised learning, one needs to select the size of H to balance the trade-off between approximation error and estimation error.

2.7.2 Hypothesis Space Selection

Practically, a good hypothesis space should have a small approximation error and a small estimation error. The problem of choosing a good hypothesis space is central to the performance of the learning algorithm, but often requires specific domain knowledge or assumptions of the world. It is assumed that there is a set of candidate hypothesis spaces. If one only observes a single prediction problem $\mathbf{X} \to \mathbf{Y}$ on the underlying domain $\mathbf{X}$, then a standard approach to hypothesis space selection is by cross validation. If one observes multiple prediction problems on the same underlying domain, then it is possible to better estimate the underlying hypothesis space by considering these problems simultaneously. Consider m learning problems indexed by $l \in \{1, \ldots, m\}$, each with N_l samples $(\mathbf{x}_i^l, \mathbf{y}_i^l)$ indexed by $i \in \{1, \ldots, N_l\}$, which are independently drawn from a distribution D_l. For each problem l, it can assumed that we have a set of candidate hypothesis spaces $H_{l,\theta}$ indexed by a common structural parameter $\theta \in \Gamma$, which is shared among the problems. For the lth problem, a predicator $f_l : \mathbf{X} \to \mathbf{Y}$ should be found in $H_{l,\theta}$ which minimizes the expected loss over D_l. Given a fixed structural parameter θ, the predictor for each problem can be estimated using empirical risk minimization (ERM) over the hypothesis space $H_{l,\theta}$:

$$\widehat{f}_{l,\theta} = \arg \min_{f \in H_{l,\theta}} \sum_{i=1}^{N_l} L(f(\mathbf{x}_i^l), \mathbf{y}_i^l), (l = 1, \ldots, m). \qquad (2.107)$$

If the cross-validation is adopted for structural parameter selection, it can be immediately noticed that a more stable estimate of the optimal θ can be obtained by considering multiple learning tasks together. Thus, more data can be obtained for the purpose of selecting the optimal shared hypothesis space structure. This implies that even if the sample sizes are small for the individual problems, as long as m is large, the optimal θ can be found accurately.

Assume that for each problem l, a learning algorithm A_l is to take a set of training data $S_l = \{(\mathbf{x}_i^l, \mathbf{y}_i^l)\}_{i=1,\ldots,N_l}$ and a structural parameter $\theta \in \Gamma$, and produce a predictor $\widehat{f}_{l,\theta} : \widehat{f}_{l,\theta} = A_l(S_l, \theta)$. It should be noted that if the algorithm estimates the predictor from a hypothesis space $H_{l,\theta}$ by empirical risk minimization, then it can be obtained $\widehat{f}_{l,\theta} \in H_{l,\theta}$. It can be further assumed that there is a procedure estimating the performance of the learned predictor $\widehat{f}_{l,\theta}$ using additional information T_l as $O_l(S_l, T_l, \theta)$. In structural learning, the $\widehat{\theta}$ is obtained by using a regularized estimator

$$\widehat{\theta} = \arg \min_{\theta \in \Gamma}[r(\theta) + \sum_{l=1}^{m} O_l(S_l, T_l, \theta)], \qquad (2.108)$$

where $r(\theta)$ is a regularization parameter that encodes the belief on what θ value is preferred. This is the fundamental estimation method for structural learning. Once an estimate $\widehat{\theta}$ of the structural parameter is obtained, the learning algorithm $A_l(S_l, \theta)$ can be used to obtain predictor $\widehat{f}_{l,\theta}$ for each l.

2.7.3 Algorithm for Multi-task Learning

A specific multi-task learning algorithm is introduced in this section. The basis of this learner is joint empirical risk minimization. The linear prediction models are considered because they have been demonstrated to be effective in many practical applications. Naturally, with respect to both the predictors $\{f_l\}$ and the structural parameter θ, we can consider the model given by equation Eq. (2.107) and formulate it as a joint optimization problem over the m problems, where θ is the shared structural parameter:

$$[\widehat{\theta}, \{\widehat{f}_l\}] = \arg \min_{\theta \in \Gamma, \{f_l \in H_{l,\theta}\}} \sum_{l=1}^{m} \frac{1}{N_l} \sum_{i=1}^{N_l} L(f_l(\mathbf{x}_i^l), \mathbf{y}_i^l). \qquad (2.109)$$

To derive a practical algorithm from Eq. (2.109), a specific model should be considered and solved numerically. In particular, a linear prediction model is employed for the multiple tasks, and underlying structure is assumed in a shared low-dimensional subspace. This model leads to a simple and intuitive computational procedure.

Given the input space $\mathbf{X}$, a linear predictor is not necessarily linear on the original space, but rather can be regarded as a linear functional on a high dimensional feature space $\mathbf{F}$. It can be assumed there is a known feature mapping $\Phi : \mathbf{X} \to \mathbf{F}$. A linear predictor f is determined by a weight vector $\mathbf{u} : f(x) = \mathbf{u}^T \Phi(\mathbf{x})$. In order to apply the structural learning framework, a parameterized family of feature maps is considered. In this setting, the goal of structural learning may be regarded as learning a good feature map. Therefore, it can be assumed that the overall feature map contains two components: one is with a known high-dimensional feature map, and the other component is a parameterized low-dimensional feature map. That is, the linear predictor has a form

$$f(\mathbf{x}) = \mathbf{u}^T \Phi(\mathbf{x}) + \mathbf{v}^T \Psi_\theta(\mathbf{x}), \qquad (2.110)$$

where $\mathbf{u}$ and $\mathbf{v}$ are weight vectors specific for each prediction problem, and θ is the common structure parameter shared by all problems.

To simplify the linear predictor, Eq. (2.110) can be rewritten as

$$f_\Theta = \mathbf{u}^T \Phi(\mathbf{x}) + \mathbf{v}^T \Theta \Psi(\mathbf{x}) \qquad (2.111)$$

where $\Psi_\theta(\mathbf{x}) = \Theta \Psi(\mathbf{x})$. Based on Eq. (2.108), we obtain the specific objective function for multi-task learning:

$$[\{\widehat{\mathbf{u}}_l, \widehat{\mathbf{v}}_l\}, \widehat{\Theta}] = \arg \min_{\{\mathbf{u}_l, \mathbf{v}_l\}, \Theta} [r(\Theta) + \sum_{l=1}^{m} (g(\mathbf{u}_l, \mathbf{v}_l) + \frac{1}{N_l} \sum_{i=1}^{N_l} L(f_\theta(\mathbf{u}_l, \mathbf{v}_l; \mathbf{x}_i^l), \mathbf{y}_i^l))],$$
$$(2.112)$$

where $g(\mathbf{u}, \mathbf{v})$ is an appropriate regularization condition on the weight vector $(\mathbf{u}, \mathbf{v})$, and $r(\Theta)$ is the appropriate regularization condition on the structural parameter Θ.

2.7.4 Solution by Alternative Optimization

The alternative optimization is an appropriate choice for solving Eq. (2.111). With fixed Θ, the computation of $\{\mathbf{u}_l, \mathbf{v}_l\}$ for each problem l becomes decoupled. We consider a special case of Eq. (2.112) with a simple iterative solution. Let $\Phi(\mathbf{x}) = \Psi(\mathbf{x}) = \mathbf{x} \in \mathbf{R}^p$ with square regularization of weights vectors. Then, we have

$$[\{\widehat{\mathbf{u}}_l, \widehat{\mathbf{v}}_l\}, \widehat{\Theta}] = \arg\min_{\{\mathbf{u}_l, \mathbf{v}_l\}, \Theta} \sum_{l=1}^{m} \left(\frac{1}{N_l} \sum_{i=1}^{N_l} L((\mathbf{u}_l + \Theta^{\mathbf{T}}\mathbf{v}_l)^{\mathbf{T}}\mathbf{x}_i^l, \mathbf{y}_i^l) + \lambda_l \|\mathbf{u}_l\|_2^2\right),$$

$$\text{s.t.} \Theta\Theta^{\mathbf{T}} = \mathbf{I}_{h \times h}$$

$$(2.113)$$

with given constraints $\{\lambda_l\}$. In this formulation, the regularization condition $r(\Theta)$ in Eq. (2.112) is integrated into the orthonormal constraint $\Theta\Theta^{\mathbf{I}} = \mathbf{T}_{h \times h}$. To solve this optimization problem, an auxiliary variable $\mathbf{q}_l$ for each problem l such that $\mathbf{q}_l = \mathbf{u}_l + \Theta^{\mathbf{T}}\mathbf{v}_l$. Thus, $\mathbf{u}$ can be estimated using $\mathbf{q}$ to obtain

$$[\{\widehat{\mathbf{q}}_l, \widehat{\mathbf{v}}_l\}, \widehat{\Theta}] = \arg\min_{\{\mathbf{q}_l, \mathbf{v}_l\}, \Theta} \sum_{l=1}^{m} \left(\frac{1}{N_l} \sum_{i=1}^{N_l} L(\mathbf{q}_l^{\mathbf{T}}\mathbf{x}_i^l, \mathbf{y}_i^l) + \lambda_l \|\mathbf{q}_l - \Theta^{\mathbf{T}}\mathbf{v}_l\|_2^2,\right.$$

$$\text{s.t.} \Theta\Theta^{\mathbf{T}} = \mathbf{I}_{h \times h}$$

$$(2.114)$$

At the optimal solution, we let $\widehat{u}_l = \widehat{q}_l - \widehat{\Theta}^{\mathbf{T}}\widehat{\mathbf{v}}_l$. To solve Eq. (2.114), the following optimization procedure can be adopted: (1) Fix $(\Theta, \mathbf{v})$, and optimize Eq. (2.114) with respect to $\mathbf{q}$; (2) Fix $\mathbf{q}$, and optimize Eq. (2.114) with respect to $(\Theta, \mathbf{v})$; (3) Repeat until convergence. In this alternating optimization procedure, we shall focus on the second step, which is crucial for the derivation of this method. It is easy to see that the optimization of Eq. (2.114) with fixed $\{\mathbf{q}_l\} = \{\widehat{\mathbf{q}}_l\}$ is equivalent to the following problem:

$$[\{\widehat{\mathbf{v}}_l, \widehat{\Theta}\}] = \arg\min_{\{\mathbf{v}_l\}, \Theta} \sum_l \lambda_l \|\widehat{\mathbf{q}} - \Theta^{\mathbf{T}}\mathbf{v}_l\|_2^2 \text{ s.t.} \Theta\Theta^T = \mathbf{I}_{h \times h}. \qquad (2.115)$$

From this formula, we know with fixed Θ,

$$\min_{\mathbf{v}_l} \|\widehat{\mathbf{q}} - \Theta^{\mathbf{T}}\mathbf{v}_l\|_2^2 = \|\widehat{\mathbf{q}}_l\|_2^2 - \|\Theta\widehat{\mathbf{q}}_l\|_2^2 \qquad (2.116)$$

and the optimal value is achieved at $\widehat{\mathbf{v}}_l = \Theta\widehat{\mathbf{q}}_l$. To estimate $\mathbf{v}_l$ and use the above equation, Eq. (2.115) can be rewritten as

$$\widehat{\Theta} = \arg\max_{\Theta} \sum_{i=1}^{m} \lambda_l \|\Theta\widehat{\mathbf{q}}_l\|_2^2, \text{ s.t.} \Theta\Theta^{\mathbf{T}} = \mathbf{I}_{h \times h}. \qquad (2.117)$$

Let $\mathbf{Q} = [\sqrt{\lambda_1}\widehat{\mathbf{q}}_1, \ldots, \sqrt{\lambda_m}\widehat{\mathbf{q}}_m]$ be an $p \times m$ matrix, we can have

$$\widehat{\Theta} = \arg\max_{\Theta} \mathbf{tr}(\Theta\mathbf{Q}\mathbf{Q}^{\mathbf{T}}\Theta^{\mathbf{T}}), \text{ s.t.} \Theta\Theta^{\mathbf{T}} = \mathbf{I}_{h \times h}. \qquad (2.118)$$

It is apparent that the solution of this problem is given by the Singular Value Decomposition (SVD) of $\mathbf{Q}$. The algorithm introduced in this part can be summarized in the following contents, which solves Eq. (2.114) by alternating optimization of $\mathbf{q}$ and $(\Theta, \mathbf{v})$.

Input: training data $\{(\mathbf{x}_i^l, \mathbf{y}_i^l)\}(l = 1, \ldots, m)$

Parameters: h and $\lambda_1, \ldots, \lambda_m$

Output: $h \times p$ dimensional matrix Θ

Initialize: $\mathbf{q}_l = 0(l = 1, \ldots, m)$ and arbitrary Θ

Iterate

for $l = 1$ to m do

with fixed Θ and $\mathbf{v}_l = \Theta\mathbf{q}_l$, approximately solve for $\widehat{\mathbf{u}}_l$:

$$\widehat{\mathbf{u}}_l = \arg\min_{\mathbf{u}_l} [\tfrac{1}{N_l} \textstyle\sum_{i=1}^{N} L(\mathbf{u}_l^{\mathrm{T}}\mathbf{x}_i^l + (\mathbf{v}_l^{\mathrm{T}}\Theta)\mathbf{x}_i^l, \mathbf{y}_i^l) + \lambda_l \|\mathbf{u}_l\|_2^2].$$

Let $\mathbf{q}_l = \widehat{\mathbf{u}} + \Theta^{\mathrm{T}}\mathbf{v}_l$.

endfor

Compute the SVD of $\mathbf{Q} = [\sqrt{\lambda_1}\mathbf{q}_1, \ldots, \sqrt{\lambda_m}\mathbf{q}_m]$:

$\mathbf{Q} = \mathbf{V}_1 \mathbf{D} \mathbf{V}_2^{\mathrm{T}}$ (with diagonals of $\mathbf{D}$ in descending order).

Let the rows of Θ be the first h rows of $\mathbf{V}_1^{\mathrm{T}}$.

Until Converge

It should be noted that since the objective value in Eq. (2.114) decreases at each iteration, the procedure produces parameters $\{\widehat{\mathbf{u}}_l, \widehat{\mathbf{v}}_l\}, \Theta$ with converging objective values. Generally, the parameters $\{\widehat{\mathbf{u}}_l, \widehat{\mathbf{v}}_l\}, \Theta$ will also converge (to a local optimal solution). However, in reality, it is usually sufficient to use the Θ parameter from the first iteration of the procedure. This is because the performance of this model is not very sensitive to a small perturbation of the structural parameter Θ. The main dimensional reduction effect is already well captured by SVD in the first iteration.

2.8 CHAPTER SUMMARY

This chapter introduces a group of modern machine learning techniques including manifold learning; spectral clustering and graph cuts; ensemble manifold learning; multiple kernel learning; multiview subspace learning and multiview distance metric learning. For manifold learning, we introduce a novel framework called patch alignment framework [261] which unifies all existing manifold learning [41, 293, 257, 282, 284] into it. For spectral clustering and graph cuts, we explain the close connections between these two fields. For ensemble manifold learning and multiple-kernel learning, we introduce a group of state-of-the-art techniques in this area, which successfully achieve linear combination in estimating data distribution. For multiview subspace learning and multiview distance metric learning, we introduce how to learn an efficient subspace or distance metric from multiview features. The applications of these modern machine learning techniques in animation research will be introduced in Chapters 3 and 4.

CHAPTER 3

ANIMATION RESEARCH: A BRIEF INTRODUCTION

2D and 3D computer animation, for many people, is synonymous with big-screen events such as Monkey King (2D), MULAN (2D), The Smurfs (2D&3D), Transformers (3D), Toy Story (3D), and so on. Figure 3.1 presents the posters of these movies. Computer games also take advantage of state-of-the-art computer graphics techniques, and desktop computer animation is now possible at a reasonable cost. Computer animation on the Web is routine. Digital simulators for training pilots, SWAT teams, and nuclear reactor operators are commonplace. The distinguishing characteristics of these various media types are the cost, the desired image quality, and the amount and type of interaction allowed.

Excellent introductions to the field of computer animation are presented by Parent [218] and Pina et al. [231]. Computer animation is a time-intensive process, and this is true for both 2D and 3D cartoon animation. As a result, there has long been interest in partially automating animation [218, 231], and indeed, animation has thus far benefited greatly from applications of machine learning. The majority of the computer animation production burden is usually artistic, not scientific or computational. This is due to the fact that computer animation algorithms are eminently reusable, but the data they operate on is often custom-designed and highly stylized. This bottleneck is illustrated by computer-generated movie production (shown in Figure 3.1) in which

Modern Machine Learning Techniques and Their Applications in Cartoon Animation Research, **105**
First Edition. By Jun Yu and Dacheng Tao

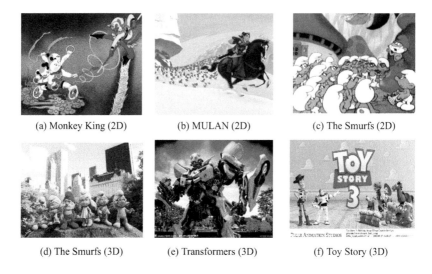

(a) Monkey King (2D)   (b) MULAN (2D)   (c) The Smurfs (2D)

(d) The Smurfs (3D)   (e) Transformers (3D)   (f) Toy Story (3D)

Figure 3.1   Posters of 2D and 3D animation movies.   (a) Monkey King (2D); (b) MULAN (2D); (c) The Smurfs (2D); (d) The Smurfs (3D); (e) Transformers (3D); (f) Toy Story (3D).

the human workload is usually more than 80 % artistic (e.g., modeling, texturing, animating, etc.).

There is therefore a need in computer animation for data transformation and modeling techniques that can synthesize and/or generalize data, thereby at least partially alleviating the data bottleneck. Machine learning techniques are proposed to fulfill this need, and they have two functions that are particularly useful to computer graphics: (1) They extract functional information from data, and (2) they synthesize new data based on existing data. Machine learning allows us to leverage existing data in a nondirect and nontrivial manner, which can save both human and computational time. For example, techniques have been developed for generating meshes of novel human bodies given a small set of example meshes. This is done by creating a generative model of the mesh data through regression.

Even when the computation workload is more important than the human workload, it is still often the case that clever synthesis and reuse of data can be beneficial. For example, some techniques [125] perform scattered data interpolation of the discrete irradiance computed for only a small subset of points in a virtual scene. This allows for the rapid generation of convincing images that do not exhibit discernible noise.

In this chapter, we survey the progress of computer animation developments including traditional animation production, computer-assisted animation production, and data-driven animation production.

3.1   TRADITIONAL ANIMATION PRODUCTION

In most cases, animation includes "live-action" puppetry such as that found in the children's television program Sesame Street, and the use of mechanical devices to articulate figures such as in animatronics. In this section, we first present the main history of traditional animation. We then introduce the procedure of animation production; the main steps in animation production are presented in this part. Finally, we will illustrate the connection between traditional animation and computer animation.

3.1.1   History of Traditional Animation Production

Traditional animation exploded in the twentieth century in the form of filming hand-drawn, two-dimensional images, which is also referred to as conventional animation. The earliest use of camera to make static things move appeared in 1896. Georges Méliès used simple camera tricks such as multiple exposures and stop-motion techniques to make objects appear, disappear, and change shape [290, 6]. Some of the earliest pioneers of film animation were Emile Cohl, J. Stuart Blackton, and Winsor McCay.

The first major technical developments in the animation process can be traced to the efforts of John Bray. In 1910, his work built the foundation for traditional animation, which still exists today. Earl Hurd, who made great progress in the field, proposed using translucent cels to compose multiple layers of drawing into an integrated image. Bray and others made further developments by enhancing the overlay idea to include the peg system for registration and drawing the background, enabling operation of the camera parallel to the plane of the background to be performed more easily. Out of Bray's studio came Max Fleischer (Betty Boop), Paul Terry (Terrytoons), George Stallings (Tom and Jerry), and Walter Lantz (Woody Woodpecker). In 1915, Fleischer patented rotoscoping, which draws images on cels by tracing over previously recorded live action. Several years later, Bray experimented with color in animation production.

In the late 1920s, Walt Disney became the new force in animation production. In the history of traditional animation, Walt Disney is the overpowering force. Disney's innovations in animation technology include:

- The usage of storyboard to review the story and pencil sketches to review motion.

- The usage of sound and color in animation.

- Study of the live action sequences to create more realistic motion in his films.

- Development of the multiplane camera, which consists of a camera mounted above multiple planes, each of which holds an animation cell. Each plane can move in six directions, and the camera can move closer or farther away.

In the art of animation, Disney perfected the ability to impart unique, endearing personalities to his characters, such as those exemplified in Mickey Mouse, Pluto,

Goofy, the Three Little Pigs, and the Seven Dwarfs. He promoted the idea that the mind of the character was the driving force of the action and that a key to believable animated motion was the analysis of real-life motion.

The 1930s saw the proliferation of animation studios, among them Fleischer, Iwerks, Van Beuren, Universal Pictures, Paramount, MGM, and Warner Brothers. The technological advances that are of concern here were mostly complete by this period. The differences between the various studios and their contributions have to do more with the artistic aspects of animation than with the technology involved in producing animation.

3.1.2 Procedures of Animation Production

It is beneficial to understand the detail of the animation production procedure. Traditionally, a piece of animation is usually generated through a four-level hierarchy, and this procedure has been used widely in traditional animation and computer animation. We will outline the whole procedure from top-down. First, the entire project is referred to as the "production." Typically, productions are separated into several parts called sequences. Each sequence is a major episode and is frequently identified by an associated staging area; the number of sequences in a production generally ranges from one to a dozen. A sequence is composed of several shots, which represent the continuous camera recording. Finally, the shot is composed of an individual frame of film; each frame is a single recorded image. This hierarchy has been clearly presented in Figure 3.2.

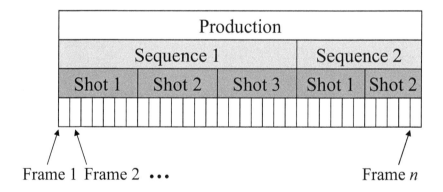

Figure 3.2 Hierarchy of the animation production procedure.

The production of a piece of animation comprises several components:

- To record the main story for the animation, a storyboard is designed to describe the action scenes by sketching the representative frames. The frames are accompanied by text, which elaborates the action taking place. This method can be used to present and review the action as well as to supervise character development.

- A model sheet is developed consisting of a number of drawings for each figure in various poses, and this is used to ensure that each figure's appearance is consistent as it is repeatedly drawn during the animation process.

- The exposure sheet records information for each frame including sound track cues, camera moves, and compositing elements. A route sheet records the statistics and responsibility for each scene.

- An animatic, or story reel, is produced in which the storyboard frames are recorded. This method creates a rough estimation of the timing.

- Master animators are responsible for identifying and producing the keyframes, which can be used to aid to confirm character development and image quality.

- Assistant animators make up the frames between the keyframes, a process called "inbetweening."

- Testing shots, which are short sequences rendered in full color, are used to verify the rendering and motions. To fully test the motion, a pencil test, which is an extended sequence using low-quality images such as pencil sketches, is used.

- In animation, sound is critical. There are three forms of sound used in animation: music, special effects, and voice.

3.1.3 Relationship between Traditional Animation and Computer Animation

Traditional man-made animation can be considered as the precursor to computer animation; therefore, a close relationship exists between computer animation and traditional animation. A close comparison can be made between computer animation and some stop-motion techniques, such as clay and puppet animation. For example, the initial step of three-dimensional animation is modeling. Similarly, clay and puppet animation use three dimensional characters in separate stages. After the three-dimensional characters are created, they are arranged in a three-dimensional scene. A camera is positioned to view the environment and capture the image. To create various animation scenarios, one or more characters are manipulated, and the camera may be repositioned to record the images from different viewpoints. This process can be repeated to generate animation.

Lasseter [155] mentioned that the principles of traditional animation as articulated by some of the original Disney animators [290] are related to techniques which are widely used in computer animation. These principles include: squash & stretch, timing, secondary actions, slow in & slow out, arcs, follow through/overlapping action, exaggeration, appeal, anticipation, staging, and straight ahead versus pose to pose. We will explain some of the main principles in detail. The squash & stretch, timing, secondary actions, slow in & slow out, and arcs form the physical basis of objects in the scene. These principles can be used to simulate the distortion of shapes. Timing relates to how actions are spaced according to the weight, size, and personality of an object or character. Slow in & slow out are concerned with how things move through space. Anticipation and staging concern how an action is presented to the audience. Exaggeration, appeal, and follow through/overlapping action are principles that address the aesthetic design of an action or action sequence. Straight ahead versus pose to pose concerns how a motion is created.

In production, computer animation has borrowed most of the ideas from traditional animation production, including the usage of a storyboard, test shots, and pencil testing. For computer animation, the storyboard has translated directly to computer animation production carried out on-line. It still has the same functions in the animation procedure, and it is still critical in animation planning. The concept of keyframes and inbetweenings used in traditional animation has also been adopted in computer animation.

Although computer animation has adopted the concept of traditional animation production, there are still many differences between computer animation and traditional animation in creating individual frames. The model creation, the layout and motion of the models, etc., are carried out separately in computer animation production. This allows these materials (including models and lighting setups) to be reused in further productions, whereas in traditional animation, all of these processes happen simultaneously as each drawing is created.

Two main evaluation tools of traditional animation, test shots and pencil tests, have their counterparts in computer animation. A speed/quality trade-off can be made in each of the three stages of creating a frame of computer animation: model building, motion control, and rendering. By using high-quality techniques in only one or two of these stages, that aspect of the presentation can be quickly checked in a cost-effective manner. A test shot in computer animation is produced by a high-quality rendering of a highly detailed model to view a single frame, a short sequence of frames from the final product, or every nth frame of a longer sequence from the final animation. The equivalent of a pencil test can be performed by simplifying the sophistication of the models used, by using low-quality and/or low resolution renderings, or by using simplified motion.

Computer animation is well suited to producing the equivalent of test shots and pencil tests. In fact, because the quality of the separate stages of computer animation can be independently controlled, it may be even better suited for these evaluation techniques than traditional animation.

3.2   COMPUTER-ASSISTED SYSTEMS

In the late 1960s and early 1970s, computer animation was produced by a mix of researchers in university labs and individual visionary artists [288, 289]. In 1963, when Ivan Sutherland developed an interactive constraint satisfaction system on a vector refresh display, the earliest research in computer graphics and animation began. In this case, the user could construct an assembly of lines by specifying constraints between the various graphical elements. In the early 1970s, computer animation in university research labs became more widespread. As a result, several groundbreaking works in animation were created, such as an animated hand and face by Ed Catmull; a walking and talking human figure by Barry Wessler; and a talking face by Fred Parke. In 1974, the first computer animation nominated for an Academy Award, Hunger, was produced by Rene Jodoin; it was directed and animated by Peter Foldes. This piece used a system that depended heavily on object shape modification and line interpolation techniques. The system was developed by Nestor Burtnyk and Marceli Wein at the National Research Council of Canada in conjunction with the National Film Board of Canada. Hunger was the first animated story using computer animation. Others who advanced computer animation during the period were Ed Emshwiller at NYIT, who demonstrated moving texture maps in Sunstone (1979); Jim Blinn, who produced the Voyager flyby animations at the Jet Propulsion Laboratory (1979); Don Greenberg, who used architectural walk-throughs of the Cornell University campus (1971); and Nelson Max at Lawrence Livermore Laboratory, who animated space-filling curves (1978).

In the early 1980s Daniel Thalmann and Nadia Magnenat-Thalmann started work in computer animation at the University of Montreal. Over the years, their labs have produced several impressive animations, including Dream Flight, Tony de Peltrie, and Rendez-vous à Montréal.

Nowadays, as modeling, rendering, and animation have become more sophisticated and hardware has become faster and inexpensive, quality computer graphics have spread to the Internet, television commercials, computer games, and standalone game units. The two-dimensional animation technique, morphing, should be mentioned here because of its use in some films and its high impact in television commercials. This is essentially a 2D procedure that warps feature lines of one image into the feature lines of another image while the images themselves are blended. In the next section, we will introduce several popular computer-assisted systems.

3.2.1   Computer Animation Techniques

Most early computer animation systems are keyframe systems [56, 57, 62]. The design of these systems is based on the standard procedure used for hand-drawn animation, which was introduced in Section 3.1.2. The keyframes of animations are defined and drawn by master animators, while the task of drawing inbetweenings is completed by assistant animators. We first introduce the details about keyframe systems.

3.2.1.1 Keyframing Systems   The term "keyframing" in computer animation is generalized to apply to variables whose value is fixed and for which the values for inbetweenings are interpolated according to specific procedure. Frequently, the keyframing system will offer an interactive interface, with which the cartoonist can assign the key values and conduct the interpolation.

Since the keyframing system adopts the interpolation between two-dimensional shapes, the elementary operation is to interpolate one curve into another curve. The prerequisite of conducting the interpolation is to obtain the correspondence between lines. Thus, each pair of lines can be interpolated on a point-to-point basis to generate lines in inbetweenings. This interpolation requires that for each pair of curves in the keyframes, the curves have the same number of points (shown in Figure 3.3 and Figure 3.4).

Keyframe   Keyframe

Figure 3.3   Keyframes in which each curve of a frame has the same number of points as its counterpart in the other frame.

Keyframe   Keyframe

Figure 3.4   Keyframes and three inbetweenings with interpolation of a specified feature point.

Point-by-point correspondence information is usually not known, and even if it is, the resulting correspondence is not necessarily what the user wants. The best one can expect is for the curve-to-curve correspondence to be known. The problem, given two arbitrary curves in keyframes, is to interpolate a curve as it should appear in inbetween frames. Therefore, if the point-to-point correspondence has been built, we should reconstruct the curve correspondence based on it. Next, we propose our stroke reconstruction algorithm to build correspondence of strokes which are of different number and length in two keyframes, based on the obtained feature point correspondence.

3.2.1.2 *Stroke Correspondence Construction via Stroke Reconstruction Algorithm*   In this section, the curve reconstruction algorithm is presented to build correspondence of curves which are of different number and length in two keyframes, based on the obtained feature point correspondence. It aims to minimize the sensitivity of point matching accuracy and establish correct curve matching for inbetween generation. In practice, inbetween generation should be based on accurate correspondence of curves which describe the shapes of objects in the drawings.

It means that the curves representing the same part of corresponding objects from two keyframes should be matched. When artists draw keyframes freely, however, the same part of corresponding objects may be composed of a different number of strokes of different lengths. Thus, "many to many" and "part to whole" curve mapping is necessary to preserve the shape of corresponding objects during inbetweening. These complex mappings will cause robustness problems during inbetweening. As our solution, we propose compound curves to realize optimal curve correspondence where only "one to one" correspondence exists. A compound curve consists of a list of segments derived from the original curves. Figure 3.5 illustrates an example of curve reconstruction.

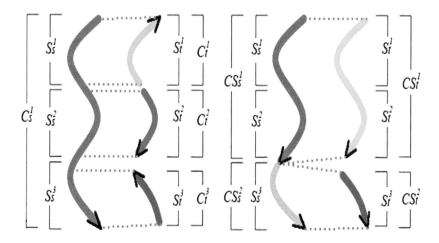

Figure 3.5   Illustration of curve reconstruction. C_s and C_t denote source and target original curves, S_s and S_t denote source and target segments, and CS_s and CS_t denote source and target compound curves.

Here, one keyframe is named as the source frame and the other as the target frame. C_s^1 is the original curve in the source frame; and C_t^1, C_t^2, and C_t^3 are the original curves in the target frame. In the curve reconstruction algorithm, the original curves in the source frame are checked one by one. For each original source curve, the best matching can be found in a curve from the target frame. Based on this mapping, one source segment of the source stroke is created. For example, a source segment S_s^1 and a target segment S_t^1 form a best match. Recursively, the best matching target segments can be found for all the remaining segments of the source curve. After searching for all the source curves, the matching segments are grouped into a list according to their connectivity. The segments which are of approximate G_1 continuity with one another and matched to the same original curve are put into the same list, e.g., segment S_t^1 and S_t^2. Finally, one list of matching segments composes a compound stroke, e.g., segment S_t^1 and S_t^2 composing compound stroke CS_t^1. In Figure 3.5, the arrows show the directions of the curves. The direction of the generated compound curve is determined based on parameter changes along the source curve. For instance, when going through the points along source segment S_s^3, the parameters increase, while those of the matched points decrease on the corresponding target segment S_t^3. Thus, the directions of S_t^3 and CS_t^2 are set as the same as S_s^3.

The evaluation of a match is defined as follows:

$$rate = \left(\frac{N^s}{N_c^s} + \frac{N^t}{N_c^t} \right) \times \alpha_1 + \frac{\min\left(L^s, L^t\right)}{\max\left(L^s, L^t\right)} \times \alpha_2. \tag{3.1}$$

The first and second parts are the ratio of matching point numbers and the ratio of the matching segment lengths, with respective weights α_1 and α_2. N is the numbers of matching points, N_c is the total number of feature points, and L is the length of a matching segment. s and t denote the source and the target respectively. With this condition, segments with relatively more matched points and of similar length tend to be evaluated as a better match.

In some situations, a few segments may be partially matched but are not evaluated as a best match. Thus, they do not constitute any of the compound curves. After all the curves are processed, postprocessing is applied to the remaining unmatched segments. An unmatched segment is appended to a matched segment if the two meet approximate G1 continuity. Otherwise, its point correspondence is reexamined. Our stroke reconstruction algorithm can be described by the pseudo codes given below:

1 for each original curve in the source frame **do**

2 Get feature points on the curve

3 Get matched points in the target frame based on point correspondence

4 while number of unmatched source points > 0 **do**

5 Find matched points with consecutive index to form candidate matched segments

6 Find the best matched source and target segments by Eq. (3.1)

7 Record matched segments

8 Remove matched feature points

9 end while

10 end for

11 Post-processing unmatched segments

12 Construct compound curves from segment lists

The proposed curve reconstruction algorithm successfully handles the problem of "many to many" and "part to whole" mapping of original curves and obtains one-to-one correspondence of compound curves. In the next section, we will introduce the interpolation techniques used to obtain the inbetweening based on the one-to-one curve correspondence.

3.2.1.3 *Interpolation Techniques*   For the purpose of illustration, we consider the simple case in which the keyframes k_1 and k_2 consist of a single curve. The curve in frame k_1 is referred to as $S(u)$, and the curve in frame k_2 is referred to as $Q(v)$. This single curve will be interpolated for each frame between the keyframes. Some basic assumptions are used to guarantee reasonable interpolation. For example, if the curve is a continuous open segment in frames k_1 and k_2, this curve should remain a continuous open segment in all the inbeweens. In addition, the top point of $S(t)$, $S(0)$ should interpolate to the top point in $Q(t)$,$Q(0)$. When both curves are generated with the cubic Bezier curve interpolation information, then inbetween curves can be generated by interpolating the control points and reapplying the Bezier interpolation [247]. Next, we will provide the basic interpolation definitions and present the Bezier interpolation.

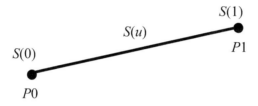

Figure 3.6   Illustration for linear interpolation

Figure 3.6 and Eq. (3.2) show the simple linear interpolation. Here, the weights $1 - \alpha$ and α sum to one. It can be guaranteed that the interpolating curve falls within the convex hull of the geometric entities being interpolated. In this case, the convex hull is the straight line.

$$S(u) = (1 - u) \cdot S0 + u \cdot S1. \tag{3.2}$$

In general, the above equation can be rewritten as in Eq. (3.3). Here $F0$ and $F1$ are called blending functions. This is referred to as the geometric form.

$$S(u) = F_0(u) \cdot S0 + F_1(u) \cdot S1. \tag{3.3}$$

Two other general equations for linear interpolation are

$$S(u) = (S1 - S0) \cdot u + S0, \tag{3.4}$$

$$S(u) = a1 \cdot u + a0. \tag{3.5}$$

In addition, these forms can be written in a matrix representation. The curves discussed below can all be written in this form. Of course, depending on the actual curve type, the matrices will contain different values:

$$S(u) = \begin{bmatrix} F_0(u) \\ F_1(u) \end{bmatrix} \cdot \begin{bmatrix} S0 & S1 \end{bmatrix} = \mathbf{FS^T}, \tag{3.6}$$

$$S(u) = \begin{bmatrix} u & 1 \end{bmatrix} \begin{bmatrix} a1 \\ a0 \end{bmatrix} = \mathbf{U}^{\mathbf{T}}\mathbf{A}, \tag{3.7}$$

$$S(u) = \begin{bmatrix} u & 1 \end{bmatrix} \begin{bmatrix} -1 & 1 \\ 1 & 0 \end{bmatrix} \begin{bmatrix} S0 \\ S1 \end{bmatrix} = \mathbf{U}^{\mathbf{T}}\mathbf{MB}. \tag{3.8}$$

Next, we introduce the Bezier interpolation method, which has been widely used in animation systems. The example shown in Figure 3.4 is achieved using this method. Generally, the cubic Bezier curve can be defined by the start point and end point; two interior points are adopted to control the shape of the curve. The Bezier form uses the auxiliary control points to define tangent vectors. The form of a cubic curve is represented by four points: PT_0, PT_1, PT_2, PT_3. For the curve, the beginning and ending points are PT_0 and PT_3, respectively. The interior control points, which are used to control the shape of the curve and define the beginning and ending tangent vectors, are PT_1 and PT_2.

The continuity between adjacent Bezier segments can be controlled by colinearity of the control points on either side of the shared beginning/ending point of the two curve segments (Figure 3.7).

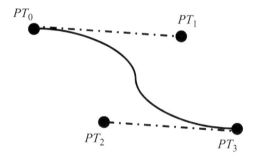

Figure 3.7 The representation of cubic Bezier curve in four points PT_0, PT_1, PT_2, PT_3.

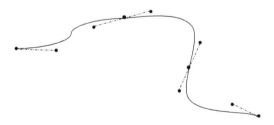

Figure 3.8 Tangents and collinear control points for composite cubic Bezier curve.

Normally, an animator hopes for better control over the interpolation of keyframes than provided by the standard interpolating splines. To achieve better control of the shape of an interpolating curve, Kochanek [141] suggests a parameterization of the internal tangent vectors based on the three values tension, continuity, and bias. The three parameters are explained by decomposing each internal tangent vector into an incoming part and an outgoing part. These tangents are referred to as the left and right parts, respectively. Tension controls the sharpness of the bend of the curve. It achieves this by means of a scale factor that changes the length of both the incoming and outgoing tangents at the control point. The continuity parameter gives the user control over the continuity of the curve at the control point where the two curve segments join. The incoming (left) and outgoing (right) tangents at a control point are defined symmetrically with respect to the chords on either side of the control point. Bias defines a common tangent vector, which is a blend between the chord left of the control point and the chord right of the control point. At the default value, the tangent is an even blend of these two, resulting in a Catmull-Rom type of internal tangent vector.

The most flexible and useful type of curve is the B-spline curve; however, this type of curve is hard to operate intuitively. The formulation includes Bezier curves as a special case. The B-spline curve's formulation decouples the number of control points from the degree of the resulting polynomial. A typical simple type of B-spline curve is a uniform cubic B-spline curve, which is formulated by four control points over the interval zero to one (Figure 3.8). Thus, the compound curve can be generated from an arbitrary number of control points by constructing a curve segment from each four-tuple of adjacent control points: PT_i, PT_{i+1}, PT_{i+2}, PT_{i+3}, for $i = 1, 2, \cdots, n-3$, where n is the total number of control points. Each segment of the curve is generated by multiplying the same 4×4 matrix, and four adjacent control points with an interpolating parameter between zero and one.

$$PT(u) = \frac{1}{6} \begin{bmatrix} -1 & 3 & -3 & 1 \\ 3 & -6 & 3 & 0 \\ -3 & 0 & 3 & 0 \\ 1 & 4 & 1 & 0 \end{bmatrix} \begin{bmatrix} PT_i \\ PT_{i+1} \\ PT_{i+2} \\ PT_{i+3} \end{bmatrix}. \tag{3.9}$$

NURBS, or Non-uniform rational B-splines are even more flexible than basic B-splines. NURBS allow for the exact representation of circular arcs, whereas Bezier and non-rational B-splines do not. This is often important in modeling, but for the purpose of animation, the basic periodic, uniform cubic B-spline is usually sufficient.

3.3 CARTOON REUSE SYSTEMS FOR ANIMATION SYNTHESIS

Cartoon reuse is an emerging technique for generating animations. As mentioned in Section 3.1, traditional cartoon generation is generally labor intensive and includes the steps of keyframing, inbetweening, painting, and so on. Though these conventional techniques can produce smooth and fluent animations, the cost of production is high because of the large amount of manual work. To improve the efficiency of animation generation, a group of reuse methods has recently been proposed in facial animation, character animation and cartoon animation. These techniques are gradually replacing the technique of "Interpolation" to produce high quality animations.

In facial animation, facial movement is captured from the source face and retargeted onto the new target faces. Similarly, in character animation, the motion is captured and retargeted onto the new characters. By adopting the reuse method, the cost of cartoon making can evidently be reduced and efficiency can be improved. In the next section, we present reuse techniques proposed in cartoon animation. The reuse details in facial and character animation will be introduced in Section 3.4.

3.3.1 Cartoon Texture for Animation Synthesis

The system of "Cartoon Texture" [131] is proposed for creating novel animations from a library of existing cartoon data. The idea of reusing the cartoon images is inspired by video texture [245], which combines similar-looking cartoon data into a user-directed sequence. The goal of "Cartoon Texture" is to re-sequence cartoon data to create new motion from the original data that retains the same characteristics and exposes similar or new behaviors.

By using "Cartoon Texture," the number of behaviors for new sequences is restricted by the amount of data in the cartoon library. Starting with a small amount of cartoon data, an unsupervised learning method for nonlinear dimensionality reduction [287] is used to discover a lower-dimensional structure of the data. The specified start and end frames are selected by users, and the system traverses this lower-dimensional manifold to re-organize the data into a new animation. The main procedures of "Cartoon Texture" are introduced briefly below.

3.3.1.1 Cartoon Library Construction The data collected in a cartoon library comes from 2D animated cartoon videos, as shown in Figure 3.9. The background of the video is removed and the character is registered relative to a fixed location through the sequence. Though several automatic methods can be conducted to achieve the background subtraction, the segmentation is manually conducted in "Cartoon Texture." Since the cartoon data representation is model free, it is unnecessary to identify any specific region of character. Thus, it does not matter that the characters may undergo deformation. In this method, the registration is conducted by using the centroid of the character in each frame and repositioning it to the center of the image, facilitating the later computation of a distance matrix.

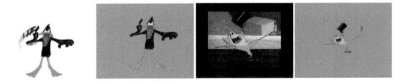

Figure 3.9   A cartoon frame from the library before and after background segmentation.

3.3.1.2 Manifold Building Manifold learning finds an embedding of the cartoon data into a lower-dimensional space. In "Cartoon Texture," a modified ISOMAP is used to perform the manifold-based nonlinear dimensionality reduction. The ISOMAP preserves the intrinsic geometry of the data as captured in the geodesic manifold distances between all pairs of data points. The algorithm is listed below:

1. Calculate the local neighborhoods based on the distances $\mathbf{D}_P(i, j)$ between all-pairs of points i, j in the input space P based on a chosen distance metric.

2. Coordinate $\mathbf{D}_P(i, j)$ to account for temporal neighbors.

3. Estimate geodesic distances into a full distance matrix $\mathbf{D}(i, j)$ by computing all-pairs shortest paths from $\mathbf{D}_P$, which contains the pairwise distances.

4. Apply MDS to construct a d-dimensional embedding of the data.

If the data is sufficiently dense, ISOMAP can form a single connected component, which is important in representing the data as a single manifold structure. The connected components of a graph represent the distinct pieces of the graph. Two data points (nodes in the graph) are in the same connected component if and only if there exists some path between them.

3.3.1.3 Distance used in Similarity Estimation
The distance metric is critical in creating a good manifold embedding of the cartoon data. In "Cartoon Texture," three different distance metrics are adopted: the L2 distance, the cross-correlation between pairs of images, and an approximation to the Hausdorff distance.

- The first distance metric is the L2 distance between all-pairs of images. Here, two input images I_i and I_j are given, and the distance is calculated as

$$d_{L_2}(I_i, I_j) = \sqrt{\|I_i\|^2 + \|I_j\|^2 - 2 * (I_i \cdot I_j)}. \qquad (3.10)$$

The L2 distance is calculated based on the luminance of images. The L2 distance metric is simple and works well for large data sets with incremental changes between frames. However, it is unable to handle cartoon data because of the exaggerated deformations between frames.

- The second distance metric is based on the cross-correlation between the luminance of a pair of images. Given two input images I_i and I_j, we obtain

$$c_{i,j} = \frac{\sum_m \sum_n (I_{i_{mn}} - \bar{I}_i)(I_{j_{mn}} - \bar{I}_j)}{\sqrt{(\sum_m \sum_n (I_{i_{mn}} - \bar{I}_i)^2)(\sum_m \sum_n (I_{j_{mn}} - \bar{I}_j)^2)}} \qquad (3.11)$$

- The third distance metric is an approximation of the Hausdorff distance. An edge map and a distance map of each image are adopted and the Hausdorff distance between a pair of images I_i and I_j is calculated as

$$D_{Haus}(i, j) = \frac{\sum_{(x,y) \in E_i \equiv 1} X_j(x, y)}{\sum_{(x,y) \in E_i \equiv 1} E_i(x, y)}, \qquad (3.12)$$

where E_i is the edge map of image I_i , X_j is the distance map of image I_j , and (x, y) denote the pixel coordinates for each image.

3.3.1.4 New Animations Generation   To generate a new animation, the user selects a start frame and an end frame, and the system traverses the ISOMAP embedding space to find the shortest cost path through the manifold. This path gives the indices of the images used for the resulting animation, which is created by re-sequencing the original, unregistered images. Dijkstra's algorithm is used to find the shortest cost path through the manifold. The dimensionality of the embedding space used for re-sequencing, i.e., for traversing the neighborhood graph, varies for each data set.

3.3.2   Cartoon Motion Reuse

In this section, we briefly introduce a technique called "cartoon capture and retargeting" [53], which is used to track the motion from conventionally animated cartoons and retarget the motion onto new 2D or 3D characters. By using animation as a source, the new animations can be produced with expressive, exaggerated or nonrealistic motions. Based on the mixture of affine transformation and keyframe interpolation, cartoon capture tracks non-rigid shape changes in cartoon layers.

The technique of cartoon capture transfers the cartoon motion style into a representation that can be used in the same style as standard motion capture. This technique can be applied in the fields of game development, film production, and more. It allows conventional animators to animate on paper and transfer the motion to a 2D or 3D character. The overview chart of the technique is shown in Figure 3.10. The input of cartoon capture is the digitized video and a set of keyframes selected from the source sequence. This system transfers the digitized cartoon into a cartoon motion representation, in which the motion is composed of the combination of affine transformation and key-weights vectors. In this way, a wide range of motion and non-rigid shape deformations can be described. In order to retarget the captured cartoon motion, the correspondence should be built between the input and output keyframes. Details of these techniques are presented in the following subsections.

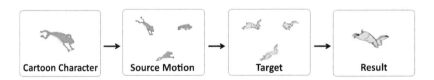

| Cartoon Character | Source Motion | Target | Result |

Figure 3.10   Overview chart for the technique of cartoon motion capture and retargeting.

3.3.2.1 Motion Representation of Cartoon Characters   The motion of cartoon characters comes from the velocity of the character body with its deformations of stretches and squashes in different directions. The motion can be formulated by the moving speed of the body, the moving path of the body, the rotation of the body from frame to frame, the level of the deformation in squashes and stretches, and the timing of the squash and stretch. As mentioned in Ref. [53], the character s can be deformed to a shape $V(t)$ at time frame t with affine parameters $\zeta(t) = [p_1, p_2, p_3, p_4, d_x, d_y]$. Thus, the $V(t)$ can be represented as

$$V = \zeta(t) \cdot \mathbf{S} = \begin{bmatrix} p_1 & p_2 & d_x \\ p_3 & p_4 & d_y \end{bmatrix} \cdot \mathbf{S}, \qquad (3.13)$$

where p_1, p_2, p_3 and p_4 describe rotation, x/y scale, and shear and d_x and d_y represent the x/y translation. The $\mathbf{S}$ in the form of $3 \times N$ matrix $\mathbf{s}_1, ..., \mathbf{s}_N$ represents N points in homogeneous form $\mathbf{s}_i = [x_i, y_i, 1]^T$. For example, a set of points along the edge of character can form the shape S. It can be assumed that if a new shape is used to replace S, and the same parameters $\zeta(1), ..., \zeta(t)$ are applied, the resulting shapes $V(1), ..., V(t)$ remain the same.

By using these affine parameters, the coarse motion can be approximated, although several important deformations will be lost. In this system, several shapes, including all possible extreme deformations, are selected by users and are used to cover these deformations. In this case, the proposed motion representation can be extended to

$$V = \zeta(t) \cdot \sum_k w_k \mathbf{S}_k = \begin{bmatrix} p_1 & p_2 & d_x \\ p_3 & p_4 & d_y \end{bmatrix} \cdot \sum_k w_k \mathbf{S}_k, \qquad (3.14)$$

so the character V is parameterized by $6 + K$ variables including the 6 affine parameters and the K keyframe interpolation weights.

3.3.2.2 The Methods of Motion Capture

To capture the motion, a sequence of cartoon contours $V(1), ..., V(t)$, and the keyframes $S_1, ..., S_k$ are used as input. Based on Eq. (3.14), the parameters V can be obtained; however, the proposed motion model will not perfectly fit the input. Thus, the parameters V can be estimated by using the error term:

$$\left\| V - \begin{bmatrix} p_1 & p_2 & d_x \\ p_3 & p_4 & d_y \end{bmatrix} \cdot \sum_k w_k \mathbf{S}_k \right\|^2. \qquad (3.15)$$

Estimating the affine motion of contours can be done with a closed-form solution. We measure the affine motion in minimizing the following error term:

$$\mathbf{Err}_{aff} = \left\| V - \begin{bmatrix} p_1 & p_2 & d_x \\ p_3 & p_4 & d_y \end{bmatrix} \cdot \mathbf{S}_1 \right\|^2. \qquad (3.16)$$

The standard least-squares solution can be

$$\begin{bmatrix} p_1 & p_2 & d_x \\ p_3 & p_4 & d_y \end{bmatrix} = \mathbf{V} \cdot \mathbf{S}^T (\mathbf{S} \cdot \mathbf{S}^T)^{-1}. \qquad (3.17)$$

Subsequently, a set of weights $w_1, ..., w_k$ for keyframes should be found by minimizing the error in Eq. (3.16). In this case, additional constraints can be used to improve the results: (1) All the weights are added to 1; (2) weights must lie in a margin.

3.3.2.3   The Methods of Motion Retargeting   The obtained motion can be applied with different output media, including 2D cartoon characters, 3D CG models and photo-realistic output. For each domain, a specific input keyframe should be modeled. In this subsection, the method of 2D cartoon character retargeting, which is related with the main topic of this book, is introduced.

For each keyframe used in the keyframe deformation, a corresponding 2D frame is drawn in the output domain. The corresponding control points between the different output keyframes are labeled. The main procedure of retargeting can be shown as follows: First, the affine motion of each output keyframes with respect to some reference frames can be obtained through Eq. (3.16). Then, the chosen interpolation function is applied to the affine adjusted keyframes using weights obtained from Eq. (3.17). Finally, the affine motions of the input cartoon characters are added to the resulting keyframes to produce the final animation.

3.3.3   Motion Capture Data Reuse in Cartoon Characters

In 2007, Hornung et al. [115] proposed another interesting method of reusing the motion capture data to efficiently generate cartoon animations. In this section, we will briefly introduce this method. The key idea of this method is to drive the 2D character directly in the image space using 3D mocap data [7]. The mocap data consists of a series of poses of a predefined human skeleton model; the positions and orientations of the skeleton bones and joints are registered in each pose. Firstly, the mocap data is fixed to the 2D character by building a proper camera model and a model pose that best fits the 2D character. This is achieved by asking the user to artificially build the correspondence between a 2D character and 3D human skeleton. Based on the 2D to 3D correspondences, the camera project and best-fitting pose can be formed, providing the closest possible fit to the user-selected pose in 2D. Second, the animation is prepared by fitting the initial model of a generalized shape template to the user-selected pose of the character. In this way, every part of the character's body corresponds to a set of layers in each template, all of which are combined into a single nonmanifold triangular mesh. The main steps of this approach are briefly introduced below. Finally, the animation is achieved by adopting projected motion sequence to control deformation of the 2D shape in the image space.

3.3.3.1   Data Preprocessing   To build the correspondences between the character's 2D shape and 3D skeleton, the user is asked to select joint positions in the input image. In this approach, the manual method allows users to conveniently animate cartoon characters.

A camera projection model P should be computed to use the 3D motion data to animate the 2D shape. The project model here describes the mapping from 3D joint positions to 2D image space. The best 3D pose X_0 which is closest to the selected 2D pose should be found in the motion sequence, and an appropriate initial solution for the subsequent animation will be obtained.

3.3.3.2   2D Character Deformation   To create convincing animations of a 2D character, the character's shape should be deformed in a reasonable way, to keep the effort of generating animations to a minimal level. Here, a set of generic shape templates are used to represent the topological changes of a generalized character model for different viewpoints of the camera. These templates are fitted in a semi-automatic approach to the character. For example, when animating characters from a side view, we have to consider different layers for separately moving parts of the body, for instance, one layer for the foremost arm, one for the body and the foremost leg, and one for the remaining arm and leg, respectively (see Figure 3.11).

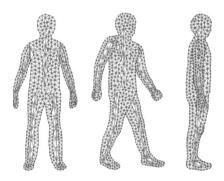

Figure 3.11   Representation of three generic templates used for animation.

In Figure 3.11, each layer consists of a triangulated set of vertices representing the shape boundary and skeleton joints. Additional vertices are added inside each layer, which allows us to generate more realistic animations by "inflating" the shape templates prior to animation. For a given image, a shape template can be automatically selected by exploiting the reconstructed extrinsic camera data in relation to the best-matching model pose. For the deformation of the template, the shape manipulation technique as-rigid-as-possible (ARAP) [119] is used. This technique allows for flexible deformations of the character's shape, and at the same time it preserves the size and aspect ratios of the character's body to bound the distortion.

The remaining steps for generating a final shape used for animation proceed as follows. The shape template for a given image is first fitted to the user-selected joint positions using a single ARAP deformation step. Depending on the mismatch between the contour of the template and the character in the input image, the boundaries of the deformed shape are "snapped" to the character's silhouette using a 2D-snakes approach [134]. Those parts of the silhouette which do not contain enough information for a stable convergence, such as occluded regions of the body, can be manually improved by the user. This refined shape is defined as the final aligned shape.

3.3.3.3   *Character Driven in 2D image*   Based on the ARAP technique [119], the textured shape can be easily animated by constraining the bone vertices to the 2D positions obtained by sequentially projecting the poses from the motion dataset into the image plane. However, ARAP aims at the rigid preservation of the original 2D triangle shapes which will not lead to plausible deformations because perspective scaling and distortion effects are completely ignored. This leads to unrealistic distortions, such as thinning or thickening of the character's limbs when they change orientation relative to the image plane. A possible solution is to generalize the ARAP technique to an ASAP(as similar as possible) technique. The details of this technique can be found in Ref. [119]. Finally, it should be mentioned that new animations can be generated trivially by simply exchanging the 3D motion.

3.4 GRAPHICAL MATERIALS REUSE: MORE EXAMPLES

In Section 3.3, we presented cartoon reuse techniques which are used to efficiently generate animations. Aside from these techniques, the idea of refurbishing (reusing) has been widely used in many different areas, such as video texture [245], to synthesize a new, similar-looking video of arbitrary length from existing video clips; motion texture [336], which can synthesize complicated human-figure motion that is statistically similar to the original motion captured data; and motion graph [46], which can generate novel animation by using both the original motion and automatically generated transitions. In this section, we provide more examples of graphical material reuse.

3.4.1 Video Clips Reuse

In video texture [245], a new type of video producing technique is proposed. This new technique provides a continuous, infinitely varying stream of video images which repeat visual patterns in similar, quasi-periodic ways. The video texture is synthesized from a finite set of images by randomly rearranging (and possibly blending) original frames from a source video.

3.4.1.1 Existing Problems To create video textures and apply them in all these ways, a number of problems need to be solved. First, it is difficult to locate potential transition points in video sequences, i.e., places where the video can be looped back on itself in a minimally obtrusive way. Second, a big challenge is to find a sequence of transitions that respects the global structure of the video. A third challenge is to smooth visual discontinuities at the transitions. This problem has been solved by using morphing techniques in video texture. Fourth, problems exist in automatically factoring video frames into different regions that can be analyzed and synthesized independently.

3.4.1.2 Frameworks for Video Clips Synthesis The general approach of the video texture is to find places in the original video where a transition can be made to some other place in the video clip without introducing noticeable discontinuities. This system is organized into three major components. The first component of the system analyzes the input video to find the good transition points and stores these in a small data table that becomes part of the video texture representation. This analysis component may also optionally trim away parts of the input video that are not needed, or segment the original video into independently moving pieces, in order to more easily analyze these individual regions.

The second part of the system synthesizes new video from the analyzed video clip by deciding in what order to play the original video frames. Two different approaches are developed to perform this sequencing. The first approach randomly plays the existing video clips and uses a stochastic technique to decide the order of playing, based on the similarity distance matrix. The second approach selects a small number of transitions to take in such a way that the video is guaranteed to loop after a specified number of frames. The obtained video loop can then be played iteratively.

If the set of frames to be played has been selected, the rendering component puts together the frames in a way that is visually pleasing. This process may be as simple as just displaying or outputting the original video frames, or it may involve cross-fading or morphing across transitions and/or blending independently moving regions. The whole framework is shown in Figure 3.12.

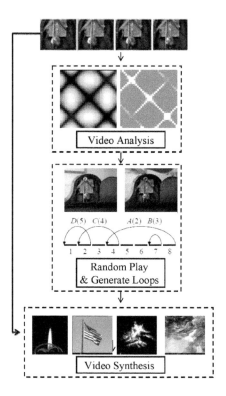

Figure 3.12   Framework for the system of video texture.

3.4.2 Motion Captured Data Reuse by Motion Texture

Motion captured data can also be reused to create novel animation. In this section, we describe the novel technique-motion texture [336] for synthesizing complicated motion which is similar to the original motion captured data. In this approach, the motion texture is composed of a group of motion textons. The characteristics of the captured motion are recorded through the distribution of the textons and a linear dynamic system(LDS) is used to model a motion texton. The learned motion texture can then be used to generate new animations automatically. The details of this approach are introduced below.

3.4.2.1 Motion Data Preprocessing In this approach, N_t motion textons $T = \{T_1, T_2, ..., T_{N_t}\}$ are constructed and represented by respective texton parameters $\Theta = \{\theta_1, \theta_2, ..., \theta_{N_t}\}$. The motion sequence can be initially separated into N_s segments, in which each segment can be represented by one of the N_t textons. Thus, texton distribution, or the relationship between any pair of textons, can be described by counting how many times a texton is switched to another. The length of each segment may be different, and all N_t textons are learned from the entire sequence of N_s segments, $N_t \leq N_s$ must hold.

Here, each motion texton is represented by an LDS with the following state-space model:

$$P_{t+1} = A_t P_t + V_t, Q_t = C_t P_t + W_t, \tag{3.18}$$

where P_t is the hidden state variable, Q_t is the observation, and V_t and W_t are independent Gaussian noises at time t. The texton must have T_{min} frames so that local dynamics can be captured.

In motion texture, it is assumed that the distribution of textons satisfies the first-order Markov dynamics, represented by a transition matrix $M_{ij} = P(l_k = j|l_{k-1} = i)$. This transition matrix has been widely used in Ref. [233] to indicate the likelihood of switching from one discrete state to another. The transition matrix has also been used in video texture, whereby transition points are found so that the video can be looped back to itself in a minimally obtrusive way.

To give $Q_{1:T} = \{Q_1, Q_2, ..., Q_T\}$, or the observation Q_t from frame 1 to frame T, the system of motion texture learns the parameters $\{\Theta, M\}$ through the maximum likelihood solution

$$\{\Theta', M'\} = \arg \max_{\{\Theta, M\}} P(Q_{1:T}|\Theta, M). \tag{3.19}$$

The greedy approach can be used to incrementally initialize the model. First, T_{min} frames is used to suit an LDS i, and incrementally label the subsequent frames to segment i until the error is above a threshold. The existing LDS learnt from all preceding segments are tested on the remaining unlabeled frames, and the best LDS is chosen. When the smallest error exceeds the given threshold, a new LDS will be introduced and the above process repeated.

3.4.2.2 Automatic Motion Synthesis New motions can be synthesized based on the obtained motion texture, and the motion can be edited interactively both at the texton level and at the distribution level. Two steps have been proposed in motion texture to synthesize the new motions. First, a texton path needs to be generated in the state space. A straightforward approach is to randomly sample the texton distribution to obtain an infinitely long texton sequence. The user can also be asked to edit the texton path interactively. Based on two textons and their related poses, the motion texture can produce a most likely texton sequence that passes through those key poses. Once the texton sequence has been obtained, the next step in synthesis is conceptually straightforward. In principle, given a texton and its key poses (the first two frames, to be exact), a motion sequence can be synthesized frame by frame with the learnt LDS and sampled noise. However, the prediction power of LDS decreases after some critical length of the sequence as LDS approaches its steady state. The key poses of the texton next to the synthesized one can be used to achieve a smooth motion transition between two neighboring textons.

3.4.3 Motion Capture Data Reuse by Motion Graph

In this section, we introduce a novel motion synthesis approach-motion graph [145], which creates realistic and controllable motions. Based on the motion capture data, this approach builds a directed graph to encapsulate connections in the database, and a group of graph walks can be built to meet the user's specifications.

The goal of proposing motion graph [145] is to preserve the realism of motion capture while also providing the ability to control and direct the character. By using this approach, for instance, a character can be driven to walk around a room without considering a piece of motion data that contains the correct number of steps, and will travel in the right direction.

The motion graph is a directed graph in which the edges contain either pieces of original motion data or automatically generated transitions. The nodes of the graph act as choice points where these small bits of motion join seamlessly. Transitions between motions can be automatically detected and created in motion graph; thus, users need not capture motions specifically designed to connect to one another. If necessary, the user can modify the high-level structure of the motion path to produce the desired degrees of connectivity among different parts, converting the motion graph from a motion synthesis problem into a sequence of nodes selection problem.

3.4.3.1 Flowchart for Constructing Motion Graph In this section, the procedures for constructing the motion graph from a database of clips are presented. A clip of motion is defined as a regular sampling of the character's parameters, consisting of the position of the root joint and quaternions representing the orientations of each joint.

Motion graph construction can be separated into three steps. First, a set of candidate transition points will be detected. Then, the selection and blending among these candidate transitions will be explained. Finally, the pruning method will be introduced to eliminate the problematic edges.

1. **Candidate Transitions Detection** In a motion graph, the motion capture data is represented as vectors of parameters specifying the root position and joint

rotations of a skeleton on each frame. One might attempt to locate transition points by computing a vector norm to measure the difference between poses at each pair of frames. To calculate the distance $D(F_i, F_j)$ between two frames F_i and F_j, the point clouds formed over two windows of frames of user defined length k will be considered. This means that each point cloud is the composition of smaller point clouds representing the pose at each frame in the window. The size of the windows is the same as the length of the transitions, so $D(F_i, F_j)$ is affected by every pair of frames that form the transition. The distance between F_i and F_j can be calculated by computing a weighted sum of squared distances between corresponding points in the two point clouds. To solve the problem of finding coordinate systems for these point clouds, the minimal weighted sum of squared distances can be calculated

$$\min_{\theta, x_0, z_0} \sum_i w_i \left\| P_i - T_{\theta, x_0, z_0} P_i' \right\|^2, \tag{3.20}$$

where the linear transformation T_{θ, x_0, z_0} rotates a point p around the vertical axis by θ degrees and then translates it by x_0, z_0. The objective function in Eq. (3.20) can be simply solved by using partial derivatives of the parameters θ, x_0, z_0.

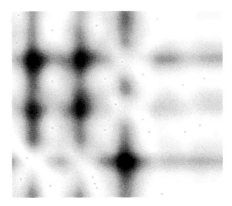

Figure 3.13   An example error function for two motions. The entry at (i, j) records the error for making a transition from the ith frame of the first motion to the jth frame of the second. Here, the white values correspond to lower errors and black values to higher errors. The colored dots represent local minima.

The distance defined above can be computed for every pair of frames in the database, and form a sampled 2D error function. The results have been shown in Figure 3.13. In order to make the transition model more compact, all the local minima of this error function can be found (shown in Figure 3.13).

2. **Transition Points Selection**

A local minimum in the distance function does not necessarily imply a high-quality transition; it only implies a transition better than its neighbors. To find the local minima with small error values, the simplest approach is to only accept local minima below an empirically determined threshold. However, in most cases, users would want to configure the threshold to choose a compromise between good transitions (low threshold) and high connectivity (high threshold). Besides, different kinds of motions have different requirements; therefore, the motion graph permits users to adopt flexible thresholds for different kinds of motions.

3. **Transitions Generations** If $D(F_i, F_j)$ meets the threshold requirements, a transition in blending frames F_i to F_{i+k-1} with frames F_{j-k+1} to F_j, is created. Initially, the appropriate alignment is applied to 2D transformation to motion F_j. We then linearly interpolate the root positions and perform spherical linear interpolation on joint rotations. The use of linear blends means that constraints in the original motion may be violated; for instance, one of the character's feet may slide when it ought to be planted. This can be corrected by using constraint annotations in the original motions. In addition, the graph should be pruned to generate arbitrarily long streams of motion of the same type so that as much of the database as possible is used.

3.4.3.2 *Motion Synthesis from Motion Graph*
At this stage, the motion extraction that satisfies the user constraints is achieved in the motion graph. This can be formulated as an optimization problem. In motion graph, every edge represents a piece of motion, and the graph walk corresponds to the motion generated by placing these pieces one after another. The key point is to arrange each piece in the correct location and orientation. The use of linear blends to create transitions can cause artifacts; however, every graph walk is automatically annotated with constraint information, and these constraints are specified directly in the original motions. The constraints may be satisfied using a variety of methods, such as Ref. [91] or Ref. [159]. In motion graph, the method described in Ref. [146] is used.

3.5 CHAPTER SUMMARY

Computer graphics and animation have created a revolution in visual effects. Advances continue to be made, and new effects are finding a receptive audience, yet there is more potential to be realized as players in the entertainment industry demand their own special look and desire a competitive edge. Computer animation has come a long way since the days of its invention. Viewed as another step in the development of animation, the use of digital technology is indeed both a big and an important step in the history of animation. With the advent of low-cost computing and desktop video, animation is now within reach of more people than ever. It remains to be seen how the limits of the technology will be pushed as new and interesting ways to create moving images are explored.

CHAPTER 4

ANIMATION RESEARCH: MODERN TECHNIQUES

In this chapter, we introduce various kinds of machine learning techniques that can be applied in modern animation making approaches. The contents of this chapter include the application of the semi-supervised learning algorithm into the correspondence construction, which is the prerequisite for keyframe-based animation. We will also present the usage of multiview learning in refurbishing existing cartoon images, which is a convenient and efficient cartoon generation technique. These researches show that the merger of machine learning and computer graphics techniques is incipient in the computer animation field.

4.1 AUTOMATIC CARTOON GENERATION WITH CORRESPONDENCE CONSTRUCTION

The prerequisite for achieving high quality auto-inbetweening and auto-coloring in cartoon animation is the construction of accurate correspondences between keyframe objects, with which inbetween frames can be generated by interpolation so that corresponding objects and colors can be propagated. In practice, there are several difficulties that make effective correspondence construction challenging for both theoretical study and implementation. First, the objects in keyframes are complex in

Modern Machine Learning Techniques and Their Applications in Cartoon Animation Research, **131**
First Edition. By Jun Yu and Dacheng Tao
Copyright © 2013 by The Institute of Electrical and Electronics Engineers, Inc. Published 2013 by John Wiley & Sons, Inc.

shape and can be either closed or open, as shown in the enlarged pictures in Figure 4.1. Second, the structures of the objects are complicated. There are always many details in the composition of a hierarchical structure such as the monkey face in Figure 4.1. Third, to map the objects from keyframes accurately, the optimization process is computationally expensive. In recent years, researches on correspondence construction have been proposed in both computer animation and image processing areas; however, there are quite a few limitations to previous works which make these methods unsuitable for our problem of correspondence construction of objects in keyframes.

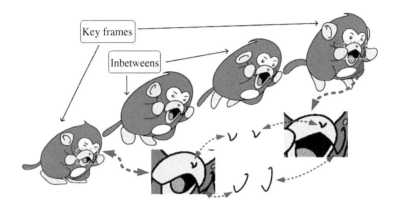

Figure 4.1 Two inbetweens with colors are generated according to two keyframes. The enlarged parts show the corresponding objects with complex and open shapes.

4.1.1 Related Work in Correspondence Construction

In correspondence construction, popular descriptors can be classified into two groups: contour-based and region-based. Considering the application of 2D animation, objects are defined by curves only (without loss of generality, curve is used instead of contour) in keyframes at the inbetweening stage. Thus, only contour-based methods are related. Of these, most approaches assume that objects are represented by a single closed contour, such as integral and differential descriptors. However, in animation production, objects in keyframes usually have complex structures which consist of multiple curves, and most of those curves are of open shapes due to occlusion, or for artistic reasons, as shown by the enlarged parts in Figure 4.1. Thus, the shape descriptor, "shape context" [34], is most suitable for the application because it uses related distribution to model complex objects.

For matching methods, the assignment linear programming Hungarian algorithm is applied to shape context matching. However, it can only obtain one-to-one correspondence, so equalizing the number of sampling points becomes a problem. Early spectral methods on correspondence construction, such as those discussed in [246] and [271], directly apply eigendecomposition on an adjacent matrix. Because of high dimensionality and data redundancy, these methods are not robust and accurate. Moreover, similar to the Hungarian algorithm and the SVD-based methods, they can only obtain one-to-one correspondence. To seek improvement, different techniques are combined with spectral graph theory [70]. In Ref. [60], clustering is used to create many-to-many correspondence, and linear projection is applied to generate a low dimensional subspace. However, linear subspace construction cannot discover manifold properties of data distribution, and building subspaces separately for targeting objects and aligning them afterward does not effectively construct the best common subspace for those objects.

4.1.2 Introduction of the Semi-supervised Correspondence Construction

Writers on spectral graph approaches [70] have discussed the importance of the intrinsic structure of data distribution for the performance of spectral graph techniques. Some methods have demonstrated that in estimating the data distribution, manifold structure is important [31]; however, global information should still be considered in estimating data structures. The "Patch Alignment" Framework (PAF) introduced in Section 2.1 unifies the existing classic spectral graph techniques in a general framework and consists of two parts: local patch construction and whole alignment. A local patch can be constructed according to specific applications, while the whole alignment is shared by all methods. Equally, semi-supervised learning [365] has successfully been employed in many applications due to its utilization of user input as labels or pairwise constraints. For animation production software, user assistance has become popular for achieving good performance on auto-inbetweening and auto-coloring. To take advantage of both spectral learning and semi-supervised learning, user input is introduced to the PAF and a Semi-supervised Patch Alignment Framework (Semi-PAF) for correspondence construction is developed. Since objects in keyframes can be sampled as a point set which is a general representation for both raster image and vector graphics, our framework aims to build accurate correspondences between objects represented by points.

4.1.2.1 *Shape Descriptor* The application of cartoon correspondence building requires accurately matching objects with complicated structures and open shapes. Shape context is used because it describes the relative spatial distribution (distance and orientation) of landmark points around feature points. For the shape context descriptor, two shapes P and Q are defined by the feature points as $\{p_1, p_2, \ldots, p_n\}$ and $\{q_1, q_2, \ldots, q_m\}$, respectively. The shape context of p_s is defined as a histogram h_s of the remaining $n-1$ points of the shape P under a global coordinate system: $h_s(c) = \#\{p_j : j \neq s, p_j - p_s \in bin(c)\}$, in which the bins uniformly divide the log-polar space. Similarly, $h_t(c) = \#\{q_j : j \neq t, q_j - q_s \in bin(c)\}$ is the shape context of q_t. An illustration of shape context is given in Figure 4.2(b). The distance between the shape contexts of p_s and q_t is defined as

$$D\left(p_s, q_t\right) = \frac{1}{2} \sum_{c=1}^{C} \frac{\left[h_s\left(c\right) - h_t\left(c\right)\right]^2}{h_s\left(c\right) + h_t\left(c\right)}. \tag{4.1}$$

The value of parameter c indicates the number of bins of the histogram. In our experiments, this value is set to 60.

4.1.2.2 Algorithm Introduction In this section, a new Semi-supervised Patch Alignment Framework (Semi-PAF) for correspondence construction is introduced. To better present the details of the proposed Semi-PAF technique, important notations used are provided below. Capital letter $\mathbf{X}$ represents the data matrix including all the feature points from shapes in the original feature space $\mathbf{R}^m$, and $\mathbf{Y}$ represents the corresponding new feature space $\mathbf{R}^d$. Lower case letter $\mathbf{x}_i$ represents the vector of ith feature point in $\mathbf{X}$, and $\mathbf{y}_i$ represents the corresponding new representation of $\mathbf{x}_i$. Figure 4.2 explains Semi-PAF. In particular, step 1 shows the input (a pair of keyframes) of Semi-PAF. In step 2, these two frames are sampled into feature points that form the data matrix $\mathbf{X} \in \mathbf{R}^m$. Here, we use the shape context as the visual feature to describe the relative spatial distribution of landmark points around the feature points. The dimension m is set to 60. Subsequently, local patches are built from feature points $\mathbf{x}_s$ and $\mathbf{x}_t$, and pairwise constraint patches are built between feature points $\mathbf{x}_s$, $\mathbf{x}_q$ and $\mathbf{x}_t$, $\mathbf{x}_p$ in steps 3 and 4, where a global alignment matrix for patches is obtained. In step 5, a linear mapping matrix $\mathbf{U}$ is obtained by eigendecomposition to project the feature points (e.g., $\mathbf{x}_s$, $\mathbf{x}_t$, $\mathbf{x}_p$ and $\mathbf{x}_q$) from the original feature space $\mathbf{X} \in \mathbf{R}^m$ onto the new feature space $\mathbf{Y} \in \mathbf{R}^d$ (e.g., $\mathbf{y}_s$, $\mathbf{y}_t$, $\mathbf{y}_p$ and $\mathbf{y}_q$) through $\mathbf{Y} = \mathbf{U}^T\mathbf{X}$. We decrease the dimensionality to reduce the possibility of subsequent matching model overfitting to noises and increase the model's robustness. In step 6, those feature points in corresponding regions of the two keyframes are respectively grouped into the same clusters, while points of mouths are grouped erroneously. In this case, to improve the clustering performance, Human Computer Interactions are introduced in step 7 to refine the data distribution estimation by adding new pairwise constraints. In step 8, final correspondences between sample points are constructed from the clustering result by using the nearest neighbor rule.

4.1.2.3 Local Patch Construction for Correspondence Construction
The details of the patch alignment framework have already been introduced in Section 2.1. In this subsection, we aim to integrate this framework into the specific correspondence construction applications. According to Section 2.1, the $\mathbf{L}_i$ is calculated from the patch built by the data $\mathbf{x}_i$ and its related neighbors $\mathbf{x}_{i_1}, \ldots, \mathbf{x}_{i_k}$, it is critical to choose the k related neighbors. The aim of the Semi-PAF is to group similar points from two keyframes into one cluster, as shown in Figure 4.2(f), and to build correspondences from it. Therefore, the local geometry is integrated in local patch construction as follows. For patch $\mathbf{x}_i$, the k related data can be found in following way: $\mathbf{x}_{i_j}$ can be added into $\mathbf{x}_i$'s patch, if $\mathbf{x}_{i_j}$ is one of the k_1 nearest neighbors of $\mathbf{x}_i$ in keyframe 1, or $\mathbf{x}_{i_j}$ is one of the k_2 nearest neighbors of $\mathbf{x}_i$ in keyframe 2. Figure

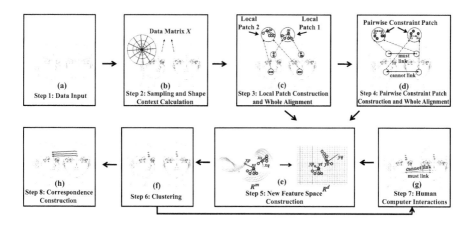

Figure 4.2   Semi-supervised patch alignment framework for correspondence construction. (a) Data input. (b) Sampling and shape context calculation. (c) Local patch construction and whole alignment; two local patches are illustrated here, within which the f points are from two keyframes. (d) Pairwise constraint patch construction and whole alignment; two pairs of constraints are illustrated in the enlarged circles where the arrows and corresponding feature points displayed with the same colors indicate the correspondences. (e) New feature space construction; the manifold represents the original feature space and the submanifold represents the obtained low dimensional feature space. (f) Clustering, the points with the same color form one cluster. (g) Additional human computer interactions indicated by arrows. (h) Correspondence construction; the lines indicate the final correspondences.

4.2(c) shows the process of local patch construction where k equals $k_1 + k_2$, and k_1, k_2 can be determined by a user. The optimization over the patch is defined by

$$\arg\min_{\mathbf{y}_i} \sum_{j=1}^{k} \left\| \mathbf{y}_i - \mathbf{y}_{i_j} \right\|^2 (\mathbf{w}_i)_j , \qquad (4.2)$$

where $\mathbf{y}_{i_j}$, $j = 1, \cdots, k$, are the k connected data of the given $\mathbf{y}_i$. As shown in Figure 4.2(c), the k connected data are from points acquired from two keyframes. $\mathbf{w}_i$ is the k dimensions column vector calculated by

$$(\mathbf{w}_i)_j = \exp\left(-D\left(\mathbf{x}_i, \mathbf{x}_{i_j}\right)/t \right) , \qquad (4.3)$$

where $D\left(\mathbf{x}_i, \mathbf{x}_{i_j}\right)$ is calculated by Eq. (4.1). Equation (4.3) aims to preserve the local geometry of the patch in low-dimensional space as shown in Figure 4.2(e). It means that feature points $[\mathbf{x}_i, \mathbf{x}_{i_1}, \ldots, \mathbf{x}_{i_k}]$ gathered in one patch will be projected closely in the low dimensional feature space as $[\mathbf{y}_i, \mathbf{y}_{i_1}, \ldots, \mathbf{y}_{i_K}]$. The optimization in Eq. (4.3) implicitly emphasizes the natural clusters in the data. So via subsequent clustering, the data in one patch will be grouped into the same cluster. Equation (4.3) can be rewritten as

$$\arg\min_{\mathbf{y}_i} \mathbf{tr} \left(\begin{bmatrix} (\mathbf{y}_i - \mathbf{y}_{i_1})^{\mathbf{T}} \\ \vdots \\ (\mathbf{y}_i - \mathbf{y}_{i_k})^{\mathbf{T}} \end{bmatrix} [\mathbf{y}_i - \mathbf{y}_{i_1}, \cdots, \mathbf{y}_i - \mathbf{y}_{i_k}] \, diag\,(\mathbf{w}_i) \right)$$

$$= \arg\min_{\mathbf{Y}_i} \mathbf{tr} \left(\mathbf{Y}_i \begin{bmatrix} -\mathbf{e}_k^{\mathbf{T}} \\ \mathbf{I}_k \end{bmatrix} diag\,(\mathbf{w}_i)\,[-\mathbf{e}_k\ \mathbf{I}_k]\,\mathbf{Y}_i^{\mathbf{T}} \right)$$

$$= \arg\min_{\mathbf{Y}_i} \mathbf{tr} \left(\mathbf{Y}_i \mathbf{L}_i \mathbf{Y}_i^{\mathbf{T}} \right),$$

(4.4)

where $\mathbf{Y}_i = [\mathbf{y}_i, \mathbf{y}_{i_1}, \cdots, \mathbf{y}_{i_k}]$; $\mathbf{e}_k = [1, \cdots, 1]^{\mathbf{T}} \in \mathbf{R}^k$; $\mathbf{I}_k$ is an $k \times k$ identity matrix and $diag\,(\mathbf{w}_i)$ constructs a $k \times k$ diagonal matrix. The $\mathbf{L}_i$ for each patch in our application is formulated as

$$\mathbf{L}_i = \begin{bmatrix} -\mathbf{e}_k^{\mathbf{T}} \\ \mathbf{I}_k \end{bmatrix} diag\,(\mathbf{w}_i)\,[-\mathbf{e}_k\ \mathbf{I}_k] = \begin{bmatrix} \sum_{j=1}^{k}(\mathbf{w}_i)_j & -\mathbf{w}_i^{\mathbf{T}} \\ -\mathbf{w}_i & diag\,(\mathbf{w}_i) \end{bmatrix}. \quad (4.5)$$

Take the character shown in Figure 4.2(c) for example. Given a specified feature point $\mathbf{x}_i = [\ 0\ \ 9\ \ 6\ \ \cdots\ \ 2\ \ 0\ ]^{\mathbf{T}} \in \mathbf{R}^{60}$, the parameters k_1 and k_2 are determined to be 2, so the 4 nearest feature points of $\mathbf{x}_i$ in the character are

$$[\mathbf{x}_{i_1}, \mathbf{x}_{i_2}, \mathbf{x}_{i_3}, \mathbf{x}_{i_4}]^{\mathbf{T}} = \begin{bmatrix} 0 & 4 & 8 & \cdots & 1 & 2 \\ 0 & 2 & 10 & \cdots & 1 & 0 \\ 0 & 2 & 10 & \cdots & 1 & 0 \\ 0 & 0 & 4 & \cdots & 0 & 0 \end{bmatrix}^{\mathbf{T}} \in \mathbf{R}^{60 \times 4}.$$

These five feature points construct a local patch. Thus, by using Eq. (4.3), the column vector $\mathbf{w}_i$ can be calculated as

$$\mathbf{w}_i = [\ 0.9624\ \ 0.9629\ \ 0.9635\ \ 0.9611\ ]^{\mathbf{T}}.$$

By using Eq. (4.5), the matrix $\mathbf{L}_i$ for this local patch can be calculated as a 5×5 matrix as

$$\begin{bmatrix} 3.8499 & -0.9624 & -0.9629 & -0.9635 & -0.9611 \\ -0.9624 & 0.9624 & 0 & 0 & 0 \\ -0.9629 & 0 & 0.9629 & 0 & 0 \\ -0.9635 & 0 & 0 & 0.9635 & 0 \\ -0.9611 & 0 & 0 & 0 & 0.9611 \end{bmatrix}.$$

With $\mathbf{L}_i$, the alignment matrix $\mathbf{L}$, which is equal to the Laplacian matrix used in LE, can be constructed. Based on the assumption of linearization that $\mathbf{Y} = \mathbf{U}^{\mathbf{T}}\mathbf{X}$, the projection matrix $\mathbf{U}$ can be resolved according to the whole alignment trick.

4.1.2.4 *Pairwise Constraint Patch Construction for Correspondence Construction*   Besides integrating the local geometry in local patch construction,

pairwise constraints are added during whole alignment to enhance the data estimation. As shown in Figure 4.2(d), it is natural and convenient for users to add two such groups of pairwise constraints: the positive constraints (must link $P : (\mathbf{x}_i, \mathbf{x}_j) \in P$) and negative constraints (cannot link $D : (\mathbf{x}_i, \mathbf{x}_j) \in D$), which form the pairwise constraint patch. The feature points in the positive pairwise constraint patch are similar to each other so they should be close in the low-dimensional feature space. Thus, the optimization can be defined as

$$\arg\min_{\mathbf{y}_i} \sum_{(\mathbf{x}_i, \mathbf{x}_j) \in P} \|\mathbf{y}_i - \mathbf{y}_j\|^2 . \tag{4.6}$$

The optimization in Eq. (4.6) aims to find the best low dimensional representation for feature points belonging to the same cluster, and thus the distance between their low dimensional representations will be small. Based on the assumption of linear mapping $\mathbf{Y} = \mathbf{U}^T\mathbf{X}$, the linear mapping matrix $\mathbf{U}$ can be obtained as

$$\begin{aligned}
&\arg\min_{\mathbf{y}_i} \sum_{(\mathbf{x}_i, \mathbf{x}_j)\in P} \|\mathbf{y}_i - \mathbf{y}_j\|^2 \\
&= \arg\min_{\mathbf{U}} \sum_{(\mathbf{x}_i, \mathbf{x}_j)\in P} (\mathbf{x}_i - \mathbf{x}_j)^T \mathbf{U}\mathbf{U}^T (\mathbf{x}_i - \mathbf{x}_j) \\
&= \arg\min_{\mathbf{U}} \mathbf{tr} \left\{ \mathbf{U}^T \left[\sum_{(\mathbf{x}_i, \mathbf{x}_j)\in P} (\mathbf{x}_i - \mathbf{x}_j) (\mathbf{x}_i - \mathbf{x}_j)^T \right] \mathbf{U} \right\}
\end{aligned} \tag{4.7}$$

In contrast with the positive constraint, the link of a negative constraint indicates two dissimilar points, and these two points in the negative pairwise constraint patch should be kept far away in the low dimensional feature space. Thus, the optimization can be defined as

$$\arg\max_{\mathbf{y}_i} \sum_{(\mathbf{x}_i, \mathbf{x}_j) \in D} \|\mathbf{y}_i - \mathbf{y}_j\|^2 . \tag{4.8}$$

The optimization in Eq. (4.48) aims to find the best low dimensional representation for feature points belonging to different clusters, and thus the distance between their low dimensional representations will be large. According to Eq. (4.48), the linear mapping matrix $\mathbf{U}$ can be obtained as

$$\begin{aligned}
&\arg\max_{\mathbf{y}_i} \sum_{(\mathbf{x}_i, \mathbf{x}_j)\in D} \|\mathbf{y}_i - \mathbf{y}_j\|^2 \\
&= \arg\max_{\mathbf{U}} \mathbf{tr} \left\{ \mathbf{U}^T \left[\sum_{(\mathbf{x}_i, \mathbf{x}_j)\in D} (\mathbf{x}_i - \mathbf{x}_j) (\mathbf{x}_i - \mathbf{x}_j)^T \right] \mathbf{U} \right\}
\end{aligned} \tag{4.9}$$

According to the PAF, Eq. (4.7) can be rewritten as

$$\begin{aligned}
&\arg\min_{\mathbf{U}} \mathbf{tr} \left\{ \mathbf{U}^T \left[\sum_{(\mathbf{x}_i, \mathbf{x}_j)\in P} (\mathbf{x}_i - \mathbf{x}_j) (\mathbf{x}_i - \mathbf{x}_j)^T \right] \mathbf{U} \right\} \\
&= \arg\min_{\mathbf{U}} \mathbf{tr} \left\{ \mathbf{U}^T \left[\sum_{i=1}^{N_P} \tfrac{1}{2} (\mathbf{x}_i - \mathbf{x}_j) (\mathbf{x}_i - \mathbf{x}_j)^T \right] \mathbf{U} \right\} \\
&= \arg\min_{\mathbf{U}} \sum_{i=1}^{N_P} \mathbf{tr} \left[\mathbf{U}^T \tfrac{1}{2} \left(\mathbf{X}_i^P \begin{bmatrix} 1 \\ -1 \end{bmatrix} \right) \left(\mathbf{X}_i^P \begin{bmatrix} 1 \\ -1 \end{bmatrix} \right)^T \mathbf{U} \right] \\
&= \arg\min_{\mathbf{U}} \sum_{i=1}^{N_P} \mathbf{tr} \left[\mathbf{U}^T (\mathbf{X}_i^P) \mathbf{L}_i^P (\mathbf{X}_i^P)^T \mathbf{U} \right],
\end{aligned} \tag{4.10}$$

where N_P represents the number of points in the positive set P and $\mathbf{L}_i^P$ equals

$$\mathbf{L}_i^P = \begin{bmatrix} \frac{1}{2} & -\frac{1}{2} \\ -\frac{1}{2} & \frac{1}{2} \end{bmatrix}. \tag{4.11}$$

By using the alignment trick, the problem in Eq. (4.10) becomes

$$\arg\min_{\mathbf{U}} \mathbf{tr}\left[\mathbf{U}^{\mathbf{T}}\left(\mathbf{X}^P\right)\mathbf{L}^P\left(\mathbf{X}^P\right)^{\mathbf{T}}\mathbf{U}\right] \tag{4.12}$$

Similar to Eq. (4.10), Eq. (4.9) which is for the "cannot link" sets, can be rewritten as:

$$\arg\max_{\mathbf{U}} \mathbf{tr}\left[\mathbf{U}^{\mathbf{T}}\left(\mathbf{X}^D\right)\mathbf{L}^D\left(\mathbf{X}^D\right)^{\mathbf{T}}\mathbf{U}\right]. \tag{4.13}$$

Finally, by integrating the pairwise constraints into the whole optimization, the objective function for Semi-PAF can be formulated as

$$\arg\min_{\mathbf{U}} \mathbf{tr}\left\{\mathbf{U}^{\mathbf{T}}\left[\mathbf{XLX}^{\mathbf{T}} + \left(\mathbf{X}^P\right)\mathbf{L}^P\left(\mathbf{X}^P\right)^{\mathbf{T}} - \mu\left(\mathbf{X}^D\right)\mathbf{L}^D\left(\mathbf{X}^D\right)^{\mathbf{T}}\right]\mathbf{U}\right\},$$
$$\text{s.t. } \mathbf{U}^{\mathbf{T}}\mathbf{U} = \mathbf{I}_d \quad , \tag{4.14}$$

where μ is defined as

$$\mu = \mathbf{tr}\left[\mathbf{XLX}^{\mathbf{T}} + \left(\mathbf{X}^P\right)\mathbf{L}^P\left(\mathbf{X}^P\right)^{\mathbf{T}}\right] / tr\left[\left(\mathbf{X}^D\right)\mathbf{L}^D\left(\mathbf{X}^D\right)^{\mathbf{T}}\right]. \tag{4.15}$$

The linearization matrix $\mathbf{U}$ can be obtained through generalized or standard eigenvalue decomposition on $\mathbf{XLX}^{\mathbf{T}} + \left(\mathbf{X}^P\right)\mathbf{L}^P\left(\mathbf{X}^P\right)^{\mathbf{T}} - \mu\left(\mathbf{X}^D\right)\mathbf{L}^D\left(\mathbf{X}^D\right)^{\mathbf{T}}$. The solution of $\mathbf{U}$ is the d eigenvectors associated with d smallest eigenvalues.

To further improve the performance of dimension reduction, Additional Human Computer Interactions(HCI) are adopted into this framework. HCI carry abundant information contained in relevant or irrelevant inputs marked by users. Their ability to boost the performance of algorithms has been proved in many tasks. As mentioned above, although the pairwise constraints have been added to enhance the estimation of the data distribution, some parts of the correspondence results may still be unsatisfactory to users (such as the eyebrows shown in Figure 4.2(f)). For such cases, our framework allows users to add more pairwise constraints as additional HCI (as shown in Figure 4.2(g)), which will be applied to update $\mathbf{X}^P$ and $\mathbf{X}^D$ in Eq. (4.14) to improve the final correspondence construction.

4.1.3   Stroke Correspondence Construction via Stroke Reconstruction Algorithm

In this section, the stroke reconstruction algorithm is presented to build a correspondence of strokes which are of different number and length in two keyframes, based on the obtained feature point correspondence. It aims to minimize the sensitivity of point matching accuracy and establish correct stroke matching for inbetween generation. In practice, inbetween generation should be based on the accurate match of strokes which describe the shapes of objects in the drawings; i.e., the strokes representing the same part of corresponding objects from two keyframes should be matched. When artists draw keyframes freely, however, the same parts of corresponding objects may be composed of a different number of strokes of different lengths. Thus, "many to many" and "part to whole" stroke mapping is necessary to preserve the shape of corresponding objects during inbetweening. During inbetweening, these complex mappings will cause robustness problems. As our solution, we proposed compound strokes to realize optimal stroke correspondence where only "one to one" mapping exists. A compound stroke consists of a list of segments from the original strokes. Figure 3.5 illustrates an example of stroke reconstruction.

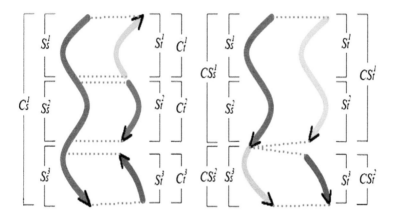

Figure 4.3   Illustration of stroke reconstruction. C_s and C_t denote source and target original strokes, S_s and S_t denote source and arget segments, CS_s and CS_t denote source and target compound strokes. .

Here, one keyframe is named as the source frame and the other as the target frame. C_s^1 is the original stroke in the source frame and $C_t^1; C_t^2; C_t^3$ are the original strokes in the target frame. In the stroke reconstruction algorithm, the original strokes in the source frame are checked one by one. For each original source stroke, the best match can be found in a stroke from the target frame. Based on this mapping, one source segment of the source stroke is created; for example, a source segment S_s^1 and a target segment S_t^1 form a best match. Recursively, the best matching target segments can be found for all the remaining segments of the source stroke. After searching for all the source strokes, the matching segments are grouped into a list according to connectivity between one another. The segments of approximate G_1 continuity between one another and matched to the same original stroke are put into the same list, e.g., segment S_t^1 and S_t^2. Finally, one list of matching segments composes a compound stroke, e.g., segment S_t^1 and S_t^2 composing compound stroke CS_t^1. In Figure 4.3, the arrows show the directions of the strokes. The direction of the generated compound stroke is determined according to parameter changes along the source stroke. For instance, when going through the points along source segment S_s^3, the parameters increase, while those of the matched points decrease on the corresponding target segment S_t^3. Thus, the directions of S_t^3 and CS_t^2 are set the same as S_s^3.

The evaluations of a match is defined as follows:

$$rate = \left(\frac{N^s}{N_C^s} + \frac{N^t}{N_C^t} \right) \times \alpha_1 + \frac{\min(L^s, L^t)}{\max(L^s, L^t)} \times \alpha_2. \qquad (4.16)$$

The first and second parts are the ratio of the matching point numbers and the ratio of the matching segment lengths, with respective weights α_1 and α_2. N is the numbers of matching points, N_C is the total number of feature points, and L is the length of a matching segment. s and t denote the source and the target respectively. With this condition, segments with relatively more matched points and of similar lengths tend to be evaluated as a better match.

In some situations, a few segments may be partially matched but are not evaluated as being the best match. Thus, they do not constitute any of the compound strokes. After all the strokes are processed, post-processing is applied to the remaining unmatched segments. An unmatched segment is appended to a matched segment if it meets approximate G1 continuity. Otherwise, its point correspondence is reexamined. Our stroke reconstruction algorithm can be described by the pseudo codes given below:

1 for each original stroke in the source frame **do**

2 Get feature points on the stroke

3 Get matched points in the target frame based on point correspondence

4 while number of unmatched source points > 0 **do**

5 Find matched points with consecutive index to form candidate matched segments

6 Find the best matched source and target segments by Eq. (4.16)

7 Record matched segments

8 Remove matched feature points

9 end while

10 end for

11 Post-processing unmatched segments

12 Construct compound strokes from segment lists

The proposed stroke reconstruction algorithm successfully handles the problem of "many to many" and "part to whole" mapping of original strokes and obtains one-to-one correspondence of compound strokes. Each compound stroke is in fact a piecewise disk Bézier curve. Inbetweens of two piecewise disk Bézier curves are generated.

4.1.4 Simulation Results

In this section, results and comparisons of testing data and data from real world animation productions are provided.

4.1.4.1 Data Set Construction   Experiments are conducted on data sets from real-world 2D animation production, in which characters are usually separated into different layers. Consequently, each test dataset in our experiments consists of two keyframes and each frame has one layer. Figure 4.4(a) shows six data sets including the faces, hair, and whole bodies of cartoon characters. Figure 4.4(b) presents the points for each data set after sampling. For shape context calculation, the number of bins is 60; thus, for each point, a 60-dimensional feature vector is obtained to represent this point in the original shape context feature space.

The local shape context is invariant to rotations and uses the ordering information of points along curves to construct a consistent local coordinate system. Complex shapes used in our experiments consist of multiple curves, and the directions of curves may be different from one another, thus the ordering information is insufficient to form a consistent local coordinate system. Supervised information is applied to aligning shapes to achieve the rotational invariance.

4.1.4.2 Parameters Configurations   The performance of Semi-PAF for correspondence construction is evaluated by using two metrics: Cluster Built Rates(CBR) and Correspondence Built Percentages(CBP). CBR is the ratio of successfully built clusters over all clusters. CBR is used to evaluate the effectiveness of the first step in correspondence construction (shown in Figure 4.2(f)). A high CBR is the precondition for subsequent operations. If all points within one cluster are from an identical keyframe, then the algorithm fails to build correspondence inside this cluster. In this case, we consider this cluster to be constructed unsuccessfully. Otherwise, if points in a cluster are from different keyframes, this cluster is valid. Sometimes, points from two different keyframes are grouped in one cluster but the subsequent matching of those points is incorrect. Figure 4.2(g) shows that one point of the character's mouth in the side view is mismatched to one point of the character's nose in the front view during the final correspondence construction within clusters. Therefore, CBP is needed to evaluate the effectiveness of the final step in the correspondence construction. CBP is the ratio of correctly built final correspondences over all constructed mappings. This metric is commonly used in shape matching for performance evaluation.

The following experiments are conducted on the six datasets and all experiments are divided into two parts. First, the performance of Semi-PAF on CBR is evaluated and compared with representative spectral graph algorithms: PCA, ISOMAP, LPP, and LTSA. Unsupervised Patch Alignment Framework (Unsup-PAF) is implemented

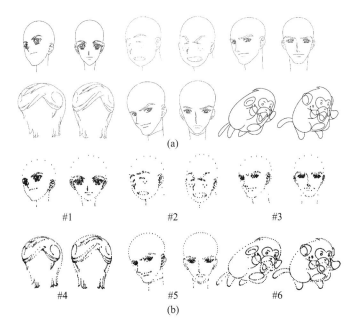

Figure 4.4   The real-world data sets for performance evaluation: (a) four pairs of faces, one pair of hair and one pair of bodies for cartoon characters; (b) the corresponding data points obtained by sampling.

by directly discarding pairwise constraints. Therefore, we have six algorithms, including Semi-PAF, Unsup-PAF, PCA, LPP, LTSA, and ISOMAP, to transform the data into low dimensional spaces. Clusters are obtained by using the classical K-Means algorithm. To demonstrate the effectiveness of dimension reduction, the results acquired by performing K-Means in the original feature space are also given as a baseline.

In our experiments, we observe that the proposed algorithm and selected baseline algorithms are insensitive to small k values with a wide range. CBR varies with dimensionality, which increases from 5 to 60 with step 5 ($[5, 10, \cdots, 60]$). For each dimension, experiments are conducted 20 times and the average CBR is recorded. In the second stage, point correspondence is built based on the clustering results and the CBP is calculated to evaluate the performance of each method. In this stage, we focus on comparing the performance of Semi-PAF on correspondence building with the Hungarian method, which is a classic algorithm widely used in shape matching and shape retrieval, and the CBP is also recorded, varying with dimensionality which increases from 5 to 60.

4.1.4.3 *Experimental results on CBR*   Figure 4.5 shows the CBR of different algorithms. In all six subfigures, the dimensionality increases from 5 to 60 with step 5, and all subfigures show that Semi-PAF achieves the highest CBR value. This indicates that clustering performance is improved by integrating the local geometry

(encoding the data distribution information) and the pairwise constraints (encoding the semi-supervised information). Figure 4.5 shows that Semi-PAF maintains high CBR value with a wide range of dimensionality from 5 to 20.

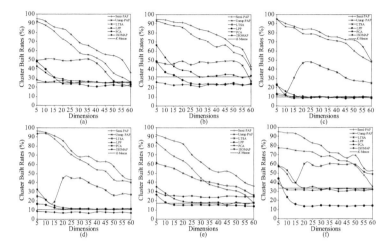

Figure 4.5   Cluster built rates (CBR) vs. subspace dimension on our data sets: (a) results of data set 1; (b) results of data set 2; (c) results of data set 3; (d) results of data set 4; (e) results of data set 5; and (f) results of data set 6.

4.1.4.4   *Experimental Results on CBP*   Semi-PAF is compared with the Hungarian method on CBP. Figure 4.6 shows that Semi-PAF's CBP increases with increasing the dimensionality from 5 to 20 but decreases with further increasing dimensionality from 50 to 60. Additionally, the CBP of the Hungarian method is 64% and is higher than Semi-PAF below dimensionality 15. However, when the dimensionality is between 20 and 50, Semi-PAF's CBP is around 80% and is higher than that obtained by the Hungarian method. On the remaining data sets, we have similar results as shown in Figures 4.6(b) to Figures 4.6(f). Therefore, Semi-PAF is effective in eliminating the redundant information and improving the performance of correspondence construction.

Based on the experimental results shown in Figure 4.5 and Figure 4.6, it can be observed that Semi-PAF achieves satisfactory performance when the dimensionality is around 20. Therefore, the results of the final correspondence construction with dimensionality 20 will be presented in the next section.

4.1.4.5   *Comparison of the Correspondence Construction*   Figure 4.6 illustrates the constructed correspondences of the six datasets using Semi-PAF and the Hungarian method. The figure contains six subfigures for the six respective data sets. Each subfigure contains two rows to compare Semi-PAF and the Hungarian method. Each row consists of three example groups of correspondences for the most difficult parts of the data set. To demonstrate the improvement of Semi-PAF

for correspondence construction, we show the clustering results on those parts by marking points from the same cluster in red.

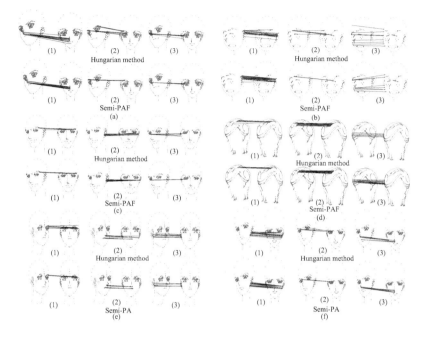

Figure 4.6 Correspondences constructed using Semi-PAF and the Hungarian method on real-world data sets. In each result, straight lines are used to display the obtained correspondences between points.

Figure 4.6 shows the correspondences that are built between the lower-right view and the front view of the character's face. We compare Semi-PAF and the Hungarian method on correspondence construction for the three most difficult parts of data set #1. The second row suggests that Semi-PAF maps the corresponding points in the two frames perfectly. However, the Hungarian method mismatches several points, such as in the first plot of the first row in Figure 4.6(a), where some points of the nose of the down-right view are wrongly matched to those of the left eye and the mouth of the front view. Figure 4.6(b) to Figure 4.6(f) suggest similar results based on the other five data sets.

In addition, the third column of plots in Figure 4.6(b) shows that the Hungarian method can only build one-to-one correspondence, while Semi-PAF can build many-to-many correspondences.

4.1.4.6 Stroke Correspondence Construction Results
In Figure 4.7, stroke correspondence results on three sets of data are given in three subfigures. In each subfigure, the upper picture shows the original strokes from two keyframes. The middle picture shows the feature point correspondence built by our method. The bottom

picture demonstrates the final compound stroke correspondence. The correspondences of several pairs of feature points are highlighted by small circles and straight lines with arrows, while several compound stroke correspondences are highlighted by straight lines with arrows.

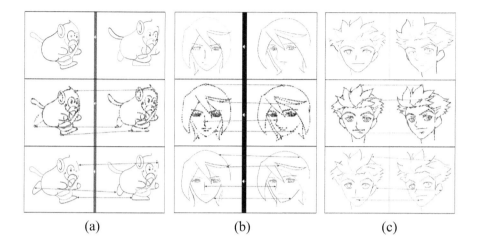

(a)   (b)   (c)

Figure 4.7   Stroke correspondence construction for real-world data. The upper picture shows the original strokes. The middle picture shows the feature point correspondence construction result. The bottom picture shows the final compound stroke correspondence.

In Figure 4.7(a), the correspondence construction result of one set of data from real world production is provided. In this example, the number of strokes between two keyframes is different and there is complex correspondence between original strokes, such as that between the strokes forming the main body contour, the right hand and the tail. Moreover, the right ear does not exist in the left keyframe but appears in the right keyframe. Our method not only converts all original complex correspondence to simple "one to one" compound stroke mapping, but also matches the right ear in the right frame with one automatically generated compound stroke in the left frame, which is a segment of the body contour. The advantage of this will be demonstrated by the following inbetweening results.

Figure 4.7(b) shows the results of another more complex real-world example where the anime character was drawn in two layers: face layer and hair layer. The motion between these two keyframes involves 3D rotations as the character turns to the left and a little downwards. We built stroke correspondence for the two layers separately. In Figure 4.7(b), the results of the two layers are combined to save space. We can see that all parts of the character are matched correctly and the complicated correspondences between the original strokes, such as the strokes of the right strip of hair and the face contour, are simplified to "one to one" mapping between compound strokes. More real world examples are given in Figure 4.7(c). These examples are also handled with layering and all strokes are correctly matched. More inbetweening results are presented in Figure 4.8.

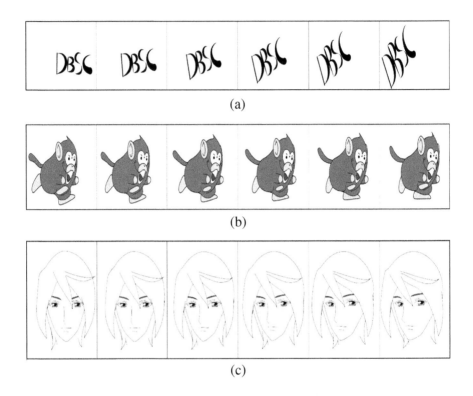

(a)

(b)

(c)

Figure 4.8   Generated inbetweens based on compound stroke correspondence. The first and last pictures of each row are keyframes, and those between them are generated inbetweens.

4.2   CARTOON CHARACTERS REPRESENTED BY MULTIPLE FEATURES

How can we retrieve cartoon characters accurately? Or how can we synthesize new cartoon clips smoothly and efficiently from the cartoon library? These two questions are important for animators and cartoon enthusiasts to enable them to design and create new cartoons by utilizing existing cartoon materials. The first key issue in answering these questions is to find a proper representation that effectively describes both cartoon character geometry and gesture. In this section, we propose multiple features: color histogram, Hausdorff edge feature and skeleton feature, to represent cartoon characters with different motions. Each visual feature reflects a unique characteristic of a cartoon character and they are complementary to one another for retrieval and synthesis. However, how the three visual features should be combined is another key issue for these applications. Simply concatenating them into a long vector will result in the so-called "curse of dimensionality," let alone the fact that their heterogeneity will be embedded in different visual feature spaces. Inspired from the multiview subspace learning algorithm presented in Section 2.5, we propose multiview learning methods for cartoon retrieval and synthesis, details of which will be presented in Section 4.4.

4.2.1 Cartoon Character Extraction

The prerequisite for multiple feature extraction is the segmentation of cartoon characters from videos which contain a large number of celebrated characters (e.g., "Monkey-King," "Tom," and "Jerry"). Several approaches are commonly used in background segmentation; for example, Support Vector Machine (SVM) is appropriate for segmenting Disney cartoons, which are usually easily identifiable and often made up of a few solid colors. However, it is hard to extract "Monkey-King," a famous Chinese cartoon character, using SVM. The colors used in Chinese cartoons are more flexible than those used in Disney cartoons. In Figure 4.9(a), for example, "Monkey-King" is painted with seven colors, and at the same time the background color changes gradually, so SVM cannot be used to classify these images. Another common approach, single/multi-level threshold, is also incapable of producing acceptable results, because the color used in the image is flexible and the threshold is hard to determine.

When the animator makes a cartoon, a sketch is painted before colorization, so the edge around the character is easily detectable. We adopt a method based on edge detection to extract the character precisely. This method is based on Laplacian of Gaussian filter (LOG), in which the Gaussian suppresses noise and Laplacian estimates the second-order derivative of the noise-suppressed image. LOG filter can be derived as follows:

$$G = \frac{1}{2\pi\sigma^2} e^{-\frac{x^2+y^2}{2\sigma^2}}, \qquad (4.17)$$

$$L = \nabla^2 = \nabla \circ \nabla = \frac{\partial^2 f}{\partial x^2} + \frac{\partial^2 f}{\partial y^2}, \qquad (4.18)$$

in which G is Gaussian filter and L is Laplace operator (both in two dimensions). The symbolic derivation of LOG is as follows:

$$L \circ G = \nabla^2 G = \frac{1}{\pi\sigma^4} \left(\frac{x^2+y^2}{2\sigma^2} - 1 \right) e^{-\frac{x^2+y^2}{2\sigma^2}}. \qquad (4.19)$$

Since the LOG response approximates second-order derivatives of the smoothed image, edges can be located at zero-crossings, which are local maxima or minima of the first-order derivative. The main advantage compared to techniques based on the first-order derivative is that no explicit threshold is needed: All zero-crossings are equally important. Firstly, all the edges in the image are processed using LOG, whose response is controlled by the standard deviation parameter σ. By varying σ, edges at different scales are focused. In our experience, the constant $\sigma = 1.25$ is usually sufficient for most images. The detection results are shown in Figure 4.9(b). In order to refine it, the edge image $A_{Ma \times Na}$ is filtered by using two-dimensional convolution with a filter$F_{5 \times 5}$:

$$F = \begin{bmatrix} 0 & 0 & 0 & 0 & 0 \\ 0 & 1 & 1 & 1 & 0 \\ 0 & 1 & 1 & 1 & 0 \\ 0 & 1 & 1 & 1 & 0 \\ 0 & 0 & 0 & 0 & 0 \end{bmatrix} \tag{4.20}$$

and the convolution process is

$$C(i,j) = \sum_{m=0}^{Ma-1} \sum_{n=0}^{Na-1} A(m,n) * F(i-m, j-n) \tag{4.21}$$

where $0 \le i < Ma + 4$and $0 \le j < Na + 4$. The central part of the Matrix C of the same size of A is chosen as the final result. The filtered results are shown in Figure 4.9(c), in which the edge of the character forms a continuous closed part. In the resultant image, the edge that has the largest length, or is larger than a preset value, is likely to be the edge of the character. Figure 4.9(d) shows the result after edge removal, and the remaining edge is the largest. Since the character's edge forms a closed region, the flood fill algorithm is adopted to fulfill the region and finally the character "Monkey King" can be successfully extracted (Figures 4.9(e) and 4.9(f)). This method is suitable for both traditional Chinese cartoons and Disney cartoons.

After obtaining the cartoon characters $\mathbf{X} = [\mathbf{x}_1, \cdots, \mathbf{x}_N]$, we extract the Color Histogram $\mathbf{x}_i^{CH}$, Hausdorff Edge Feature $\mathbf{x}_i^{HEF}$, Motion Feature $\mathbf{x}_i^{MF}$ and Skeleton Feature $\mathbf{x}_i^{SF}$ to represent the cartoon character.

4.2.2   Color Histogram

Color Histogram(CH) is an effective representation of the color information. It is defined as the distribution of the number of pixels for each quantized bin. We adopt the RGB color space to model the cartoon character. Since RGB is a linear space, we quantize each component of RGB color space uniformly into four bins (0-63, 64-127, 128-191, and 192-255). Therefore, CH comprises a total of 64 ($4 \times 4 \times 4$) bins. In this case, each component of CH for cartoon character $\mathbf{x}_i$ is defined as $\mathbf{x}_i^{CH}(j) = c_j / C_i$, $j = 1, 2, \ldots, 64$, wherein c_j is the number of pixels with value j, and C_i is the total number of pixels in $\mathbf{x}_i$.

4.2.3   Hausdorff Edge Feature

Humans can recognize line drawings as accurately as gray level pictures. Edge features, which contain information about the shapes of objects, are frequently used to measure the dissimilarity between objects. To efficiently represent a character's

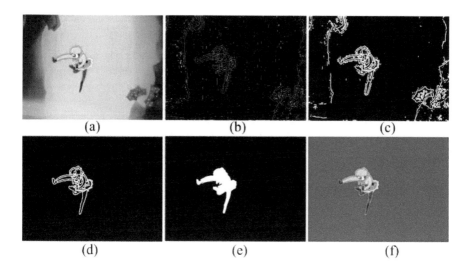

Figure 4.9   Workflow for cartoon character extraction: (a) image input; (b) edge detection; (c) noise removal; (d) closed edge selection; (e) silhouette preservation; (f) background subtraction.

shape, we use a modified Hausdorff distance to calculate the edge distance. Let E_i be the edge points set of the cartoon character $\mathbf{x}_i$. Given two cartoon characters $\mathbf{x}_i$ and $\mathbf{x}_j$, $h\left(E_i, E_j\right)$ is

$$h\left(E_i, E_j\right) = \left(\sum_{p_a \in E_i} \min_{p_b \in E_j} \left(\|p_a - p_b\|\right)\right) \Big/ |E_i|, \qquad (4.22)$$

where $\|p_a - p_b\|$ is the Euclidean distance between the coordinates of the two edge points p_a and p_b. This $|E_i|$ represents the total number of edge points on E_i. Thus, the Hausdorff edge distance is

$$Haus\_Dist_{ij} = \begin{cases} \max\left(h\left(E_i, E_j\right), h\left(E_j, E_i\right)\right) & i \neq j, \\ 0, & i = j. \end{cases} \qquad (4.23)$$

By calculating the Hausdorff distance in the whole data set, we obtain the edge dissimilarity matrix $\mathbf{W}_{edge} \in R^{N \times N}$, wherein $\mathbf{W}_{edge}\left(i, j\right)$ is the dissimilarity between a pair of cartoon images. Then, we use Multi-Dimensional Scaling (MDS) to obtain a unified vector representation $\mathbf{x}_i^{HEF}$ for each cartoon character according to the edge dissimilarity. It is

$$\mathbf{A} = -\frac{1}{2}\mathbf{P}\mathbf{W}_{edge}\mathbf{P}, \qquad (4.24)$$

where $\mathbf{P} = \mathbf{I} - \frac{1}{N}\mathbf{1}_N\mathbf{1}_N^{\mathbf{T}}$ is the centering matrix. Thus we have

$$\mathbf{A} = \mathrm{H}\Lambda\mathrm{H}^{\mathbf{T}}, \tag{4.25}$$

where $\Lambda = diag\,(\lambda_1,\ldots,\lambda_N)$ is the diagonal matrix of the eigenvalues of $\mathbf{A}$, and $\mathrm{H} = (h_1,\ldots,h_N)$ is the matrix of corresponding eigenvectors. The vectors of the Hausdorff edge features (HEF) for all cartoon characters are then given by

$$\left[x_1^{HEF}, x_2^{HEF}, \ldots, x_N^{HEF}\right]^{\mathbf{T}} = \mathrm{H}\Lambda^{1\!/2}. \tag{4.26}$$

4.2.4 Motion Feature

In most cases, characters having similar edges may represent different gestures, which can generate errors and visual incontinuity in cartoon retrieval and synthesis. If the gesture similarity is taken into account, the incontinuity can be easily solved. As the cartoon data are unstructured, recognizing the character's gesture in each frame is hard to achieve. However, it is well known that in animation, the gesture of the character should correspond to the character's current motion, so the gesture recognition problem can be converted into a motion tracking problem. If the character moves in the opposite direction in two consecutive frames, it is impossible for their gestures to be similar in those frames.

In cartoon videos, the character's motion can be synthesized from its motion relative to the camera and the camera's own motion. To calculate a character's relative motion, two characters are extracted from a pair of successive frames I_i and I_{i+1} (Figures 4.10(a), 4.10 (b)) by using the edge detection method. Based on these characters, their centroids can easily be calculated as C_i and C_{i+1} as shown in Figure 4.10 (c). The relative motion direction for the character in image I_i (shown in Figure 4.10 (c)) is represented by

$$\overrightarrow{M_r^i} = \overrightarrow{C_iC_{i+1}}. \tag{4.27}$$

In cartoon animation, the camera's motions are mainly translation, which can be calculated by reversing the background's motion. For two successive images I_i and I_{i+1} the optical flow for I_i is calculated as shown in Figure 4.10(d). The optical flow o from image I_i to image I_{i+1} is a vector field that encodes, for each pixel of I_i, the displacement of the corresponding pixel on I_{i+1}. Many methods can be used to calculate optical flow; here, an algorithm comparing the cross-correlation between image patches is adopted. To find the pixel location on image I_{i+1} that corresponds to a location (x_0, y_0) on image I_i, a square window is defined and the neighborhood of (x_0, y_0) is searched on I_{i+1} for a pixel (x, y) that maximizes the cross-correlation r between the window centered at (x_0, y_0) on I_i and the windows centered at (x, y) on I_{i+1}. r is defined by

$$r = \frac{\sum_{m,n}\left(W_i\,(m,n) - \overline{W_i}\right)\left(W_{i+1}\,(m,n) - \overline{W_{i+1}}\right)}{\sqrt{\sum_{m,n}\left(W_i\,(m,n) - \overline{W_i}\right)^2 \cdot \sum_{m,n}\left(W_{i+1}\,(m,n) - \overline{W_{i+1}}\right)^2}}, \tag{4.28}$$

where W_i and W_{i+1} are the windows on I_i and I_{i+1} and $\overline{W_k}$ is the mean intensity (color) in W_k.

After carrying out the optical flow, the motion of the pixels in the character is not consistent with the pixels in the background, as shown in Figure 4.10(d). To calculate the background's motion, the optical flows of those pixels on character are taken away (Figure 4.10(e)). If the optical flows are calculated explicitly at each pixel in the background, the results are highly redundant and some outliers emerge at pixels whose neighborhoods take on a uniform color (e.g., the blue sky in the middle of Figure 4.10(e)). It is well known that optical flow is most accurate at corner points due to the aperture problem, so optical flows can be calculated at corners in the background shown in Figure 4.10(f). The background motion in I_i is calculated from the average of the Vector Addition of the motion of the corner points

$$\overrightarrow{M_b^i} = \frac{1}{n} \sum_{a=0}^{n} \overrightarrow{M_{P_a}}, \tag{4.29}$$

where P_a is a certain corner point in I_i and $\overrightarrow{M_{P_a}}$ represents a corner point's motion calculated by optical flow. n represents the number of corner points detected in the background. Since the background's motion is opposite to the camera's motion, the motion of the character (shown in Figures 4.10(g) and 4.10(h)) is synthesized by

$$\overrightarrow{M_c^i} = \overrightarrow{M_r^i} - \overrightarrow{M_b^i}. \tag{4.30}$$

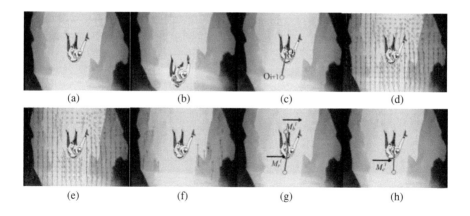

Figure 4.10   Synthesis of character's motion.

4.2.5 Skeleton Feature

The skeleton, which integrates both the geometrical and topological features of an object, is an important descriptor for object representation. In order to integrate the properties of cartoon characters, we adopt Discrete Curve Evolution(DCE) [26] to extract the skeleton of cartoon characters and obtain a new visual feature. Figure 4.11 shows the endpoints of the skeleton that are located on the edge. The number of skeleton endpoints differs from one character to another, so we use MDS to obtain a unified vector representation $\mathbf{x}_i^{SK}$ for each cartoon character according to the skeleton dissimilarity.

We apply the graph matching algorithm [25] to estimate the skeleton dissimilarity. In Ref. [25], the shortest path between a pair of endpoints is called a skeleton path, as shown by red lines in Figure 4.11. In the character x_i, each endpoint has the skeleton paths to all other endpoints, but these skeleton paths are useful for distinguishing characters having different geometric structures rather than the motion or gesture of characters with similar geometric structures. Instead, we use the relative angle to represent the relationship between endpoints; for example, in x_i, the endpoint v_i^0 can be described by a group of skeleton paths $sp\left(v_i^0, v_i^1\right), sp\left(v_i^0, v_i^2\right), \ldots, sp\left(v_i^0, v_i^8\right)$, where $sp\left(v_i^s, v_i^t\right)$ denotes the skeleton path from v_i^s to v_i^t. After obtaining the descriptor for each endpoint, we apply the optimal subsequence bijection (OSB) [25] to calculate the distance value $c\left(v_i^s, v_j^t\right)$ of two endpoints v_i^s in $\mathbf{x}_i$ and v_j^t in $\mathbf{x}_j$. The distance matrix between endpoints in $\mathbf{x}_i$ and $\mathbf{x}_j$ can then be obtained:

$$
\mathbf{C}\left(\mathbf{x}_i, \mathbf{x}_j\right) = \begin{bmatrix} c\left(v_i^0, v_j^0\right) & \cdots & c\left(v_i^0, v_j^7\right) \\ \vdots & & \vdots \\ c\left(v_i^8, v_j^0\right) & \cdots & c\left(v_i^8, v_j^7\right) \end{bmatrix}. \tag{4.31}
$$

To conduct the Hungarian algorithm on $\mathbf{C}\left(\mathbf{x}_i, \mathbf{x}_j\right)$, the correspondence can be constructed between endpoints in $\mathbf{x}_i$ and $\mathbf{x}_j$, as shown in Figure 4.11. The intuition for using the Hungarian algorithm is that we need a globally consistent one-to-one assignment. This means that some of the endpoints will be assigned to dummy points. For endpoints $\left(v_i^1, v_i^2, \ldots, v_i^8\right)$ in $\mathbf{x}_i$, the corresponding endpoints in $\mathbf{x}_j$ can be represented by $\left(M\left(v_i^1\right), M\left(v_i^2\right), \ldots, M\left(v_i^8\right)\right)$. Therefore, we can adopt two successive endpoints $\left(v_i^k, v_i^{k+1}\right)$ and the centroid c_i of character $\mathbf{x}_i$ to construct the relative angle A_i^k:

$$
A_i^k = \cos^{-1}\left(\frac{\overrightarrow{c_i v_i^k} \bullet \overrightarrow{c_i v_i^{k+1}}}{\left|\overrightarrow{c_i v_i^k}\right|\left|\overrightarrow{c_i v_i^{k+1}}\right|}\right), \tag{4.32}
$$

where $\overrightarrow{c_i v_i^k}$ is a vector and $\left|\overrightarrow{c_i v_i^k}\right|$ represents the length of the vector. As shown in Figure 4.11, the relative angle can be used to effectively represent the geometric structures of the character. The corresponding relative angle of A_i^k in character c_j is

$$
M\left(A_i^k\right) = \cos^{-1}\left(\frac{\overrightarrow{c_j M\left(v_i^k\right)} \bullet \overrightarrow{c_j M\left(v_i^{k+1}\right)}}{\left|\overrightarrow{c_j M\left(v_i^k\right)}\right|\left|\overrightarrow{c_j M\left(v_i^{k+1}\right)}\right|}\right) \tag{4.33}
$$

By using these angles, the character $\mathbf{x}_i$ in Figure 4.11 can be represented as $\left(A_i^1, A_i^2, \ldots A_i^8\right)$, and the character $\mathbf{x}_j$ can be represented as $\left(M\left(A_i^1\right), M\left(A_i^2\right), \ldots, M\left(A_i^8\right)\right)$. Thus, the skeleton dissimilarity can be measured by

$$Dist\left(\mathbf{x}_i, \mathbf{x}_j\right) = \frac{1}{N} \sum_{k \in N} \left\| A_i^k - M\left(A_i^k\right) \right\|, \tag{4.34}$$

where N is the number of corresponding points. In this way, we can obtain the skeleton dissimilarity matrix $\mathbf{W}_{skel} \in \mathbf{R}^{N \times N}$, where $\mathbf{W}_{skel}\left(i, j\right)$ is the value of skeleton dissimilarity between every pair of cartoon characters. According to the MDS method, the skeleton feature vectors for all cartoon characters can be obtained as $\left[\mathbf{x}_1^{SK}, \mathbf{x}_2^{SK}, \ldots, \mathbf{x}_N^{SK}\right]^{\mathbf{T}}$.

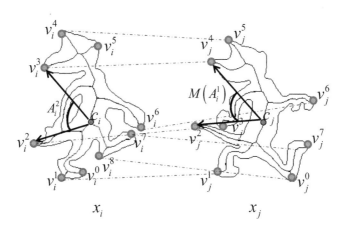

Figure 4.11   Cartoon characters represented by skeletons. The red line represents the shortest path between two endpoints. The blue points represent the endpoints of the skeleton located on the edge. The dashed lines between these two characters represent the constructed correspondence. The bold arrows describe the relative angles used in representing the geometric structures of the characters.

4.2.6 Complementary Characteristics of Multiview Features

In this section, we utilize three kinds of features, including 64-dimensional CH vector, 100-dimensional HEF vector and 96-dimensional SF vector, to describe the complementary characteristics of these features in cartoon character representation. For example, in Figures 4.12(a) and 4.12(e), the distance between the HEFs of M1 and M3 is 0.09, which indicates that these two characters have little difference between their edges. However, from the viewpoint of color and motion, these two characters are completely different, and the distance on CH and that on SF, as shown in Figure 4.12(d) and Figure 4.12(f), is 0.56 and 0.18, respectively. In this case, both CH and SF play more important roles than HEF in measuring dissimilarity between M1 and

M3. Another example is given in Figure 4.12(a), in which characters M1 and M2 are dissimilar in shape. However, as reported in Figure 4.12(d), their distance on CH is 0.05, which cannot separate M1 from M2. That means the distance between these two characters cannot be measured accurately by using CH; thus, it is necessary to consider the cartoon character's shape and motion information. Figures 4.12(b) and 4.12(h) show that J1 cannot be separated from character J3 according to their distance on HEF, although their color and motions are very different. Thus, taking the motion information and color information into account will be helpful.

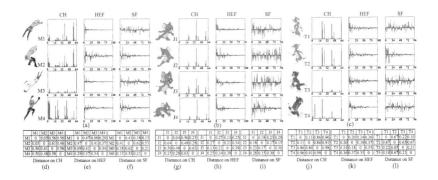

Figure 4.12 Complementary characteristics of multiview features in cartoon character representation. For each cartoon character, the extracted multiview features include: Color Histogram (CH) encoded in a 64-dimensional vector, Hausdorff Edge Feature (HEF) encoded in a 100-dimensional vector and Skeleton Feature (SF) encoded in a 96-dimensional vector. The distance matrix calculated on multiview features is presented, and all the distances are normalized in the range [0, 1]. (a) Multiview features for characters of Monkey King; (b) multiview features for characters of Jerry; (c) multiview features for characters of Tom; (d)-(f) distance calculation on CH, HEF and SF for characters of Monkey King; (g)-(i) distance calculation on CH, HEF and SF for characters of Jerry; (j)-(l) distance calculation on CH, HEF and SF for characters of Tom.

4.3 GRAPH-BASED CARTOON CLIPS SYNTHESIS

Cartoons today are used widely in entertainment, education, advertising, and so on; therefore, large amounts of cartoon data exist. Cartooning is an amazing art which has the power to attract both children and adults; however it is a very tedious and time consuming job requiring animators who are also art professionals. To improve efficiency in cartoon generation, the Graph-based Cartoon Clip Synthesis(GCCS) system is proposed. The aim of this system is to combine similar cartoon characters into a user directed sequence. Based on dissimilarity measurement, GCCS builds a graph and generates a new cartoon sequence by finding the shortest path. One typical GCCS system is "Cartoon Texture" [131]. This system creates novel animations from a library of existing cartoon data by combining similar-looking data into a user-directed sequence. A nonlinear dimensionality reduction method, ISOMAP, is adopted to build an embedding of the data into a manifold space. Some results from "Cartoon Texture" are unreasonable, however, because only the distance between two characters' edges are taken into account when constructing the lower-dimensional space, and the character's other factors (e.g., gesture) are neglected. In some cases, two characters containing similar edges may have totally opposite gestures. If they are connected in the reordering process, an obvious break occurs in the animation. In this section, a novel GCCS method is proposed to fuse the features of edges and gestures in cartoon clip synthesis.

4.3.1 Graph Model Construction

As mentioned above, this novel GCCS approach aims to provide inbetween frames to generate novel animation, which is a transition from the start frame to the end frame. The cartoon data have very complex relations in the original high-dimensional image space, in which a smooth transition between any two frames is hard to find. ISOMAP finds an embedding of the data into a lower-dimensional space, and its main objective is to preserve the global structure and the geodesic distances of the manifold in which any points (two cartoon frames) are connected by a number of paths. The points in one of the paths may form a satisfying transition. We use a standard ISOMAP to perform the manifold-based nonlinear dimensionality reduction. The algorithm is listed below:

1 Compute the local neighborhoods based on the distances $D_X(i,j)$ between all pairs of points i, j in the input space X based on a chosen distance metric.

2 Estimate the geodesic distances into a full distance matrix $D(i,j)$ by computing all-pairs shortest paths from D_X, which contains the pairwise distances.

3 Apply MDS to construct a d-dimensional embedding of the data.

4.3.2 Distance Calculation

In ISOMAP the distance calculation between two data points decides each point's nearest neighbors, which are the inputs in calculating the distance matrix. As the animation is generated from the paths of two points, calculated based on the matrix, the distance calculation has a great effect in animation. Several methods have been used to calculate distance between images, e.g., the L2 distance and the Hausdorff distance. Before comparing two images, the characters in the images are normalized into the same scale, including size and position. By implementing Hausdorff distance, the edge difference between two images can be efficiently calculated. However, the gesture difference is not clearly defined; for example, two images I_i and I_j are shown in Figures 4.13 (a)and 4.13(b). By using Hausdorff distance, I_j is chosen to be the neighbor of I_i based on a cartoon library L. When constructing a path, I_i and I_j are connected successively and the visual break will occur. This problem can be easily solved by adding the gesture difference into distance calculation. After motion synthesis, the character's motion in I_i and I_j are $\overrightarrow{M_c^i}$ and $\overrightarrow{M_c^j}$ shown in Figures 4.13(a) and 4.13(b). We adopt the following equation to calculate the distance between I_i and I_j

$$D\left(I_i, I_j\right) = \alpha D_H'\left(I_i, I_j\right) + \left(1 - \alpha\right) D_G\left(I_i, I_j\right), \qquad (4.35)$$

where $D_G\left(I_i, I_j\right)$ calculates two images' distance according to gestures, and $D_H'\left(I_i, I_j\right)$ calculates the edge distance.

$$D_G\left(I_i, I_j\right) = \frac{1}{\pi} \cos^{-1}\left(\frac{\overrightarrow{M_c^i} \bullet \overrightarrow{M_c^j}}{\left|\overrightarrow{M_c^i}\right| \left|\overrightarrow{M_c^j}\right|}\right), \qquad (4.36)$$

$$D_H'\left(I_i, I_j\right) = \frac{D_H(I_i, I_j) - \min_{I_n \in (L - \{I_i\})}\left(D_H(I_i, I_n)\right)}{\max_{I_m \in L} D_H\left(I_i, I_m\right) - \min_{I_n \in (L - \{I_i\})}\left(D_H(I_i, I_m)\right)}, \qquad (4.37)$$

where L represents the cartoon data library and both the edge and gesture distances are normalized into the same range [0, 1] before being combined.

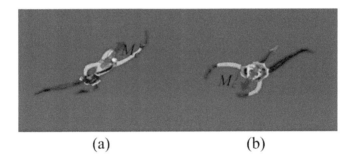

(a)   (b)

Figure 4.13   Two characters with similar edges, containing totally different gestures.

4.3.3 Simulation Results

4.3.3.1 Cartoon Library Construction   For the "Monkey King" library, 21 clips are manually chosen from the cartoon video. Each clip, in which the camera's motions are continually recording the character's motion in varied length. The sampling rate is 5 frames/s, meaning that the library contains 460 frames. These cartoon data are preprocessed before reuse to remove the background, so that each character's motion vector can be built. The characters in each frame are normalized and transformed to the center of the image. Several metrics used for performance measurement are elaborated below:

Transition Length records the number of inbetween frames which are constructed for a designated pair of start and end frames.

Edge Distance implements the Hausdorff algorithm to calculate the distances between two images according to their edges.

Gesture Distance calculates the distance between two images based on gestures.

4.3.3.2 *Experiment Configuration*
According to the ISOMAP algorithm, three issues are important for constructing the experiment platform. In the first step, distances are calculated between the data according to Eq. (4.35), so the weight α must be determined. When α is 1, it simulates De Juan and Bodenheimer's work [131], which only takes into account a character's edge. When α is between 0 and 1, the evaluation of visual differences is related to both edge distance and gesture distance.

Another issue is the neighbor number. Before finding the transition between two images, a single connected component should exist in these data. Increasing the neighbor size ensures that a single connected component is formed regardless of the sparseness of the data. However, too many neighbors will ruin ISOMAP's main objective of preserving the global structure and the geodesic distances of the manifold.

The third issue is to determine the dimensionality of the embedding space. Choosing a dimensionality that is too low or too high will affect the result's coherence. The intrinsic dimensionality of the data estimates the lower-dimensional space where the high-dimensional data actually "lives." In ISOMAP, the residual variance is computed using the intrinsic manifold differences, which take into account possible nonlinear folding or twisting. The true dimensionality of the data can be estimated from the decrease in residual variance error when the dimensionality of the embedding space is increased. The point, at which the residual variance does not significantly decrease with added dimensions is chosen to be the dimensionality. Figure 4.14 shows the residual variances when the neighbor number is 5. Note that the Monkey King data set can be reduced to approximately five dimensions by using ISOMAP.

In the experiment, 100 pairs of start and end frames are determined. When the lower-dimensional space is constructed, the weight α increases linearly from 0 to 1 ([0, 0.2 ... 1]), while the neighbor number increases from 3 to 10 ([3, 4 ... 10]); therefore, the lower-dimensional space is reconstructed 40 times by varied weight and neighbor. With a specific lower-dimensional space, 100 shortest paths between the determined start and end frames are built. The performance measurements, including mean transition length, mean edge distance and mean gesture distance, are collected. Mean transition length calculates the average length of these 100 paths, while mean edge distance and gesture distance calculate the average distance between two successive frames in the path.

4.3.3.3 *Performance Evaluations*
Figure 4.15 presents the mean transition length in six series, in which the weight linearly increases from 0 to 1. Each series shows that the value decreases when the neighbor number increases from 3 to 10. However, from neighbors 9 to 10, it does not decrease significantly. Additionally the mean transition length in the series 0.8 is larger than other series, especially that of [131] (series 1.0). The animation with larger length is more likely to be accepted by

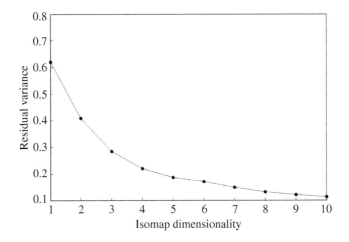

Figure 4.14   Decreases of the residual variance when the neighbor is 5, and α is 0.5.

human perception, since the transition between two frames is more easily smoothed when the number of inbetween frames is large.

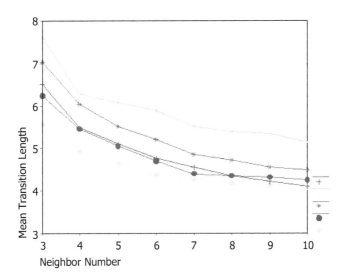

Figure 4.15   Mean transition length by varying the weight and neighbor number.

In Figure 4.16, the mean edge distance is presented in six series, in which the value keeps rising slowly with the increase of neighbor number from 3 to 10. It can be seen that the increase in neighbor number has the effect of enlarging the mean edge distance; however, this effect is small. Additionally, the six series show that the weights, which increase from 0 to 1, cause the decrease in the mean edge distance. When the weight is 0.8, performance on the mean edge distance is close to the series with weight 1.

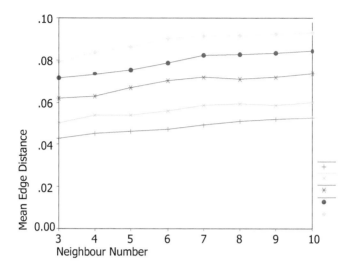

Figure 4.16   Mean edge distance by varying the weight and neighbor number.

The mean gesture distance is another factor in determining the visual difference. The six series in Figure 4.17 show that the mean gesture distance remains stable with the increase of neighbor number, which means the neighbor number has little effect on changing the gesture distance. Additionally, when the weight increases from 0 to 1, the values keeps rising. When the weight increases from 0 to 0.8, the mean gesture distance rises quite slowly, whereas the value increases nearly 15 times from weight 0.8 to 1. It can be seen that when the weight is 1, the transition created will have serious gesture incontinuity, since its mean gesture distance is so large.

In Figure 4.18 the transitions are created between frames 177 and 298. When constructing the lower-dimensional space, the neighbor number is 5. Each row in the figure shows the frames in the shortest path built between frames 177 and 298 in the lower-dimensional space when the weight α is varied linearly. In the top row (α is 1.0), five frames are generated and a serious visual incontinuity exists between frame 341 and frame 298. These two frames are similar on edge, but have totally different gestures. The second row shows that when α is 0.8, a different transition with nine frames is created. It can be seen that this transition is much smoother than the last. Any two successive frames are similar not only on edge, but also on gesture, which is more easily accepted by human perception. The following rows show another four transitions created by decreasing the weight. Though the incontinuities on gestures are not serious, they are not as smooth as the transition shown in the second row. In Figure 4.19, the visual incontinuity also occurs between frames 14 and 355 in the top row, while the second row with weight 0.8 is longer and smoother than other

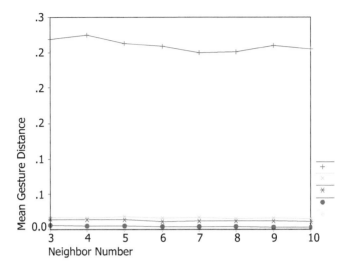

Figure 4.17 Mean gesture distance by varying the weight ahd neighbor number.

transitions. From these examples, it can be seen that the weight 0.8 is the best choice in creating transition.

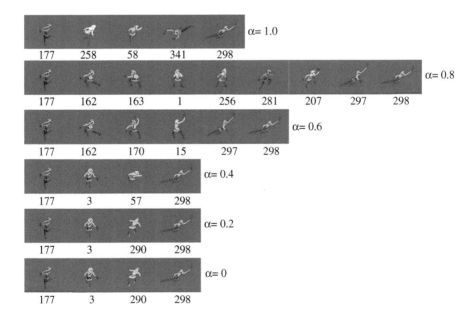

Figure 4.18 Transitions between frames 177 and 298 by varying α from 0 to 1.

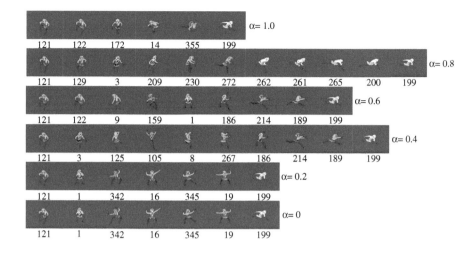

Figure 4.19   Transitions between frames 121 and 199 by varying α from 0 to 1.

4.3.3.4   Discussions   The experiment results show that weight α has a larger effect on the measurement metrics compared to neighbor number, so weight determination is critical in creating a transition which can be accepted by human perception. When α is 1, it simulates the work in Ref. [131], which evaluates the visual difference between two successive frames by using edge distance. Although it reduces the edge distance to the lowest value, which is just a little lower than other series (Figure 4.16), its gesture distance is more than 15 times larger than others (Figure 4.17). From the experiment results, weight 0.8 is a compatible value, which takes both the edge distance and gesture distance into consideration. It achieves the best mean transition length while keeping both the mean edge distance and gesture distance within satisfactory values. By using the weight 0.8, the constructed transition will be smoother and more easily accepted by human perception. Two examples in Figures 4.18 and 4.19 also demonstrate this.

4.4   RETRIEVAL-BASED CARTOON CLIPS SYNTHESIS

Retrieval-based Cartoon Clips Synthesis (RCCS) is another typical cartoon synthesis method. With this system, the user can reuse a cartoon image in the database to produce a new cartoon frame. A database image which is similar to the one in the current frame is retrieved and then used to produce a new cartoon frame. The system can also generate new cartoon clips, in an interactive way, by synthesizing the database cartoon images and the background image. The user only needs to provide the initial frame and specify the moving path of the cartoon character. The system then retrieves database cartoon images similar to the one in the current frame as candidates to synthesize the next frame. To design the RCCS, we mainly focus on two basic but important issues which can significantly affect the smoothness of the synthesized cartoons.

First, in order to synthesize new cartoons from the existing cartoon data, the ways in which the different features affect the similarity should be explored. Intuitively, their impacts on cartoon similarity vary from one feature to another. Hence, selecting the appropriate features turns out to be an important research topic. In fact, we have already discussed this problem in Section 4.2.

Second, after extracting the features, it is important to deliver a proper method which can precisely estimate the similarity between cartoon frames. In this section, we shall introduce two novel methods: constrained spreading activation network and semi-supervised multiview subspace learning algorithm (semi-MSL).

We will then demonstrate how to use the RCCS in background synthesis.

4.4.1 Constrained Spreading Activation Network

The constrained spreading activation algorithm [255] is conducted by message passing on a graph model which has been testified useful in the area of information retrieval [38]. The spreading activation algorithm consists of several rounds of iterations, and during each round, every node in the graph propagates its activation to its neighbors. Constraint strategies are used to make this algorithm robust. Given an initial frame, the spreading activation algorithm selects the most similar cartoon frames in the cartoon library as candidates for the next frame. Next, we discuss the details of this approach.

4.4.1.1 Construct the Graph Model Let Ω be the cartoon frame set in database and $n = |\Omega|$ is the number of frames. To select the candidate frames for synthesizing new cartoons, we construct three graphs, namely M Graph(MG), E Graph(EG), and C Graph(CG), according to the Motion, Edge, and Color distances respectively. Below, we give the approach of constructing the MG. The other two graphs can be constructed in the same way. The MG has n nodes and a set of edges among the nodes. Each node represents a frame $I_i \in \Omega$ and the edge weight MG_{ij} is the similarity between $I_i, I_j \in \Omega$. Let D_{ij} be the Motion distance between $I_i, I_j \in \Omega$, the edge weight between them is defined in 4.38 where σ is a smoothing factor.

$$MG_{ij} = \begin{cases} \exp\left(-\left(\frac{n^2 \times D_{ij}}{\sum_{m,n} D_{mn}}\right)^2 / 2\sigma^2\right) & \text{if } i \neq j, \\ 0. & \text{if } i = j. \end{cases} \quad (4.38)$$

Here, the value is related to a smoothing factor σ. The discussion on the choice of this smoothing factor is presented in the experiment section. Similarly, we can construct EG and CG and then all the edge weights are normalized.

4.4.1.2 The Spreading Process To select the candidate frames according to the graphs, we use the Spreading Activation (SA) algorithm which is tight-knit with the supposed mode of operation of human memory. The underlying idea is to propagate activation starting from source nodes via weighted paths over the graph. The process of propagating activation from one node to adjacent nodes is called a pulse and the SA algorithm is an iterative approach that can be divided into two steps: first, one or more pulses are triggered and, second, a termination check determines if the process has to continue or to halt.

The SA process of selecting candidate frames given an initial cartoon frame can be interpreted as a vector function $f = [f_1, f_2, ..., f_n]$ which assigns a rank value to each frame in the database according to the graph models and the initial frame. In $f = [f_1, f_2, ..., f_n]$, f_i corresponds to the rank value of the frame $I_i \in \Omega$ and this process can be formulated as Eq. (4.39) in which ICF is the initial cartoon frame provided by the user. The frames with the largest rank values are selected.

$$\{ICF, MG, EG, CG, \Omega\} \to f. \tag{4.39}$$

In the SA algorithm, a single iteration of the spreading consists of a spreading process and a post adjustment phase. We first construct a Cartoon Frame Relationship Network (CFRN) by linearly combining the MG, EG and CG, as shown in Eq. (4.40) in which w_1, w_2, and w_3 are constants such that $w_1 + w_2 + w_3 = 1$.

$$CFRN = w_1 \times MG + w_2 \times EG + w_3 \times CG. \tag{4.40}$$

We use the vector $Iter$ to represent the activation level of the cartoon frames and $Iter_j(p)$ is the activation level of the jth frame $I_j \in \Omega$ at the spreading process of pth iteration. After the post adjustment process, $Iter_j(p)$ becomes $O_j(p)$. Suppose the initial cartoon frame ICF is the kth frame in the database, at the first stage of the SA algorithm, ICF is activated by

$$O_i(0) = \begin{cases} 1 & \text{if } (i = k) \\ 0 & \text{if } (i \neq k). \end{cases} \tag{4.41}$$

During the pth round of SA, the spreading process can be formulated by

$$Iter_j(p) = \sum_{i=1}^{n}(O_i(p-1) \times CFRN_{ij}). \tag{4.42}$$

4.4.1.3 *The Constrained Spreading Activation*   The pure SA model is to define $O_i(p) = Iter_i(p)$ and iterate the spreading operation according to Eq. (4.42) recursively. However, the SA model's drawbacks have not been considered. In this section, we mainly discuss the constrained spreading activation algorithm, which applies the following constraints on the spreading.

Path Constraint: activation should spread using preferential paths along which the frames are similar. This constraint is carried out by modifying the CFRN before the spreading, as shown in Eq. (4.43) in which α is a constant around 1.

$$CFRN_{ij} = \begin{cases} CFRN_{ij} & \text{if } CFRN_{ij} < \alpha \times \sum_{l,k=1}^{n} CFRN_{lk}/n^2 \\ 0 & \text{otherwise.} \end{cases} \tag{4.43}$$

Fan-out constraint: the spreading of activation should decrease at nodes with very high connectivity or fan-out, which is at nodes connected to a very large number of other nodes. To this end, we define F in Eq. (4.44) in which C_j is the number of nodes in the graph connected to node j with edges whose weights are not zero.

$$F_j = (1 - C_j/n). \tag{4.44}$$

Then, at the post adjustment phase, we get

$$O_i(p) = F_i \times Iter_i(p). \tag{4.45}$$

Distance Constraint: The spreading of activation should cease when it reaches nodes that are far away in terms of links covered to reach them from the initially activated ones. It is common to consider only first-, second-, and third-order relations and alternatively, we rewrite Eq. (4.45) in this paper, as shown in Eq. (4.46).

$$O_i(p) = \frac{F_i}{p+1} \times Iter_i(p). \tag{4.46}$$

Activation Constraint: This constraint refers to the use of the threshold function at a single node level to control the spreading of the activation on the network. Thus, Eq. (4.46) is replaced by Eq. (4.47) during the post adjustment phase, in which τ is a small constant.

$$O_i(p) = \begin{cases} 0 & \text{if } Iter_i(p) < \tau, \\ \frac{F_i}{p+1} \times Iter_i(p) & \text{otherwise.} \end{cases} \tag{4.47}$$

The algorithm is presented below:

1 Construct the MG using Eq. (4.38). The EG and the CG are constructed in the same way.

2 Normalize the edge weights of the three graphs and construct the CFRN by linearly combining them according to Eq. (4.40).

3 Initialize $O(0)$ by Eq. (4.41).

4 Iterate the following two operations till t iterations:

(i) $Iter_j(p) = \sum_{i=1}^{n}(O_i(p-1) \times CFRN_{ij})$

(ii) $O_i(p) = \begin{cases} 0 & \text{if } Iter_i(p) < \tau, \\ \frac{F_i}{p+1} \times Iter_i(p) & \text{otherwise.} \end{cases}$

5 The $f = [f_1, f_2, ... f_n]$ in (11) is given by

$$f = [f_1, f_2, ... f_n] = [O_1(t), O_2(t), ..., O_n(t)]$$

6 Let A be a Boolean vector of size n and K be the number of selected frames. A is determined by maximizing

$$\arg\max(\sum_{i=1}^{k}(A_i \times f_i))$$
$$s.t. \sum A_i = k$$

7 For each frame $I_i \in \Omega$, if $A_i = 1$, I_i is selected as a candidate frame.

4.4.2 Semi-supervised Multiview Subspace Learning

In a constrained spreading activation network, the weights of the visual features are assigned by the users manually or empirically. Thus, the optimal weights cannot be obtained. In this section, we introduce a semi-supervised multiview subspace learning method (semi-MSL) [339] to find a low-dimensional feature space in which all the visual features can be optimally integrated. This method encodes different features to form a compact low-dimensional subspace where the heterogeneity between different features is minimized. In this unified subspace, the Euclidean distance can be directly used to measure the dissimilarity between two cartoon characters. This multiview subspace learning problem is solved based on the "Patch Alignment" Framework (PAF) (introduced in Section 3.1) that has two stages: local patch construction and global coordinate alignment. The new method adopts the discriminative information from the labeled data to construct local patches and aligns these patches to obtain the optimal and unified low-dimensional subspace for each view. At the same time, unlabeled data is taken into consideration to improve the local patch construction by exploring the data distribution information. To find a low-dimensional subspace where the data distribution of each view is sufficiently smooth, the complementary characteristics of the different views are explored in semi-MSL by using the alternating optimization. Finally, a compact subspace is achieved for subsequent retrieval and synthesis.

To clearly explain the details of the proposed semi-MSL technique, the important notations used in the rest of the paper are presented. Capital letters, e.g., $\mathbf{X}$, represent the cartoon database. Lower case letters, e.g., $\mathbf{x}$, represent cartoon characters, and $\mathbf{x}_i$ is the ith cartoon character of $\mathbf{X}$. Superscript (i), e.g., $\mathbf{X}^{(i)}$ and $\mathbf{x}^{(i)}$ represents the cartoon character's feature from the ith view.

Given a multiview cartoon database with N characters and m representations: $\mathbf{X} = \left\{ \mathbf{X}^{(i)} = \left[\mathbf{x}_1^{(i)}, \cdots, \mathbf{x}_N^{(i)} \right] \in \mathbf{R}^{m_i \times N} \right\}_{i=1}^{z}$, semi-MSL obtains a subspace of $\mathbf{X}$, i.e. $\mathbf{Y} \in \mathbf{R}^{d \times N}$, wherein $d < m_i \ (1 \le i \le z)$ and d is a free parameter. Figure 4.20 shows the workflow of semi-MSL for cartoon character retrieval and clip synthesis. First, cartoon characters are represented by the multiview visual features introduced in Section 4.2. According to PAF, semi-MSL builds the local patches. There are two types of local patches: local patches for labeled characters and local patches for unlabeled characters. Based on these patches, the part optimization can be performed to obtain the optimal low-dimensional subspace for each patch. All low-dimensional subspaces from different patches are unified by the global coordinate alignment to obtain the subspace in each view. We then derive an alternating optimization-based iterative algorithm to obtain the low-dimensional subspace from multiple views.

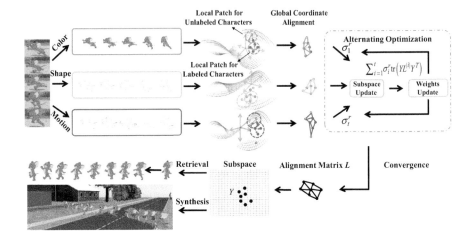

Figure 4.20 Workflow of semi-supervised Multiview Subspace Learning (semi-MSL)-based cartoon character retrieval and clip synthesis.

4.4.2.1 *Local Patches Construction for Labeled Characters*

The local patch in our approach is built by the given labeled characters and neighbors which include the characters from not only the same class but also different classes. On each patch, an objective function is designed to preserve the local discriminative information. For a given cartoon character $\mathbf{x}_j^{(i)} \in \mathbf{X}^{(i)}$, the other characters can be divided into two groups according to the class label information: characters in the same class with $\mathbf{x}_j^{(i)}$ and characters from different classes with $\mathbf{x}_j^{(i)}$. The k_1 nearest neighbors are selected from characters in the same class with $\mathbf{x}_j^{(i)}$ and termed as neighbor from an identical class: $\mathbf{x}_{j_1}^{(i)}, \ldots, \mathbf{x}_{j_{k_1}}^{(i)}$; and k_2 nearest neighbors are selected from data in different classes with $\mathbf{x}_j^{(i)}$ and termed as neighbor from different classes: $\mathbf{x}_{j_1}^{(i)}, \ldots, \mathbf{x}_{j_{k_2}}^{(i)}$. The local patch for the character $\mathbf{x}_j^{(i)}$ is constructed by putting $\mathbf{x}_{j_1}^{(i)}, \ldots, \mathbf{x}_{j_{k_1}}^{(i)}$ and $\mathbf{x}_{j_1}^{(i)}, \ldots, \mathbf{x}_{j_{k_2}}^{(i)}$ together as $\mathbf{X}_j^{(i)} = \left[\mathbf{x}_j^{(i)}, \mathbf{x}_{j_1}^{(i)}, \ldots, \mathbf{x}_{j_{k_1}}^{(i)}, \mathbf{x}_{j_1}^{(i)}, \ldots, \mathbf{x}_{j_{k_2}}^{(i)} \right]$. These local patches represent the local geometry of the characters and the discriminative information to separate characters with different labels.

For each patch $\mathbf{X}_j^{(i)}$, the output in the low-dimensional subspace is $\mathbf{Y}_j^{(i)} = \left[\mathbf{y}_j^{(i)}, \mathbf{y}_{j_1}^{(i)}, \ldots, \mathbf{y}_{j_{k_1}}^{(i)}, \mathbf{y}_{j_1}^{(i)}, \ldots, \mathbf{y}_{j_{k_2}}^{(i)} \right]$, and the distances between the given character and neighbor characters from the same class are expected to be as small as possible, so we have

$$\arg\min_{\mathbf{y}_j^{(i)}} \sum_{h=1}^{k_1} \left\| \mathbf{y}_j^{(i)} - \mathbf{y}_{j_h}^{(i)} \right\|^2 . \tag{4.48}$$

Meanwhile, the distances between the given character and neighbor characters from different classes are expected to be as large as possible, so we have

$$\arg\max_{\mathbf{y}_j^{(i)}} \sum_{p=1}^{k_2} \left\| \mathbf{y}_j^{(i)} - \mathbf{y}_{j_p}^{(i)} \right\|^2 . \tag{4.49}$$

Since patches constructed by local neighbors are approximately Euclidean, the part optimization can be formulated through the linear manipulation

$$(\mathbf{w}_i)_j = \exp\left(-D\left(\mathbf{x}_i, \mathbf{x}_{i_j} \right) /t \right), \tag{4.50}$$

where λ is a scaling factor within the range $[0, 1]$ to unify the different measures of the within class distance and the between-class distance, and the coefficients vector $\mathbf{w}_j^{(i)}$ can be defined as

$$\mathbf{w}_j^{(i)} = \left[\underbrace{1, \ldots, 1}_{k_1}, \underbrace{-\lambda, \ldots, -\lambda}_{k_2} \right]. \tag{4.51}$$

4.4.2.2 Local Patches Construction for Unlabeled Characters

Recent research results in semi-supervised learning show that unlabeled data are helpful for revealing the manifold structure of data in the original high-dimensional space. Thus, we incorporate the unlabeled cartoon characters into the local patch construction to improve the performance of subspace learning. The unlabeled characters are attached to the labeled characters of the ith view $\mathbf{X}^{(i)} = \left\{ \mathbf{x}_1^{(i)}, \ldots, \mathbf{x}_{N_l}^{(i)}, \mathbf{x}_{N_l+1}^{(i)}, \ldots, \mathbf{x}_{N_l+N_u}^{(i)} \right\}$, where the first N_l characters are labeled and the remaining N_u characters are unlabeled. The part optimization for each labeled character is presented in Eq. (4.50).

For each unlabeled character $\mathbf{x}_j^{(i)}$ $j = N_l + 1, \ldots, N_l + N_u$, its k_s nearest neighbors $\mathbf{x}_{j_1}^{(i)}, \ldots, \mathbf{x}_{j_{k_s}}^{(i)}$ both labeled and unlabeled are selected. The $\mathbf{X}_j^{(i)} = \left[\mathbf{x}_j^{(i)}, \mathbf{x}_{j_1}^{(i)}, \ldots, \mathbf{x}_{j_{k_s}}^{(i)} \right]$ is the ith patch and the associated index set is recorded in $F_j^U = [j, j_1, \ldots, j_{k_s}]$. To preserve the local geometry of the jth patch, the nearby characters should stay nearby in the low-dimensional subspace, or $\mathbf{y}_j^{(i)} \in R^d$ is close to $\mathbf{y}_{j_1}^{(i)}, \ldots, \mathbf{y}_{j_{k_s}}^{(i)}$, i.e.,

$$\arg\max_{\mathbf{y}_i} \sum_{(\mathbf{x}_i, x_j) \in D} \| \mathbf{y}_i - \mathbf{y}_j \|^2 , \tag{4.52}$$

where $\mathbf{L}_j^{U(i)} = \begin{bmatrix} k_s & -\mathbf{e}_{k_s}^T \\ -\mathbf{e}_{k_s} & \mathbf{I}_{k_s} \end{bmatrix}$, $\mathbf{e}_{k_s} = [1, \ldots, 1]^T \in R^{k_s}$, and $\mathbf{I}_{k_s}$ is the $k_s \times k_s$ identity matrix.

4.4.2.3 Global Coordinate Alignment

For each patch $\mathbf{X}_j^{(i)}$, there is a low-dimensional subspace $\mathbf{Y}_j^{(i)}$. All $\mathbf{Y}_j^{(i)}$ can be unified as a whole by assuming that the coordinate for $\mathbf{Y}_j^{(i)} = \left[\mathbf{y}_j^{(i)}, \mathbf{y}_{j_1}^{(i)}, \ldots, \mathbf{y}_{j_k}^{(i)} \right]$ is selected from the global coordinate $\mathbf{Y} = [\mathbf{y}_1, \ldots, \mathbf{y}_N]$, i.e., $\mathbf{Y}_j^{(i)} = \mathbf{Y}\mathbf{S}_j^{(i)}$, wherein $\mathbf{S}_j^{(i)} \in \mathbf{R}^{N \times (k+1)}$ is the selection matrix to encode the spatial relationship of samples in a patch in the original high-dimensional space. The $\mathbf{S}_j^{(i)}$ is

$$\left(\mathbf{S}_j^{(i)} \right)_{pq} = \left\{ \begin{array}{ll} 1, & \text{if } p = F_i, (q) \\ 0, & \text{else}, \end{array} \right. \tag{4.53}$$

where $F_i = [i, i_1, \ldots, i_k]$ is the index vector for samples in $\mathbf{Y}_j^{(i)}$. Then, we can take sum over all the local patches defined by Eq. (4.50) and Eq. (4.52):

$$\arg \sum_{j=1}^{N_l} \min_{\mathbf{Y}_j^{(i)}} \text{tr} \left(\mathbf{Y}_j^{(i)} \mathbf{L}_j^{(i)} \left(\mathbf{Y}_j^{(i)} \right)^T \right) + \beta \arg \sum_{j=N+1}^{N_l+N_u} \min_{\mathbf{Y}_j^{(i)}} \text{tr} \left(\mathbf{Y}_j^{(i)} \mathbf{L}_j^{U(i)} \left(\mathbf{Y}_j^{(i)} \right) \right)$$

$$= \arg \min_{\mathbf{Y}^{(i)}} \text{tr} \left(\mathbf{Y}^{(i)} \left(\sum_{j=1}^{N_l} \mathbf{S}_j^{L(i)} \mathbf{L}_j^{(i)} \left(\mathbf{S}_j^{L(i)} \right)^T + \sum_{j=N+1}^{N_l+N_u} \mathbf{S}_j^{U(i)} \beta \mathbf{L}_j^{U(i)} \left(\mathbf{S}_j^{U(i)} \right)^T \right) \right)$$

$$= \arg \min_{\mathbf{Y}^{(i)}} \text{tr} \left(\mathbf{Y}^{(i)} \mathbf{L}^{S(i)} \mathbf{Y}^{(i)T} \right)$$

$$\tag{4.54}$$

where β is a trade-off parameter; $\mathbf{S}_j^{L(i)} \in \mathbf{R}^{(N_l+N_u) \times (k_1+k_2+1)}$ and $\mathbf{S}_j^{U(i)} \in \mathbf{R}^{(N_l+N_u) \times (k_s+1)}$ are the selection matrices defined in Eq. (4.52), and $\mathbf{L}^{S(i)} \in \mathbf{R}^{(N_l+N_u) \times (N_l+N_u)}$ is the alignment matrix.

To explore the complementary characteristics of a cartoon character's multiview features, a set of non-negative weights $\sigma = [\sigma_1, \ldots, \sigma_t]$ is independently imposed on the different views. The σ with a larger value means the view $\mathbf{X}^{(i)}$ plays a more important role in obtaining the low-dimensional subspace. The weight for each view can be obtained through the alternating optimization presented in Subsection 2.5.3.3.

4.4.3 Simulation Results

This section focuses on a comparison of the effectiveness of semi-MSL with Unsupervised Bi-Distance Metric Learning (UBDML) [329], FCSL, DMSL [181] and Single-view Subspace Learning based on the retrieval of cartoon characters.

4.4.3.1 Cartoon Character Database

To evaluate the performance of the proposed method, the cartoon characters of Monkey King, Jerry, and Tom are collected from cartoon videos. The data are classified into three character groups. The low-dimensional subspace of each group is learned by using semi-MSL and other baseline methods. In order to annotate cartoon characters, cartoonists in our lab classified the characters with similar color, shape and motion into one category. Fifty categories of characters are obtained for each cartoon group, and the number of characters in each category is 10. Therefore, 1,500 cartoon characters are collected for this experiment. Figure 4.21 shows some samples in this database. As outlined in

Figure 4.21 Sample cartoon characters from the database.

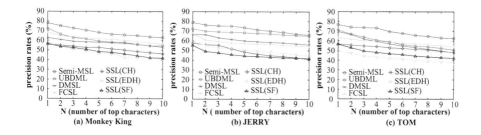

Figure 4.22 A comparison of retrieval rates among the semi-MSL, UBDML, DMSL, FCSL and SSL methods: (a) results of Monkey King database; (b) results of Jerry database; (c) results of Tom database.

Section 4.2, three types of features are extracted from the cartoon characters: Color Histogram (CH), Hausdorff Edge Feature (HEF), and Skeleton Feature (SF).

4.4.3.2 *Performance Evaluations* In this experiment, the parameters k_1, k_2 and k_s for local patch construction of labeled and unlabeled characters in semi-MSL are fixed to 5, 5, and 5, and the parameter r for calculating the weight of each view is empirically set as 5. Six samples in each category are randomly selected as the labeled samples. In FCSL, DMSL and SSL, the Laplacian Eigenmaps (LE) is adopted to calculate theLaplacian matrix for subspace learning. The k-nearest-neighbor construction in LE is fixed to 5. In addition, the subspace dimension is fixed to 10 for all methods.

The procedure of the experiment is as follows: First, the low-dimensional subspaces of the cartoon database are learned by the subspace learning algorithms including semi-MSL, UBDML, FCSL, DMSL, and SSL; second, based on each low-dimensional subspace, a standard retrieval procedure is conducted for all characters in the database. For each category, one cartoon character is selected as a query, and all other characters in the database (including other categories) are ranked according

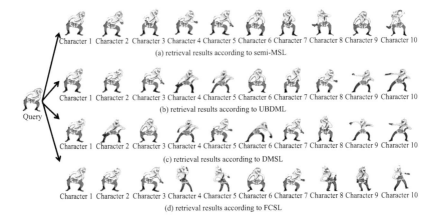

Figure 4.23   Query and top 10 retrieved characters (Monkey King): (a) In the retrieval results of semi-MSL, the Characters 8 and 10 have small differences from the Query; (b) in the retrieval results of UBDML, the Characters 4, 5, 9, and 10 are evidently dissimilar from the Query in color; (c) in the retrieval results of DMSL, the Characters 2, 4, 6, 9, and 10 are evidently dissimilar from the Query in color, shape and motion; (d) in the retrieval results of FCSL, the Characters 4, 5, 8, 9, and 10 are evidently dissimilar from the Query in color, shape and motion.

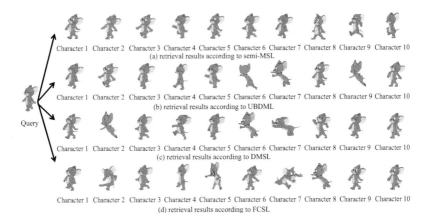

Figure 4.24   Query and top 10 retrieved characters (Jerry): (a) In the retrieval results of semi-MSL, the Characters 8 and 9 are evidently different from the Query; (b) in the retrieval results of UBDML, the Characters 4, 6, 7, and 9 are evidently dissimilar from the Query in color; (c) in the retrieval results of DMSL, the Characters 2, 4, 6, 7, and 8 are evidently dissimilar from the Query in color, shape and motion; (d) in the retrieval results of FCSL, the Characters 2, 4, 5, 7, and 8 are evidently dissimilar from the Query in color, shape and motion.

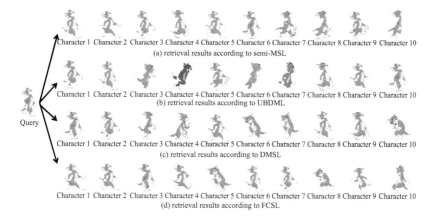

Figure 4.25   Query and top 10 retrieved characters (Tom): (a) In the retrieval results of semi-MSL, the Characters 7, 8, and 10 have small differences from the Query; (b) in the retrieval results of UBDML, the Characters 3, 4, 6, and 7 are evidently dissimilar from the Query in color; (c) in the retrieval results of DMSL, the Characters 3, 4, 6, 7, and 10 are evidently dissimilar from the Query in shape and motion; (d) in the retrieval results of FCSL, the Characters 5, 8, 9, and 10 are evidently dissimilar from the Query in shape and motion.

to the Euclidean distance to the query computed in the low-dimensional subspace. For each query cartoon character, the top N characters are obtained, among which the number of characters from the same class as the query shape is recorded. The precision rate, shown in Figure 4.22, is the ratio of the recorded number to N.

In the three subfigures of Figure 4.22, the number of top N characters increases from 1 to 10 with step 1. We first compare semi-MSL with UBDML, DMSL, and FCSL, and we can see that our method semi-MSL performs better in nearly all cases. This can be attributed to the alternating optimization algorithm, which can effectively learn the complementary characteristics of different views. In comparing the semi-MSL and SSL methods, we can see that semi-MSL performs better. This demonstrates that the performance can be successfully improved by exploring the complementary characteristics of different visual features.

To intuitively demonstrate the performance of semi-MSL, we illustrate the cartoon characters retrieval results in Figures 4.23, 4.24, and 4.25. Each figure contains four rows of characters, which are retrieved using semi-MSL, UBDML, DMSL, and FCSL, respectively. Each row consists of the top 10 characters retrieved from the database. From these three figures, we observe that the retrieval results of semi-MSL are the best. In Figure 4.23 (b), the characters 4, 5, 9 and 10 are erroneously retrieved by UBDML. The shapes and motions of these four characters are similar to the query character, but they are evidently different from the query character in terms of color. This indicates that the main disadvantage of UBDML is that it neglects the feature of color for dissimilarity estimation. In Figure 4.23(c), characters 2, 4, 6, 9, and 10 retrieved using DMSL are not only dissimilar from the query character in color, but also in shape and motion. This demonstrates that DMSL does not perform well in

Figure 4.26 Results of cartoon clips synthesis using RCCS based on the databases of Monkey King, Jerry, and Tom: (a)-(c) Performance comparison of RCCS with semi-MSL and UBDML.

exploring the complementary characteristics. Similarly, the 5 erroneously retrieved characters (4, 5, 8, 9, and 10) in Figure 4.23(d) prove that the concatenation of multiview features in FCSL is not physically meaningful. This concatenation cannot efficiently investigate the complementary characteristics of different views. Figure 4.24 and Figure 4.25 suggest similar results based on the databases of Jerry and Tom.

4.4.3.3 Clips Synthesis RCCS requires users to provide the initial character, and then retrieves cartoon characters similar to the one in the current frame as candidates to synthesize the next frame. After providing the initial frame, a set of candidates can be selected from the database by using retrieval. From the set of candidates, one character is randomly picked as the next frame. After the character is added, the newly added character can be treated as the initial character and the most appropriate character is similarly again selected. The above procedure is carried out repeatedly until a cartoon clip of the specified length is obtained. Figures 4.26(a)-(c) present the results of clips synthesis. The clips synthesized by RCCS with semi-MSL are smoother than RCCS with UBDML. Because UBDML neglects the color information in the distance metric learning, the characters in the synthesized results may have different colors. This also indicates that the three visual features, CH, HEF,

Figure 4.27   Clip synthesis results with backgrounds.

and SF, are complementary to one another in distance measure. Figure 4.27 shows that users can efficiently create cartoons by directly applying the synthesized cartoon clips to a background.

4.5   CHAPTER SUMMARY

Modern machine learning techniques are widely applied in computer animation fields. The techniques of semi-supervised learning, multiview learning and constrained spreading activation network can successfully improve the efficiency and accuracy of the algorithms in cartoon animation generation. We believe that in the future, more machine learning techniques will be applied to computer graphics and the field of animation.

REFERENCES

1. Caricature zone. http://www.magixl.com/.

2. http://www.animazoo.com/products/gypsy5.htm.

3. http://www.motionanalysis.com.

4. http://www.vicon.com.

5. Ufc soft, llc. http://ufc-soft.com/.

6. Georges méliès, 2000. http://www.wabash.edu/depart/theater/THAR4/ Melies.htm, 2000.

7. Cmu graphics lab motion capture database, 2007. http://mocap.cs.cmu.edu/.

8. M. Abboud and F. Davoine. Statistical modelling for facial expression analysis and synthesis. *Proceedings of the International Conference on Image Processing*, pages 653–656, 2003.

9. Y. Abe, C. Liu, and Z. Popovic. Momentum-based parameterization of dynamic character motion. *Graphical Models*, 68(2):194–211, 2006.

10. A. Agarwal and B. Triggs. Recovering 3d human pose from monocular images. *IEEE Transactions on Pattern Analysis and Machine Intelligence*, 28(1):44–58, 2006.

11. A. Agarwala and A. SnakeToonz. A semi-automatic approach to creating cel animation from video. *Proceedings of the 2nd international symposium on Non-photorealistic animation and rendering*, pages 139–146, 2002.

12. E. Aguiar, L. Sigal, A. Treuille, and J. Hodgins. Stable spaces for real-time clothing. *ACM Transactions on Graphics*, 29(4):1–9, 2010.

13. E. Aguiar, C. Stoll, C. Theobalt, N. Ahmed, H. Seidel, and S. Thrun. Performance capture from sparse multi-view video. *ACM Transactions on Graphics*, 27(10):1–10, 2008.

14. A. Ahmed, F. Mokhtarian, and A. Hilton. Parametric motion blending through wavelet analysis. *Proceedings of the 22nd Annual Conference of the European Association for Computer Graphics*, pages 347–353, 2001.

15. M. Alex and W. Muller. Representing animations by principal components. *Computer Graphics Forum*, 19(3):411–426, 2000.

16. B. Allen, B. Curless, and Z. Popovic. The space of human body shapes: reconstruction and parameterization from range scans. *ACM Transactions on Graphics*, 22(3):587–594, 2003.

17. R. Ando and R. Tsuruno. A particle-based method for preserving fluid sheets. *Proceedings of the 10th ACM SIGGRAPH/Eurographics Symposium on Computer Animation*, pages 7–16, 2011.

18. R. Ando and T. Zhang. A framework for learning predictive structures from multiple tasks and unlabeled data. *Journal of Machine Learning Research*, 6:1817–1853, 2005.

19. K. Anjyo, S. Wemler, and W. Baxter. Tweakable light and shade for cartoon animation. *Proceedings of the 5th International Symposium on Non-photorealistic Animation and Rendering*, pages 133–139, 2006.

20. K. Arai, T. Kurihara, and K. Anjyo. Bilinear interpolation for facial expression and metamorphosis in real-time animation. *The Visual Computer*, 12(3):105–116, 1996.

21. O. Arikan and D. Forsyth. Interactive motion generation from examples. *ACM Transactions on Graphics*, 21(3):483–490, 2002.

22. O. Arikan, D. Forsyth, and J. O'Brien. Motion synthesis from annotations. *ACM Transactions on Graphics*, 22(3):402–408, 2003.

23. R. Bach, G. Lanckriet, I. Jordan, and E. Brodley. Multiple kernel learning, conic duality, and the smo algorithm. *Proceedings of the 21st International Conference on Machine Learning*, page 6, 2004.

24. N. Badler, M. Palmer, and R. Bindiganavale. Animation control for real-time virtual humans. *Communications of the ACM*, 42(8):65–73, 1999.

25. X. Bai and J. Latecki. Path similarity skeleton graph matching. *IEEE Transactions on Pattern Analysis and Machine Intelligence*, 30(7):1282–1292, 2008.

26. X. Bai, J. Latecki, and Y. Liu. Skeleton pruning by contour partitioning with discrete curve evolution. *IEEE Transactions on Pattern Analysis and Machine Intelligence*, 29(3):449–462, 2007.

27. F. Balcan and A. Blum. An augmented pac model for semi-supervised learning. *Semisupervised learning*, pages 397–420, 2006.

28. C. Barnes, D. Jacobs, J. Sanders, D. Goldman, S. Rusinkiewicz, A. Finkelstein, and M. Agrawala. Video puppetry: A performative interface for cutout animation. *ACM Transactions on Graphics*, 27(5):1–9, 2008.

29. W. Baxter, P. Barla, and K. Anjyo. Compatible embedding for 2d shape animation. *IEEE Transactions on Visualization and Computer Graphics*, 15(5):867–879, 2009.

30. P. Beaudoin, S. Coros, M. Panne, and P. Poulin. Motion-motif graphs. *Proceedings of the 7th Symposium on Computer Animation*, pages 117–126, 2008.

31. M. Belkin and P. Niyogi. Laplacian eigenmaps and spectral techniques for embedding and clustering. *Proceedings of Conference on Advances in Neural Information Processing System*, pages 585–591, 2002.

32. M. Belkin, P. Niyogi, and V. Sindhwani. On manifold regularization. *Proceedings of the 10th International Workshop on Artificial Intelligence and Statistics*, 2005.

33. M. Belkin, P. Niyogi, and V. Sindhwani. Manifold regularization: A geometric framework for learning from labeled and unlabeled examples. *The Journal of Machine Learning Research*, 7:2399–2434, 2006.

34. S. Belongie, J. Malik, and J. Puzicha. Shape matching and object recognition using shape contexts. *IEEE Transactions on Pattern Analysis and Machine Intelligence*, 24(4):509–522, 2002.

35. P. Bennett and A. Demiriz. Semi-supervised support vector machines. *Proceedings of the conference on Advances in Neural Information Processing Systems*, pages 368–374, 1999.

36. P. Bennett, M. Momma, and J. Embrechts. A boosting algorithm for heterogeneous kernel models. *Proceedings of the 8th ACM SIGKDD International Conference on Knowledge Discovery and Data Mining*, pages 24–31, 2002.

37. E. Bergen and P. Bock. Applying collective learning systems theory to reactive actor design and control. *Proceedings of the 4th International Workshop on Multi-Strategy Learning*, pages 38–46, 1998.

38. H. Berger, M. Dittenbach, and D. Merkl. An adaptive information retrieval system based on associative networks. *Proceedings of the 1st Asian-Pacific Conference on Conceptual Modeling*, pages 27–36, 2004.

39. C. Bezdek and J. Hathaway. Some notes on alternating optimization. *Proceedings of the AFSS International Conference on Fuzzy Systems*, pages 288–300, 2002.

40. J. Bi, T. Zhang, and P. Bennett. Column-generation boosting methods for mixture of kernels. *Proceedings of the 10th ACM SIGKDD International Conference on Knowledge Discovery and Data Mining*, pages 521–526, 2004.

41. W. Bian and D. Tao. Biased discriminant euclidean embedding for content-based image retrieval. *IEEE Transactions on Image Processing*, 19(2):545–554, 2010.

42. W. Bian and D. Tao. Learning a distance metric by empirical loss minimization. *Proceedings of 22nd International Joint Conference on Artificial Intelligence*, pages 1186–1191, 2011.

43. W. Bian and D. Tao. Max-min distance analysis by using sequential sdp relaxation for dimension reduction. *IEEE Transactions on Pattern Analysis and Machine Intelligence*, 33(5):1037–1050, 2011.

44. R. Bindiganavale. *Building parameterized action representations from observation*. Doctoral Dissertation, University of Pennsylvania Philadelphia, 2000.

45. A. Blum and S. Chawla. Learning from labeled and unlabeled data using graph mincuts. *Proceedings of 18th International Conference on Machine Learning*, pages 19–26, 2001.

46. A. Blum and T. Mitchell. Combining labeled and unlabeled data with co-training. *Proceedings of the 11th Annual Conference on Computational Learning Theory*, pages 92–100, 1998.

47. D. Bradley, T. Popa, A. Sheffer, W. Heidrich, and T. Boubekeur. Markerless garment capture. *ACM Transactions on Graphics*, 37(3):Article no. 99, 2008.

48. M. Brand. Voice puppetry. *Proceedings of the 26th Annual Conference on Computer Graphics and Interactive Technique*, pages 21–28, 1999.

49. M. Brand and A. Hertzmann. Style machines. *Proceedings of the 27th Annual Conference on Computer Graphics and Interactive Techniques*, pages 399–407, 2003.

50. U. Brefeld, T. Gaertner, T. Scheffer, and S. Wrobel. Efficient coregularized least squares regression. *Proceedings of the 23rd International Conference on Machine Learning*, pages 137–144, 2006.

51. U. Brefeld and T. Scheffer. Semi-supervised learning for structured output variables. *Proceedings of the 23rd International Conference on Machine Learning*, pages 145–152, 2006.

52. C. Bregler, M. Covell, and M. Slaney. Video rewrite: driving visual speech with audio. *Proceedings of the 24th Annual Conference on Computer Graphics*, pages 353–360, 1997.

53. C. Bregler, L. Loeb, E. Chuang, and H. Deshpande. Turning to the masters: Motion capturing cartoons. *Proceedings of the 29th Annual Conference on Computer Graphics and Interactive Techniques*, pages 399–407, 2002.

54. C. Bregler and J. Malik. Video motion capture. *Computer Graphics*, 1997.

55. A. Bruderlin and L. Williams. Motion signal processing. *Proceedings of the 22nd Annual Conference on Computer Graphics and Interactive Techniques*, 19:97–104, 1995.

56. N. Burtnyk and M. Wein. Computer generated key frame animation. *Journal of the Society of Motion Picture and Television Engineers*, 8(3):149–153, 1971.

57. N. Burtnyk and M. Wein. Interactive keleton techniques for enhancing motion dynamics in key frame animation. *Communications of the ACM*, 19:564–569, 1976.

58. W. Calvert, J. Chapman, and A. Patla. Aspects of the kinematic simulation of human movement. *IEEE Computer Graphics and Applications*, 2(9):41–50, 1982.

59. Y. Cao, P. Faloutsos, and F. Pighin. Unsupervised learning for speech motion editing. *Proceedings of the ACM SIGGRAPH/Eurographics Symposium on Computer Animation*, pages 225–231, 2003.

60. M. Carcassoni and R. Hancock. Correspondence matching with modal clusters. *IEEE Transactions on Pattern Analysis and Machine Intelligence*, 25(12):1609–1615, 2003.

61. S. Carvalho, R. Boulic, and D. Thalmann. Interactive low-dimensional human motion synthesis by combining motion models and pik. *Computer Animation and Virtual Worlds*, 18(4-5):493–503, 2007.

62. E. Catmull. The problems of computer-assisted animation. *Proceedings of the 5th Annual Conference on Computer Graphics and Interactive Techniques*, 19:348–353, 1978.

63. C. Cortes, M. Mohri, and A. Rostamizadeh. A generalization bounds for learning kernels. *Proceedings of the 27th Annual International Conference on Machine Learning*, pages 247–254, 2010.

64. J. Chadwick and D. James. Animating fire with sound. *ACM Transactions on Graphics*, 30(4):Article no. 84, 2011.

65. O. Chapelle, V. Vapnik, O. Bousquet, and S. Mukherjee. Choosing multiple parameters for support vector machines. *Machine Learning*, 46(1-3):131–159, 2002.

66. H. Chen, N. Zheng, L. Liang, Y. Li, Y. Xu, and H. Shum. Pictoon: a personalized image-based cartoon system. *Proceedings of the 10th ACM International Conference on Multimedia*, pages 171–178, 2002.

67. Q. Chen, F. Tian, H. Seah, Z. Wu, J. Qiu, and M. Konstantin. Dbsc-based animation enhanced with feature and motion. *Computer Animation and Virtual Worlds*, 17:189–198, 2006.

68. Y. Chen, J. Lee, R. Parent, and R. Machiraju. Markerless monocular motion capture using image features and physical constraints. *Proceedings of the Computer Graphics International*, pages 36–43, 2005.

69. J. Cheng, M. Qiao, W. Bian, and D. Tao. 3d human posture segmentation by spectral clustering with surface normal constraint. *Signal Processing*, 91(9):2204–2212, 2011.

70. F. Chung. Spectral graph theory. *Conference Board of the Mathematical Sciences*, 92, 1997.

71. M. Cohen. Interactive spacetime control for animation. *Proceedings of the 19th Annual Conference on Computer Graphics and Interactive Techniques*, pages 293–302, 1992.

72. J. Collomosse, D. Rowntree, and M. Peter. Stroke surfaces: Temporally coherent artistic animations from video. *IEEE Transactions on Visualization and Computer Graphics*, 11(5):540–549, 2005.

73. F. Cordier and N. Magnenat-Thalmann. A data-driven approach for real-time clothes simulation. *Computer Graphics Forum*, 24(2):173–183, 2005.

74. C. Cortes, M. Mohri, and A. Rostamizadeh. L2 regularization for learning kernels. *Proceedings of the International Conference on Uncertainty in Artificial Intelligence*, pages 109–116, 2009.

75. Z. Deng and U. Neumann. efase: Expressive facial animation synthesis and editing with phoneme-isomap controls. *Proceedings of the ACM SIGGRAPH/Eurographics Symposium on Computer Animation*, pages 251–260, 2006.

76. J. Dinerstein and K. Egbert. Improved behavioral animation through regression. *Proceedings of Computer Animation and Social Agents*, pages 231–238, 2004.

77. J. Dinerstein and K. Egbert. Fast multi-level adaptation for interactive autonomous characters. *ACM Transactions on Graphics*, 24(2):262–288, 2005.

78. L. Donoho and C. Grimes. Hessian eigenmaps: New locally linear embedding techniques for high-dimensional data. *Proceedings of the National Academy of Sciences*, 100:5591–5596, 2003.

79. D. Terzopoulos. Artificial life for computer graphics. *Communications of the ACM*, 42(2):33–42, 1999.

80. C. Ennis, R. McDonnell, and C.O' Sullivan. Seeing is believing: Body motion dominates in multisensory conversations. *ACM Transactions on Graphics*, 29(4):Article no. 91, 2010.

81. T. Ezzat, G. Geiger, and T. Poggio. Trainable videorealistic speech animation. *ACM Transactions on Graphics*, 21(3):388–398, 2002.

82. J. Fekete, E. Bizouarn, E. Cournarie, T. Galas, and F. Taillefer. Tictactoon: a paperless system for professional 2d animation. *Proceedings of ACM International Conference on Computer Graphics and Interactive Techniques*, pages 79–90, 1995.

83. A. Fisher. The use of multiple measurements in taxonomic problems. *Annals of Eugenics*, 7:179–188, 1936.

84. A. Fossati, M. Dimitrijevic, V. Lepetit, and P. Fua. From canonical poses to 3d motion capture using a single camera. *IEEE Transactions on Pattern Analysis and Machine Intelligence*, 32(7):1165–1181, 2010.

85. X. Gao, N. Wang, D. Tao, and X. Li. Face sketch-photo synthesis and retrieval using sparse representation. *IEEE Transactions on Circuits and Systems for Video Technology*, 2012.

86. B. Geng, D. Tao, C. Xu, L. Yang, and X. Hua. Ensemble manifold regularization. *IEEE Transactions on Pattern Analysis and Machine Intelligence*, 34(6):1227–1233, 2012.

87. B. Geng, C. Xu, L. Yang D. Tao, and X. Hua. Ensemble manifold regularization. *Proceedings of the 22th IEEE Conference on Computer Vision and Pattern Recognition*, pages 2396–2402, 2009.

88. C. Ginsberg and D. Maxwell. Graphical marionette. *Proceedings of the ACM SIGGRAPH/SIGART interdisciplinary workshop on Motion: representation and perception*, 11:303–310, 1986.

89. P. Glardon, R. Boulic, and D. Thalmann. A coherent locomotion engine extrapolating beyond experimental data. *Proceedings of the International Conference on Computer Animation and Social Agents*, pages 73–84, 2004.

90. P. Glardon, R. Boulic, and D. Thalmann. Pca-based walking engine using motion capture data. *Proceedings of the Computer Graphics International*, pages 292–298, 2004.

91. M. Gleicher. Retargeting motion to new characters. *Proceedings of the 25th Annual Conference on Computer Graphics and Interactive Techniques*, pages 33–42, 1998.

92. M. Gleicher. Motion path editing. *Proceedings of the 5th Symposium on Interactive 3D graphics*, pages 195–202, 2001.

93. M. Gleicher and P. Litwinowicz. Constraint-based motion adaptation. *Journal of Visualization and Computer Animation*, 9:65–94, 1998.

94. M. Gleicher, J. Shin, L. Kovar, and A. Jepsen. Snap together motion: assembling run-time animations. *Proceedings of the Symposium on Interactive 3D Graphics*, pages 181–188, 2003.

95. J. Goldberger, S. Roweis, G. Hinton, and R. Salakhutdinov. Neighborhood component analysis. *Proceedings of Advances of Neural Information Processing*, 2005.

96. Y. Grandvalet and S. Canu. Adaptive scaling for feature selection in svms. *Proceedings of Conference on Advances in Neural Information Processing Systems*, pages 553–560, 2002.

97. R. Grzeszczuk, D. Terzopoulos, and G. Hinton. Neuroanimator: Fast neural network emulation and control of physics-based models. *Proceedings of the 25th Annual Conference on Computer Graphics and Interactive Techniques*, pages 9–20, 1998.

98. N. Guan, D. Tao, Z. Luo, and B. Yuan. Manifold regularized discriminative nonnegative matrix factorization with fast gradient descent. *IEEE Transactions on Image Processing*, 20(7):2030–2048, 2011.

99. N. Guan, D. Tao, Z. Luo, and B. Yuan. Non-negative patch alignment framework. *IEEE Transactions on Neural Networks*, 22(8):1218–1230, 2011.

100. S. Guy, J. Chhugani, S. Curtis, P. Dubey, M. Lin, and D. Manocha. Pledestrians: A least-effort approach to crowd simulation. *Proceedings of the ACM SIGGRAPH/Eurographics Symposium on Computer Animation*, pages 119–128, 2010.

101. S. Guy, J. Chhugani, C. Kim, M. Lin N. Satish, D. Manocha, and P. Dubey. Clearpath: Highly parallel collision avoidance for multi-agent simulation. *Proceedings of the 8th ACM SIGGRAPH/Eurographics Symposium on Computer Animation*, pages 177–187, 2009.

102. S. Guy, S. Kim, M. Lin, and D. Manocha. Simulating heterogeneous crowd behaviors using personality trait theory. *Proceedings of the ACM SIGGRAPH/Eurographics Symposium on Computer Animation*, pages 43–52, 2011.

103. W. Haevre, F. Fiore, and F. Reeth. Uniting cartoon textures with computer assisted animation. *Proceedings of the 3rd International Conference on Computer Graphics and Interactive Techniques*, pages 245–253, 2005.

104. L. Hagen and A. Kahng. New spectral methods for ratio cut partitioning and clustering. *IEEE Transactions on Computer-Aided Design of Integrated Circuits and Systems*, 11(9):1074–1085, 1992.

105. M. Haseyama and A. Matsumura. A trainable retrieval system for cartoon character images. *Proceedings of International Conference on Multimedia and Expo*, pages 393–396, 2003.

106. J. Hays and I. Essa. Image and video based painterly animation. *Proceedings of the 3rd International Symposium on Non-photorealistic Animation and Rendering*, pages 113–120, 2004.

107. X. He, D. Cai, S. Yan, and H. Zhang. Neighborhood preserving embedding. *Proceedings of 10th IEEE International Conference on Computer Vision*, pages 1208–1213, 2005.

108. X. He and P. Niyogi. Locality preserving projections. *Proceedings of Conference on Advances in Neural Information Processing System*, pages 153–160, 2004.

109. R. Heck and M. Gleicher. Parametric motion graphs. *Proceedings of the Symposium on Interactive 3D Graphics and Games*, pages 129–136, 2007.

110. C. Hecker, B. Raabe, J. Maynard, and K. Prooijen. Real-time motion retargeting to highly varied user-created morphologies. *ACM Transactions on Graphics*, 27(3):Article no. 27, 2008.

111. A. Hertzmann. Machine learning for computer graphics: A manifesto and tutorial. *Proceedings of 11th Pacific Conference on Computer Graphics and Applications*, pages 22–36, 2003.

112. E. Ho, T. Komura, and C. Tai. Spatial relationship preserving character motion adaptation. *Proceedings of the 37th Annual Conference on Computer Graphics and Interactive Techniques*, page Article no. 33, 2010.

113. J. Hodings and N. Pollard. Adapting simulated behaviors for new characters. *Proceedings of the 24th Annual Conference on Computer Graphics and Interactive Techniques*, pages 153–162, 1997.

114. J. Hong, H. Lee, J. Yoon, and C. Kim. Bubbles alive. *ACM Transactions on Graphics*, 27(3):Article no. 48, 2008.

115. A. Hornung, E. Dekkers, and L. Kobbelt. Character animation from 2d pictures and 3d motion data. *Proceedings of the 34th Annual Conference on Computer Graphics and Interactive Techniques*, page Article no. 1, 2007.

116. H. Hotelling. Analysis of a complex of statistical variables into principal components. *Journal of Educational Psychology*, 24(6):417–441, 1933.

117. E. Hsu, M. Silva, and J. Popović. Guided time warping for motion editing. *Proceedings of the 6th ACM SIGGRAPH/Eurographics Symposium on Computer Animation*, pages 45–52, 2007.

118. R. Hsu and A. Jain. Generating discriminating cartoon faces using interacting snakes. *IEEE Transactions on Pattern Analysis and Machine Intelligence*, 25(11):1388–1398, 2003.

119. T. Igarashi, T. Moscovich, and J. Hughes. As-rigid-as-possible shape manipulation. *ACM Transactions on Graphics*, 24(3):1134–1141, 2005.

120. L. Ikemoto. *Hybrid Artist- and Data-driven Techniques for Character Animation*. Electrical Engineering and Computer Sciences University of California at Berkeley, 2007.

121. L. Ikemoto, O. Arikan, and D. Forsyth. Generalizing motion edits with gaussian processes. *ACM Transactions on Graphics*, 28(1):Article no. 1, 2009.

122. S. Jain, T. Ye, and C. Liu. Optimization-based interactive motion synthesis. *ACM Transactions on Graphics*, 28(1):Article no. 10, 2009.

123. D. James, C. Twigg, A. Cove, and R. Wang. Mesh ensemble motion graphs: Data-driven mesh animation with constraints. *ACM Transactions on Graphics*, 26(4):1–21, 2007.

124. L. James and K. Fatahalian. Pre-computing interactive dynamic deformable scenes. *ACM Transactions on Graphics*, 22(3):879–887, 2003.

125. H. Jensen and P. Christensen. Efficient simulation of light transport in scenes with participating media using photon maps. *Proceedings of the 25th Annual Conference on Computer Graphics and Interactive Techniques*, pages 311–320, 1998.

126. T. Joachims. Transductive inference for text classification using support vector machines. *Proceedings of the 6th International Conference on Machine Learning*, 11:200–209, 1999.

127. B. Jonathan and L. Adrian. *Convex Analysis and Nonlinear Optimization*. Springer, 2000.

128. R. Jones. *Learning to extract entities from labeled and unlabeled text*. Carnegie Mellon University, 2005.

129. E. Ju, M. Choi, M. Park, J. Lee, K. Lee, and S. Takahashi. Morphable crowds. *ACM Transactions on Graphics*, 29(6):Article no. 140, 2010.

130. E. Ju and J. Lee. Expressive facial gestures from motion capture data. *Computer Graphics Forum*, 27:381–388, 2008.

131. D. Juan and B. Bodenheimer. Cartoon textures. *Proceedings of ACM SIGGRAPH Eurographics Symposium on Computer Animation*, pages 267–276, 2004.

132. J. Kaldor, D. James, and S. Marschner. Efficient yarn-based cloth with adaptive contact linearization. *ACM Transactions on Graphics*, 29(4):Article no. 105, 2010.

133. I. Karamouzas and M. Overmars. Simulating the local behaviour of small pedestrian groups. *IEEE Transactions on Visualization and Computer Graphics 2011*, 2011.

134. M. Kass, A. Witkin, and D. Terzopoulos. Snakes active contour models. *International Journal of Computer Vision*, 1(4):321–331, 1987.

135. G. Kawada and T. Kanai. Procedural fluid modeling of explosion phenomena based on physical properties. *Proceedings of the 10th ACM SIGGRAPH Eurographics Symposium on Computer Animation*, pages 167–176, 2011.

136. M. Kim, K. Hyun, J. Kim, and J. Lee. Synchronized multi-character motion editing. *ACM Transactions on Graphics*, 28(3):Article no. 79, 2009.

137. T. Kim, N. Thurey, D. James, and M. Gross. Wavelet turbulence for fluid simulation. *ACM Transactions on Graphics*, 27(3):Article no. 50, 2008.

138. S. King and R. Parent. Creating speech-synchronized animation. *IEEE Transactions on Visualization and Computer Graphics*, 11(3):341–352, 2005.

139. J. Kleiser. Character motion systems, course notes: Character motion systems. *Proceedings of the 20th Annual Conference on Computer graphics and Interactive Techniques*, pages 33–36, 1993.

140. M. Kloft, U. Brefeld, P. Laskov, and S. Sonnenburg. Non-sparse multiple kernel learning. *Proceedings of the NIPS Workshop on Kernel Learning Automatic Selection of Kernels*, 2008.

141. D. Kochanek. Interpolating splines with local tension, continuity and bias control. *Proceedings of the 11th Annual Conference on Computer Graphics and Interactive Techniques*, pages 33–41, 1984.

142. E. Kokiopoulou and Y. Saad. Orthogonal neighborhood preserving projections: A projection based dimensionality reduction technique. *IEEE Transactions on Pattern Analysis and Machine Intelligence*, 29:2143–2156, 2007.

143. A. Kort. Computer aided inbetweening. *Proceedings of the 2nd International Symposium on Non-photorealistic Animation and Rendering*, pages 125–132, 2002.

144. L. Kovar and M. Gleicher. Automated extraction and parameterization of motions in large data sets. *ACM Transactions on Graphics*, 23(3):559–568, 2004.

145. L. Kovar, M. Gleicher, and F. Pighin. Motion graphs. *Proceedings of the 29th Annual Conference on Computer Graphics and Interactive Techniques*, pages 473–482, 2002.

146. L. Kover, M. Gleicher, and J. Schreiner. Footskate cleanup for motion capture editing. *Proceedings of the 2002 ACM SIGGRAPH Eurographics Symposium on Computer Animation*, pages 97–104, 2002.

147. N. Kwatra, J. Gretarsson, and R. Fedkiw. Practical animation of compressible flow for shock waves and related phenomena. *Proceedings of the 9th ACM SIGGRAPH Eurographics Symposium on Computer Animation*, pages 207–215, 2010.

148. T. Kwon, Y. Cho, S. Park, and S. Shin. Two character motion analysis and synthesis. *IEEE Transactions on Visualization and Computer Graphics*, 14(3):707–720, 2008.

149. T. Kwon and J. Hodgins. Control systems for human running using an inverted pendulum model and a reference motion capture sequence. *Proceedings of the 9th ACM SIGGRAPH Eurographics Symposium on Computer Animation*, pages 129–138, 2010.

150. T. Kwon, K. Lee, J. Lee, and S. Takahashi. Group motion editing. *ACM Transactions on Graphics*, 27(3):Article no. 80, 2008.

151. Y. Lai, S. Chenney, and S. Fan. Group motion graphs. *Proceedings of ACM SIGGRAPH Eurographics symposium on Computer animation*, pages 281–290, 2005.

152. F. Lamarche and S. Donikian. Crowd of virtual humans a new approach for real time navigation in complex and structured environments. *Computer Graphics Forum*, 23(3):509–518, 2004.

153. G. Lanckriet, N. Cristianini, P. Bartlett, E. Ghaoui, and I. Jordan. Learning the kernel matrix with semidefinite programming. *Journal of Machine Learning Research*, 5:27–72, 2004.

154. M. Lasa, I. Mordatch, and A. Hertzmann. Feature-based locomotion controllers. *ACM Transactions on Graphics*, 29(4):Article no. 131, 2010.

155. J. Lasseter. Principles of traditional animation applied to 3d computer animation. *Proceedings of the 14th Annual Conference on Computer Graphics and Interactive Techniques*, pages 35–44, 1987.

156. M. Lau, J. Chai, Y. Xu, and H. Shum. Face poser interactive modeling of 3d facial expressions using facial priors. *ACM Transactions on Graphics*, 29(1):540–549, 2009.

157. M. Lau and J. Kuffner. Behavior planning for character animation. *Proceedings of the ACM SIGGRAPH Eurographics Symposium on Computer Animation*, pages 271–280, 2005.

158. J. Lee, J. Chai, P. Reitsma, J. Hodgins, and N. Pollard. Interactive control of avatars animated with human motion data. *ACM Transactions on Graphics*, 21(3):491–500, 2002.

159. J. Lee and Y. Shin. A hierarchical approach to interactive motion editing for human-like gestures. *Proceedings of the 26th Annual Conference on Computer Graphics and Interactive Techniques*, 11:39–48, 1999.

160. K. Lee, M. Choi, Q. Hong, and J. Lee. Group behavior from video: A data-driven approach to crowd simulation. *Proceedings of the ACM SIGGRAPH Eurographics Symposium on Computer Animation*, pages 109–118, 2007.

161. Y. Lee, S. Kim, and J.Lee. Data driven biped control. *ACM Transactions on Graphics*, 29(4):Article no. 129, 2010.

162. Y. Lee, K. Wampler, G. Bernstein, J. Popovic, and Z. Popovic. Motion fields for interactive character animation. *ACM Transactions on Graphics*, 29(5):Article no. 138, 2010.

163. T. Lenaerts, B. Adams, and P. Dutre. Porous flow in particle based fluid simulations. *ACM Transactions on Graphics*, 27(3):Article no. 49, 2008.

164. M. Lentine, M. Aanjaneya, and R. Fedkiw. Mass and momentum conservation for fluid simulation. *Proceedings of the 10th ACM SIGGRAPH Eurographics Symposium on Computer Animation*, pages 91–100, 2011.

165. M. Lentine, W. Zheng, and R. Fedkiw. A novel algorithm for incompressible flow using only a coarse grid projection. *ACM Transactions on Graphics*, 29(4):Article no. 114, 2010.

166. A. Lerner, Y. Chrysanthou, and D. Lischinski. Crowds by example. *Computer Graphics Forum*, 26(3):655–664, 2007.

167. A. Lerner, E. Fitusi, Y. Chrysanthou, and D. Cohen-Or. Fitting behaviors to pedestrian simulations. *Proceedings of the ACM SIGGRAPH Eurographics Symposium on Computer Animation*, pages 199–208, 2009.

168. S. Levine, Y. Lee, V. Koltun, and Z. Popovic. Space time planning with parameterized locomotion controllers. *ACM Transactions on Graphics*, 30(3):Article no. 23, 2011.

169. P. Lewis, M. Cordner, and N. Fong. Pose space deformation a unified approach to shape interpolation and skeleton driven deformation. *Proceedings of the 27th Annual Conference on Computer Graphics and Interactive Techniques*, pages 165–172, 2000.

170. T. Leyvand, D. Cohen, G. Dror, and D. Lischinski. Data driven enhancement of facial attractiveness. *ACM Transactions on Graphics*, 27(3):Article no. 38, 2008.

171. H. Li, B. Adamsy, L. Guibasz, and M. Pauly. Robust single view geometry and motion reconstruction. *ACM Transactions on Graphics*, 28(5):Article no. 175, 2009.

172. Y. Li, F. Yu, Y. Xu, E. Chang, and H. Shum. Speech driven cartoon animation with emotions. *Proceedings of the 9th ACM International Conference on Multimedia*, pages 365–371, 2001.

173. D. Liang, Y. Liu, Q. Huang, G. Zhu, S. Jiang, Z. Zhang, and W. Gao. Video2cartoon generating 3d cartoon from broadcast soccer video. *Proceedings of the 13th ACM International Conference on Multimedia*, pages 217–218, 2005.

174. S. Lim and D. Thalmann. Proactively interactive evolution for computer animation. *Proceedings of Eurographics Workshop on Animation and Simulation*, pages 45–52, 1999.

175. L. Lin, K. Zeng, H. Lv, Y. Wang, Y. Xu, and S. Zhu. Painterly animation using video semantics and feature correspondence. *Proceedings of the 9th International Symposium on Non photorealistic Animation and Rendering*, pages 73–80, 2010.

176. Y. Lin, M. Song, D. Quynh, Y. He, and C. Chen. Sparse coding for flexible and robust 3d facial expression synthesis. *IEEE Computer Graphics and Applications*, 32(2):76–88, 2012.

177. C. Liu, A. Hertzmann, and Z. Popovic. Learning physics-based motion style with nonlinear inverse optimization. *ACM Transactions on Graphics*, 24(3):1071–1081, 2005.

178. C. Liu and Z. Popovic. Synthesis of complex dynamics character motion from simple animation. *Proceedings of the 29th Annual Conference on Computer Graphics and Interactive Techniques*, pages 408–416, 2002.

179. W. Lo and M. Zwicker. Real-time planning for parameterized human motion. *Proceedings of 7th ACM SIGGRAPH Eurographics Symposium on Computer Animation*, pages 29–38, 2008.

180. N. Lockwood and K. Singh. Biomechanically-inspired motion path editing. *Proceedings of 10th ACM SIGGRAPH Eurographics Symposium on Computer Animation*, pages 267–276, 2011.

181. B. Long, S. Yu, and Z. Zhang. A general model for multiple view unsupervised learning. *Proceedings of 8th SIAM International Conference on Data Mining*, pages 822–833, 2008.

182. W. Loy and M. Zwicker. Bidirectional search for interactive motion synthesis. *Computer Graphics Forum*, 29(2):563–573, 2010.

183. J. Lu, H. Seah, and T. Feng. Computer assisted cel animation: post-processing after inbetweening. *Proceedings of ACM International Conference on Computer Graphics and Interactive Techniques*, pages 13–20, 2003.

184. H. Lutkepohl. *Handbook of Matrices*. Chichester, 1997.

185. F. Lv, J. Kang, R. Nevatia, I. Cohen, and G. Medioni. Automatic tracking and labeling of human activities in a video sequence. *Proceedings of Performance Evaluation of Tracking and Surveillance*, 2004.

186. S. Sonnenburg M. Kloft, U. Brefeld and A. Zien. Non-sparse regularization and efficient training with multiple kernels. *Machine Learning*, 2010.

187. W. Ma, S. Xia, J. Hodgins, X. Yang, C. Li, and Z. Wang. Modeling style and variation in human motion. *Proceeding of the 9th ACM SIGGRAPH Eurographics Symposium on Computer Animation*, pages 21–30, 2010.

188. B. Maeireizo, D. Litman, and R. Hwa. Cotraining for predicting emotions with spoken dialogue data. *Proceedings of the 42nd Annual Meeting of the Association for Computational Linguistics*, page 28, 2004.

189. A. Majkowska and P. Faloutsos. Flipping with physics: Motion editing for acrobatics. *Proceedings of the ACM SIGGRAPH Eurographics Symposium on Computer Animation*, pages 35–44, 2007.

190. J. McClave and T. Sincich. *Statistics, 9th edn*. Prentice Hall, Upper Saddle River, NJ, 2004.

191. R. McDonnell, M. Larkin, S. Dobbyn, S. Collins, and C. Sullivan. Clone attack! perception of crowd variety. *ACM Transactions on Graphics*, 27:26, 2008.

192. R. McDonnell, M. Larkin, B. Hernandez, I. Rudomin, and C. O'Sullivan. Eye catching crowds saliency based selective variation. *ACM Transactions on Graphics*, 28(3):55, 2009.

193. M. McGuire and A. Fein. Real time rendering of cartoon smoke and clouds. *Proceedings of the 5th International Symposium on Non-photorealistic Animation and Rendering*, pages 21–26, 2006.

194. S. Menardais, F. Multon, R. Kulpa, and B. Arnaldi. Motion blending for real-time animation while accounting for the environment. *Proceedings of the Computer Graphics International*, pages 156– 159, 2004.

195. M. Haseyama and A. Matsumura. A cartoon character retrieval system including trainable scheme. *Proceedings of International Conference on Image Processing*, pages 37–40, 2003.

196. A. Micilotta, E. Ong, and R. Bowden. Real time upper body 3d pose estimation from a single uncalibrated camera. *Proceedings of the Annual Conference of the European Association for Computer Graphics*, pages 41–44, 2005.

197. V. Mihalef, D. Metaxas, and M. Sussman. Simulation of two phase flow with subscale droplet and bubble effects. *Computer Graphics Forum*, 28(2):229–238, 2009.

198. R. Mike. *The Talking Head*. Computer Graphics World, Glender, CA, 1988.

199. T. Mitchell. *Machine Learning*. WCB McGraw-Hill, New York, 1997.

200. B. Mohar. Some applications of laplace eigenvalues of graphs, 1997.

201. H. Mori and J. Hoshino. Ica-based interpolation of human motion. *Proceedings of the 5th Computational Intelligence in Robotics and Automation*, pages 453–458, 2003.

202. A. Mosher, T. Shinar, J. Gretarsson, J. Su, and R. Fedkiw. Two way coupling of fluids to rigid and deformable solids and shells. *ACM Transactions on Graphics*, 27(3), 2008.

203. U. Muico, J. Popovic, and Z. Popovic. Composite control of physically simulated characters. *ACM Transactions on Graphics*, 30(3), 2011.

204. T. Mukai and S. Kuriyama. Geostatistical motion interpolation. *Proceedings of the 32nd Annual Conference on Computer Graphics and Interactive Techniques*, pages 1062–1070, 2005.

205. T. Mukai and S. Kuriyama. Pose timeline for propagating motion edits. *Proceedings of the 8th ACM SIGGRAPH Eurographics Symposium on Computer Animation*, pages 113–122, 2009.

206. K. Na and K. Jung. Hierarchical retargetting of fine facial motions. *Computer Graphics Forum*, 23(3):687–695, 2004.

207. R. Narain, A. Golas, S. Ming, and C. Lin. Aggregate dynamics for dense crowd simulation. *ACM Transactions on Graphics*, 28(5), 2009.

208. R. Narain, J. Sewall, M. Carlson, and M. Lin. Fast animation of turbulence using energy transport and procedural synthesis. *ACM Transactions on Graphics*, 27(5), 2008.

209. M. Neff and Y. Kim. Interactive editing of motion style using drives and correlations. *Proceedings of the 8th ACM SIGGRAPH Eurographics Symposium on Computer Animation*, pages 103–112, 2009.

210. A. Ng, M. Jordan, and Y. Weiss. On spectral clustering analysis and an algorithm. *Proceedings of Conference on Advances in Neural Information Processing Systems*, pages 849–856, 2001.

211. M. Nielsen and B. Christensen. Improved variational guiding of smoke animations. *Computer Graphics Forum*, 29(2):705–712, 2010.

212. M. Nielsen, B. Christensen, N. Zafar, D. Roble, and K. Museth. Guiding of smoke animations through variational coupling of simulations at different resolutions. *Proceedings*

of the 8th ACM SIGGRAPH Eurographics Symposium on Computer Animation, pages 217–226, 2009.

213. K. Nigam and R. Ghani. Analyzing the effectiveness and applicability of co-training. *Proceedings of 9th International Conference on Information and Knowledge Management*, pages 86–93, 2000.

214. J. Ondrej, J. Pettre, A. Olivier, and S. Donikian. A synthetic vision based steering approach for crowd simulation. *Computer Graphics Forum*, 29(4):123, 2010.

215. S. Ong, J. Smola, and C. Williamson. Hyperkernels. *Proceedings of Conference on Advances in Neural Information Processing Systems*, pages 478–485, 2002.

216. O. Ozgen, M. Kallmann, L. Ramirez, and C. Coimbra. Underwater cloth simulation with fractional derivatives. *ACM Transactions on Graphics*, 29(3):23, 2010.

217. p. Reitsma and N. Pollard. Evaluating motion graphs for character animation. *ACM Transactions on Graphics*, 26(4):18, 2007.

218. R. Parent. *Computer Animation: Algorithms and Techniques. Morgan Kaufmann.* San Francisco, 2002.

219. S. Paris, J. Pettré, and S. Donikian. Pedestrian reactive navigation for crowd simulation. *Computer Graphics Forum*, 26(3):665–674, 2007.

220. M. Park and S. Shin. Example based motion cloning. *Computer Animation and Virtual Worlds*, 15(3-4):245–257, 2004.

221. S. Park, K. Choi, and H. Ko. Processing motion capture data to achieve positional accuracy. *Graphical Models Image Process*, 61(5):260–273, 1999.

222. S. Park, H. Shin, T. Kim, and S. Shin. On-line motion blending for real-time locomotion generation. *Computer Animation and Virtual Worlds*, 15(3-4):125–138, 2004.

223. S. Park, H. Shin, and S. Shin. On-line locomotion generation based on motion blending. *Proceedings of the 1st ACM SIGGRAPH Eurographics symposium on Computer animation*, pages 105–111, 2002.

224. I. Parke. *A parametric model for human faces.* Ph.D. Thesis, University of Utah, 1974.

225. S. Patil, J. Berg, S. Curtis, D. Lin, and D. Manocha. Directing crowd simulations using navigation fields. *IEEE Transactions on Visualization and Computer Graphics*, 17(2):244–254, 2011.

226. Y. Pekelny and C. Gotsman. Articulated object reconstruction and markerless motion capture from depth video. *Computer Graphics Forum*, 27(2):399–408, 2008.

227. N. Pelechano, M. Allbeck, and I. Badler. Controlling individual agents in high-density crowd simulation. *Proceedings of the ACM SIGGRAPH Eurographics Symposium on Computer Animation*, pages 99–108, 2007.

228. D. Pierce and C. Cardie. Limitations of co-training for natural language learning from large datasets. *Proceedings of the Conference on Empirical Methods in Natural Language Processing*, pages 1–9, 2001.

229. F. Pighin, M. Cohen, and M. Shah. Modeling and editing flows using advected radial basis functions. *Proceedings of Eurographics SIGGRAPH Symposium on Computer Animation*, pages 223–232, 2004.

230. F. Pighin, J. Hecker, D. Lischinski, R. Szeliski, and H. Salesin. Synthesizing realistic facial expressions from photographs. *Proceedings of the 25th Annual Conference on Computer Graphics and Interactive Techniques*, pages 75–84, 1998.

231. A. Pina, E. Cerezo, and F. Seron. Computer animation from avatars to unrestricted autonomous actors (a survey on replication and modeling mechanisms). *Computers & Graphics 2000*, 24(2):297–311, 2000.

232. Z. Popovic and A. Witkin. Physically based motion transformation. *Proceedings of the 26th Annual Conference on Computer Graphics and Interactive Techniques*, pages 11–20, 1999.

233. L. Rabiner. A tutorial on hidden markov models and selected applications in speech recognition. *Proceedings of the IEEE*, 77(2):257–285, 1989.

234. C. Ren, L. Zhao, and S. Safonova. Human motion synthesis with optimization-based graphs. *Computer Graphics Forum*, 29(2):545–554, 2010.

235. E. Richard and A. Tovey. The simplex and projective scaling algorithms as iteratively reweighted least squares methods. *SIAM Review*, 33(2):220–237, 1991.

236. E. Riloff, J. Wiebe, and T. Wilson. Learning subjective nouns using extraction pattern bootstrapping. *Proceedings of the 7th Conference on Natural Language Learning*, pages 25–32, 2003.

237. A. Rivers, T. Igarashi, and F. Durand. 2.5d cartoon models. *ACM Transactions on Graphics*, 29(4):59, 2010.

238. B. Robertson. *Moving pictures*, volume 15. 1992.

239. A. Robinson-Mosher, R. English, and R. Fedkiw. Accurate tangential velocities for solid fluid coupling. *Proceedings of the 8th ACM SIGGRAPH Eurographics Symposium on Computer Animation*, pages 227–236, 2009.

240. C. Rose, F. Cohen, and B. Bodenheimer. Verbs and adverbs: multi-dimensional motion interpolation. *IEEE Computer Graphics and Applications*, 18(5):32–41, 1998.

241. T. Roweis and K. Saul. Nonlinear dimensionality reduction by locally linear embedding. *Science*, 290(5500):2323–2326, 2000.

242. D. Sa. Learning classification with unlabeled data. *Proceedings of the 7th Conference on Advances in Neural Information Processing Systems*, pages 112–119, 1993.

243. A. Safonova, J. Hodgins, and N. Pollard. Synthesizing physically realistic human motion in low-dimensional behavior-specific spaces. *ACM Transactions on Graphics*, 23(3):514–521, 2004.

244. D. Salesin. The need for machine learning in computer graphics. *Proceedings of 17th Conference on Advances in Neural Information Processing Systems*, 2003.

245. A. Schödl, R. Szelisk, H. Salesin, and I. Essa. Video textures. *Proceedings of the 27th Annual Conference on Computer Graphics and Interactive Techniques*, pages 489–498, 2000.

246. L. Scott and C. Longuet-Higgins. *An algorithm for associating the features of two images*, volume 244. 1991.

247. W. Sederberg and E. Greenwood. *An algorithm for associating the features of two images*. 1995.

248. J. Segen and S. Pingali. A camera-based system for tracking people in real time. *Proceedings of the 13th International Conference on Pattern Recognition*, pages 63–67, 1996.

249. A. Selle, A. Mohr, and S. Chenney. Cartoon rendering of smoke animations. *Proceedings of the 3rd International Symposium on Non-photorealistic Animation and Rendering*, pages 57–60, 2004.

250. W. Shao and D. Terzopoulos. *Autonomous Pedestrians*, volume 69. 2007.

251. J. Shi and J. Malik. Normalized cuts and image segmentation. *IEEE Transactions on Pattern Analysis and Machine Intelligence*, 22(8):888–905, 2000.

252. X. Shi, K. Zhou, Y. Tong, M. Desbrun, H. Bao, and B. Guo. Example-based dynamic skinning in real time. *ACM Transactions on Graphics*, 27(3):29, 2008.

253. H. Shin and J. Lee. Motion synthesis and editing in low-dimensional spaces. *Computer Animation and Virtual Worlds*, 17(3):219–227, 2006.

254. T. Shiratori, H. Parky, L. Sigal, Y. Sheikhy, and J. Hodginsy. Motion capture from body-mounted cameras. *ACM Transactions on Graphics*, 30(4):31, 2011.

255. J. Shrager, T. Hogg, and A. Huberman. *Observation of phase transitions in spreading activation networks*, volume 236. 1987.

256. H. Shum, T. Komura, M. Shiraishi, and S. Yamazaki. Interaction patches for multi-character animation. *ACM Transactions on Graphics*, 27(5):114, 2008.

257. S. Si, D. Tao, and K. Chan. Evolutionary cross-domain discriminative hessian eigenmaps. *IEEE Transactions on Image Processing*, 19(4):1075–1086, 2010.

258. E. Sifakis, I. Neverov, and R. Fedkiw. Automatic determination of facial muscle activations from sparse motion capture marker data. *ACM Transactions on Graphics*, 24(3):417–425, 2005.

259. V. Sindhwani, P. Niyogi, and M. Belkin. A co-regularized approach to semi-supervised learning with multiple views. *Proceedings of the 22nd ICML Workshop on Learning with Multiple Views*, 2005.

260. K. Sok, K. Yamane, and J. Hodgins. Editing dynamic human motions via momentum and force. *Proceedings of the 9th ACM SIGGRAPH Eurographics Symposium on Computer Animation*, pages 11–20, 2010.

261. D. Song and D. Tao. Biologically inspired feature manifold for scene classification. *IEEE Transactions on Image Processing*, 19(1):174–184, 2010.

262. M. Song, D. Tao, C. Chen, X. Li, and C. Chen. Color to gray: Visual cue preservation. *IEEE Transactions on Pattern Analysis and Machine Intelligence*, 32(9):1537–1552, 2011.

263. M. Song, D. Tao, X. Huang, C. Chen, and J. Bu. 3d face reconstruction from a single image by a coupled rbf network. *IEEE Transactions on Image Processing*.

264. M. Song, D. Tao, Z. Liu, X. Li, and M. Zhou. Image ratio features for facial expression recognition application. *IEEE Transactions on Systems, Man, and Cybernetics Part B*, 40(3):779–788, 2010.

265. M. Song, D. Tao, Z. Sun, and X. Li. Visual-context boosting for eye detection. *IEEE Transactions on Systems, Man, and Cybernetics Part B*, 40(6):1460–1467, 2010.

266. M. Sonka, V. Hlavac, and R. Boyle. *Image Processing-Analysis and Machine Vision*. 1999.

267. B. Stephen and V. Lieven. *Convex Optimization*. 2004.

268. M. Stoer and F. Wagner. A simple min-cut algorithm. *Journal of ACM*, 44(4):585–591, 1997.

269. C. Stoll, J. Gally, E. Aguiarz, S. Thrunx, and C. Theobalt. Video-based reconstruction of animatable human characters. *ACM Transactions on Graphics*, 29(6):32, 2010.

270. A. Sud, E. Andersen, S. Curtis, M. Lin, and D. Manocha. Real-time path planning in dynamic virtual environments using multiagent navigation graphs. *IEEE Transactions on Visualization and Computer Graphics*, 14:526–538, 2008.

271. S. Umeyama. An eigen decomposition approach to weighted graph matching problems. *IEEE Transactions on Pattern Analysis and Machine Intelligence*, 10(5):695–703, 1988.

272. M. Sung, M. Gleicher, and S. Chenney. Scalable behaviors for crowd simulation. *Computer Graphics Forum*, 23(3):519–528, 2004.

273. M. Sung, L. Kovar, and M. Gleicher. Fast and accurate goal-directed motion synthesis for crowds. *Proceedings of the ACM SIGGRAPH Eurographics symposium on Computer animation*, pages 291–300, 2005.

274. D. Sykora, J. Dingliana, and S. Collins. As-rigid-as-possible image registration for hand-drawn cartoon animations. *Proceedings of the 7th International Symposium on Non-Photorealistic Animation and Rendering*, pages 25–33, 2009.

275. D. Sýkora, J. Buriánek, and J. Zára. Unsupervised colorization of black-and-white cartoons. *Proceedings of the 3rd International Symposium on Non-photorealistic Animation and Rendering*, pages 121–127, 2004.

276. D. Sýkora, D. Sedlacek, S. Jinchao, J. Dingliana, and S. Collins. Adding depth to cartoons using sparse depth (in)equalities. *Computer Graphics Forum*, 29(2):615–623, 2010.

277. D. Sýkoray, J. Dingliana, and S. Collins. Lazybrush: Flexible painting tool for hand-drawn cartoons. *Computer Graphics Forum*, 28(2):599–608, 2009.

278. S. Takahashi, K. Yoshida, T. Kwon, K. Lee, J. Lee, and S. Shin. Spectral-based group formation control. *Computer Graphics Forum*, 28(2):639–648, 2009.

279. N. Tang, H. Tyan, C. Hsu, and H. Liao. Narrative generation by repurposing digital videos. *Proceedings of the 17th International Conference on Advances in Multimedia Modeling*, pages 503–513, 2011.

280. D. Tao, X. Li, and S. Maybank. Negative samples analysis in relevance feedback. *IEEE Transactions on Knowledge and Data Engineering*, 19(4):568–580, 2007.

281. D. Tao, X. Li, X. Wu, and S. Maybank. General tensor discriminant analysis and gabor features for gait recognition. *IEEE Transactions on Pattern Analysis and Machine Intelligence*, 29(10):1700–1715, 2007.

282. D. Tao, X. Li, X. Wu, and S. Maybank. Geometric mean for subspace selection. *IEEE Transactions on Pattern Analysis and Machine Intelligence*, 31(2):260–274, 2009.

283. D. Tao, M. Song, X. Li, J. Shen, J. Sun, X. Wu, C. Faloutsos, and S. Maybank. Bayesian tensor approach for 3-d face modeling. *IEEE Transactions on Circuits and Systems for Video Technology*, 18(10):1397–1410, 2008.

284. D. Tao, J. Sun, J. Shen, X. Wu, X. Li, S. Maybank, and C. Faloutsos. Bayesian tensor analysis. *Proceedings of IEEE International Joint Conference on Neural Networks*, pages 1402–1409, 2008.

285. D. Tao, X. Tang, X. Li, and X. Wu. Asymmetric bagging and random subspace for support vector machines-based relevance feedback in image retrieval. *IEEE Transactions on Pattern Analysis and Machine Intelligence*, 28(7):1088–1099, 2006.

286. H. Tardif. Character animation in real time, panel: Applications of virtual reality i: Reports from the field. *ACM SIGGRAPH Panel Proceedings*, 1991.

287. J. Tenenbaum, V. Silva, and J. Langford. *A Global Geometric Framework for Nonlinear Dimensionality Reduction*, volume 290. 2000.

288. N. Thalmann and D. Thalmann. Computer animation theory and practice, 1985.

289. N. Thalmann and D. Thalmann. New trends in animation and visualization, 1991.

290. F. Thomas and O. Johnson. *The Illusion of Life*. 1981.

291. P. Thompson and E. Marchant. *Testing and application of the computer model 'simulex'*, volume 24. 1995.

292. N. Thurey, C. Wojtan, G. Gross, and G. Turk. A multiscale approach to mesh-based surface tension flows. *ACM Transactions on Graphics*, 29(4):48, 2010.

293. X. Tian, D. Tao, X. Hua, and X. Wu. Active reranking for web image search. *IEEE Transactions on Image Processing*, 19(3):805–820, 2010.

294. X. Tian, D. Tao, and Y. Rui. Sparse transfer learning for interactive video search reranking. *ACM Transactions on Multimedia Computing, Communications and Applications*, 2012.

295. M. Unuma, K. Anjyo, and R. Takeuchi. Fourier principles for emotion-based human figure animation. *Proceedings of the 22nd Annual Conference on Computer Graphics and Interactive Techniques*, pages 91–96, 1995.

296. V. Vapnik. *Statistical learning theory*. Wiley-Interscience, New York, 1998.

297. M. Varma and R. Babu. More generality in efficient multiple kernel learning. *Proceedings of the 26th Annual International Conference on Machine Learning*, pages 1065–1072, 2009.

298. P. Volino and N. Magnenat. A simple approach to nonlinear tensile stiffness for accurate cloth simulation. *ACM Transactions on Graphics*, 28(4):105, 2009.

299. D. Wagner and F. Wagner. Between min cut and graph bisection. *Proceedings of the 18th International Symposium on Mathematical Foundations of Computer Science*, pages 744–750, 1993.

300. G. Walters. The story of waldo c. graphic, course notes: 3d character animation by computer. *Proceedings of the 16th Annual Conference on Computer Graphics and Interactive Techniques*, pages 65–79, 1989.

301. G. Walters. Performance animation at pdi, course notes: Character motion systems. *Proceedings of the 20th Annual Conference on Computer Graphics and Interactive Techniques*, pages 40–53, 1993.

302. K. Wampler, A. Andersen, H. Herbst, L. Lee, and P. Popovic. Character animation in two-player adversarial games. *ACM Transactions on Graphics*, 29(3):16, 2010.

303. F. Wang, C. Zhang. Label Propagation through Linear Neighborhoods. *IEEE Transactions on Knowledge and Data Engineering*,20(1):55-67,2008.

304. F. Wang, C. Zhang. Semisupervised Learning Based on Generalized Point Charge Models. *IEEE Transactions on Neural Networks*,19(7):1307-1311,2008.

305. F. Wang, C. Zhang, T. Li. Clustering with Local and Global Regularization. *IEEE Transactions on Knowledge and Data Engineering*, 21(12):1665-1678,2009.

306. F. Wang, B. Zhao, C. Zhang. Unsupervised Large Margin Discriminative Projection. *IEEE Transactions on Neural Networks*, 22(9):1446-1456,2011.

307. J. Wang, F. Wang, C. Zhang, H. Shen, L. Quan. Linear Neighborhood Propagation and Its Applications. *IEEE Transactions on Pattern Analysis and Machine Intelligence*, 31(9):1600-1615,2009.

308. J. Wang and B. Bodenheimer. An evaluation of a cost metric for selecting transitions between motion segments. *Proceedings of the 2nd ACM SIGGRAPH Eurographics symposium on Computer animation*, pages 232–238, 2003.

309. J. Wang and B. Bodenheimer. Synthesis and evaluation of linear motion transitions. *ACM Transactions on Graphics*, 27(1):1, 2008.

310. J. Wang, D. Fleet, and A. Hertzmann. Gaussian process dynamical models for human motion. *IEEE Transactions on Pattern Analysis and Machine Intelligence*, 30(2):283–298, 2008.

311. J. Wang, Y. Xu, H. Shum, and M. Cohen. Video tooning. *ACM Transactions on Graphics*, 23(3):574–583, 2004.

312. R. Wang, S. Paris, and J. Popovic. Practical color-based motion capture. *Proceeding of the 10th ACM SIGGRAPH/Eurographics Symposium on Computer Animation*, 2011.

313. X. Wang, Z. Li, and D. Tao. Subspaces indexing model on grassmann manifold for image search. *IEEE Transactions on Image Processing*, 20(9):2627–2635, 2011.

314. X. Wang, X. Ma, and W. Grimson. Unsupervised activity perception in crowded and complicated scenes using hierarchical bayesian models. *IEEE Transactions on Pattern Analysis and Machine Intelligence*, 31(3):539–555, 2009.

315. X. Wang and X. Tang. Face photo-sketch synthesis and recognition. *IEEE Transactions on Pattern Analysis and Machine Intelligence*, 31(11):1955–1967, 2009.

316. L. Wei and X. Chai. Videomocap: Modeling physically realistic human motion from monocular. *ACM Transactions on Graphics*, 29(4):42, 2010.

317. Q. Weinberger, J. Blitzer, and L. Saul. Distance metric learning for large margin nearest neighbor classification. *The Journal of Machine Learning Research*, 10:207–244, 2009.

318. T. Weise, H. Li, L. Gool, and M. Pauly. Face off: Live facial puppetry. *Proceedings of the ACM SIGGRAPH Eurographics Symposium on Computer Animation*, pages 7–16, 2009.

319. B. Whited, G. Noris, M. Simmons, R. Sumner, M. Gross, and J. Rossignac. Betweenit: An interactive tool for tight inbetweening. *Computer Graphics Forum*, 29(2):605–614, 2010.

320. M. Wicke, D. Ritchie, B. Klingner, S. Burke, J. Shewchuk, and J. Brien. Dynamic local remeshing for elastoplastic simulation. *ACM Transactions on Graphics*, 29(4):49, 2010.

321. A. Witkin and M. Kass. Spacetime constraints. *Proceedings of the 15th Annual Conference on Computer Graphics and Interactive Techniques*, pages 159–168, 1988.

322. A. Witkin and Z. Popovic. Motion warping. *Proceedings of the 22nd Annual Conference on Computer Graphics and Interactive Techniques*, pages 105–108, 1995.

323. C. Wojtan, N. Thurey, M. Gross, and G. Turk. Physics-inspired topology changes for thin fluid features. *ACM Transactions on Graphics*, 29(4):50, 2010.

324. T. Xia, D. Tao, T. Mei, and Y. Zhang. Multiview spectral embedding. *IEEE Transactions on Systems, Man, and Cybernetics, Part B*, 40(6):1438–1446, 2010.

325. B. Xie, Y. Mu, D. Tao, and K. Huang. m-sne: Multiview stochastic neighbor embedding. *IEEE Transactions on Systems, Man, and Cybernetics, Part B*, 41(4):1088–1096, 2011.

326. F. Xu, Y. Liu, C. Stoll, J. Tompkin, G. Bharaj, Q. Dai, H. Seidel, J. Kautz, and C. Theobalt. Video-based characters creating new human performances from a multiview video database. *Proceedings of the 38th Annual Conference on Computer Graphics and Interactive Techniques*, page 32, 2011.

327. K. Yamane, Y. Ariki, and J. Hodgins. Animating non-humanoid characters with human motion data. *Proceedings of the 9th Eurographics ACM SIGGRAPH Symposium on Computer Animation*, pages 169–178, 2010.

328. J. Yan and M. Pollefeys. A factorization-based approach for articulated nonrigid shape, motion, and kinematic chain recovery from video. *IEEE Transactions on Pattern Analysis and Machine Intelligence*, 30(5):865–877, 2008.

329. Y. Yang, T. Zhuang, D. Xu, H. Pan, D. Tao, and S. Maybank. Retrieval based interactive cartoon synthesis via unsupervised bi-distance metric learning. *Proceedings of the 17th ACM International Conference on Multimedia*, pages 311–320, 2009.

330. Z. Yang, M. Song, N. Li, J. Bu, and C. Chen. Visual attention analysis by pseudo gravitational field. *Proceedings of the 17th ACM International Conference on Multimedia*, pages 553–556, 2009.

331. N. Yannakakis, J. Levine, J. Hallam, and M. Papageorgiou. Performance, robustness and effort cost comparison of machine learning mechanisms in flatland. *Proceedings of the 11th Mediterranean Conference on Control and Automation*, 2003.

332. D. Yarowsky. Unsupervised word sense disambiguation rivaling supervised methods. *Proceedings of the 33rd Annual Meeting of the Association for Computational Linguistics*, pages 189–196, 1995.

333. Y. Ye and C. Liu. Animating responsive characters with dynamic constraints in near-unactuated coordinates. *ACM Transactions on Graphics*, 27(5):112, 2008.

334. Y. Ye and C. Liu. Synthesis of responsive motion using a dynamic model. *Computer Graphics Forum*, 29(2):555–562, 2010.

335. H. Yeh, S. Curtis, S. Patil, J. Berg, D. Manocha, and M. Lin. Composite agents. *Proceedings of the ACM SIGGRAPH Eurographics Symposium on Computer Animation*, pages 39–47, 2008.

336. Y. Li, T. Wang, and H. Shum. Motion texture a two level statistical model for character motion synthesis. *Proceedings of the 29th Annual Conference on Computer Graphics and Interactive Techniques*, pages 465–472, 2002.

337. J. Yu, J. Cheng, and D. Tao. Interactive cartoon reusing by transfer learning. *Signal Processing*, 92(9):2147-2158, 2012.

338. J. Yu, D. Liu, and H. Seah. Complex object correspondence construction in two dimensional animation. *IEEE Transactions on Image Processing*, 20(11):3257–3269, 2011.

339. J. Yu, D. Liu, D. Tao, and H. Seah. On combining multiple features for cartoon character retrieval and clip synthesis. *IEEE Transactions on Systems, Man and Cybernetics, Part B*, 42(5):1413-1427, 2012.

340. J. Yu, Q. Liu, and H. Seah. Transductive graph based cartoon synthesis. *Computer Animation and Virtual Worlds*, 21(3):277–288, 2010.

341. J. Yu, D. Tao, and M. Wang. Adaptive hypergraph learning and its application in image classification. *IEEE Transactions on Image Processing*, 21(7):3262-3272, 2012.

342. J. Yu, D. Tao, M. Wang, and J. Cheng. Semi-automatic cartoon generation by motion planning. *Multimedia System Journal*, 17(5):409–419, 2011.

343. J. Yu, D. Tao, Y. Rui, and J. Cheng. Pairwise Pairwise constraints based multiview features fusion for scene classification. *Pattern Recognition*, 46(2): 483-496, 2013.

344. J. Yu and G. Turk. Reconstructing surfaces of particle-based fluids using anisotropic kernels. *Proceedings of the 9th ACM SIGGRAPH Eurographics Symposium on Computer Animation*, pages 217–225, 2010.

345. J. Yu, Y. Zhuang, J. Xiao, and C. Chen. Adaptive control in cartoon data reusing. *Journal of Visualization and Computer Animation*, 18(4-5):571–582, 2007.

346. S. Yu, T. Falck, A. Daemen, C. Tranchevent, J. Suykens, B. De, and Y. Moreau. L2-norm multiple kernel learning and its application to biomedical data fusion. *BMC Bioinformatics*, 11(1):309, 2010.

347. J. Yu, M. Wang, D. Tao. Semi-supervised Multiview Distance Metric Learning for Cartoon Synthesis. *IEEE Transactions on Image Processing*, 21(11): 4636-4648, 2012.

348. Q. Zhang, Z. Liu, B. Guo, D. Terzopoulos, and H. Shum. Geometry-driven photorealistic facial expression synthesis. *IEEE Transactions on Visualization and Computer Graphics*, 12(1):48–60, 2006.

349. T. Zhang and J. Oles. A probability analysis on the value of unlabeled data for classification problems. *Proceedings of the 17th International Conference on Machine Learning*, pages 1191–1198, 2010.

350. T. Zhang, D. Tao, J. Li, and X. Yang. Patch alignment for dimensionality reduction. *IEEE Transactions on Knowledge and Data Engineering*, 21(9):1299–1313, 2009.

351. T. Zhang, J. Yang, D. Zhao, and X. Ge. Linear local tangent space alignment and application to face recognition. *Neurocomputing*, 70(7-9):1547–155, 2007.

352. Z. Zhang and D. Tao. Slow feature analysis for human action recognition. *IEEE Transactions on Pattern Analysis and Machine Intelligence*, 34(3):436–450, 2012.

353. Z. Zhang and H. Zha. Principal manifolds and nonlinear dimension reduction via local tangent space alignment. *SIAM Journal of Scientific Computing*, 26(1):313–338, 2005.

354. H. Zhao and L. Li. Human motion reconstruction from monocular images using genetic algorithms. *Computer Animation and Virtual Worlds*, 15(3-4):407–414, 2004.

355. L. Zhao, A. Normoyle, S. Khanna, and A. Safonova. Automatic construction of a minimum size motion graph. *Proceedings of the 8th Symposium on Computer Animation*, pages 27–35, 2009.

356. L. Zhao and A. Safonova. Achieving good connectivity in motion graphs. *Proceedings of 7th Eurographics ACM SIGGRAPH Symposium on Computer Animation*, pages 127–136, 2008.

357. T. Zhao and R. Nevatia. Tracking multiple humans in crowded environment. *Proceedings of the 27th Conference on Computer Vision and Pattern Recognition*, pages 406–413, 2004.

358. T. Zhao, R. Nevatia, and B. Wu. Segmentation and tracking of multiple humans in crowded environments. *IEEE Transactions on Pattern Analysis and Machine Intelligence*, 30(7):1198–1211, 2008.

359. Y. Zhao, Z. Yuan, and F. Chen. Enhancing fluid animation with adaptive, controllable and intermittent turbulence. *Proceedings of the 9th ACM SIGGRAPH Eurographics Symposium on Computer Animation*, pages 75–84, 2010.

360. C. Zheng and D. James. Harmonic fluids. *ACM Transactions on Graphics*, 28(3):37, 2009.

361. D. Zhou, O. Bousquet, T. Lal, J. Weston, and B. Schlkopf. Learning with local and global consistency. *Proceedings of Conference on Advances in Neural Information Processing System*, 2004.

362. D. Zhou, J. Huang, and B. Schlkopf. Learning with hypergraphs: Clustering, classification, and embedding. *Proceedings of the Neural Information Processing Systems*, pages 1601–1608, 2006.

363. H. Zhou, C. Zhan, and Q. Yang. Semi-supervised learning with very few labeled training examples. *Proceedings of the 22nd National Conference on Artificial Intelligence*, pages 675–680, 2007.

364. T. Zhou, D. Tao, and X. Wu. Manifold elastic net: a unified framework for sparse dimension reduction. *Data Mining and Knowledge Discovery*, 22(3):340–371, 2011.

365. J. Zhu. Semi-supervised learning literature survey, 2008.

366. X. Zhu, Z. Ghahramani, and J. Lafferty. Semi-supervised learning using gaussian fields and harmonic functions. *Proceedings of 20th International Conference on Machine Learning*, pages 912–919, 2003.

367. B. Zordan, A. Majkowska, B. Chiu, and M. Fast. Dynamic response for motion capture animation. *Proceedings of the 32nd Annual Conference on Computer Graphics and Interactive Techniques*, pages 697–701, 2005.

INDEX

Modern Machine Learning Techniques and Their Applications in Cartoon Animation Research,
First Edition. By Jun Yu and Dacheng Tao
Copyright © 2013 by The Institute of Electrical and Electronics Engineers, Inc. Published 2013 by
John Wiley & Sons, Inc.